Alvin Sloan

7/02

Gift

EIGHT KEYS TO
Greatness

EIGHT KEYS TO *Greatness*

How to Unlock Your Hidden Potential

GENE N. LANDRUM, Ph.D.

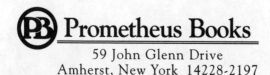

Prometheus Books

59 John Glenn Drive
Amherst, New York 14228-2197

Published 1999 by Prometheus Books

Inquiries should be addressed to
Prometheus Books, 59 John Glenn Drive, Amherst, New York 14228–2197.
VOICE: 716–691–0133, ext. 207. FAX: 716–564–2711.
WWW.PROMETHEUSBOOKS.COM

03 02 01 00 99   5 4 3 2 1

Library of Congress Cataloging-in-Publication Data

Landrum, Gene N.
    Eight keys to greatness : how to unlock your hidden potential / by Gene N. Landrum.
        p.   cm.
    Includes bibliographical references and index.
    ISBN 1–57392–686–8 (alk. paper)
    1. Success—Psychological aspects—Case studies. I. Title.
BF637.S8L344   1999
158.1—dc21   99–13588
                                                                                     CIP

Printed in the United States of America on acid-free paper

To

My Children

Glen, Gene, & Tammy

Follow Your Bliss

Contents

List of Tables and Figure

Acknowledgments

M any people contributed to this book including those creative geniuses I worked with and for over the years, most notably Nolan Bushnell, Joe Keenan, Zoltan Kiss, and Charles Muench. All of these men were entrepreneurial visionaries who proved to me there was a vast divide between true entrepreneurial genius and the average population. Others who contributed to the research material were my International College students Chantal Dehne, Amy Gesdorf, and Karen Wojtysiak. Also contributing to the research effort were the reference librarians at Naples Public Library and International College, especially Harriet Protos. Sports psychologist Marilyn Varcoe provided valuable information on the competitive nature of over-achievers.

Preface

In my extensive studies of what makes a genius, I have determined that eight specific characteristics help pave the path to success: charisma, competitiveness, confidence, drive, intuition, rebellion, risk-taking, and tenacity.

Seventy-eight subjects were used to validate these "keys to greatness." The majority of these have been quoted extensively throughout, and forty of them were used to specifically authenticate the eight paths to greatness. This book will give the reader an insight into the keys to success by using both contemporary and historical figures as examples of visionaries worthy of emulation.

I am convinced winners have bought into past *success imprints* and losers live their lives by their *failure imprints*. Passing comments like "that kid is a real worker and is destined for something big" can have a lasting impact on a child, just as "that kid is destined to be a hood" can have the reverse influence. A psychic told Freud's parents that he was destined for greatness. They began treating him like he was special and sure enough the prognostication proved to be a self-fulfilling prophecy. Environmental interactions are often the real key to success or failure in later life. In other words, greatness and ineptitude are learned, not inherited. And they are acquired along the road by buying into either success imprints or failure imprints. This book will attempt to show how these early influences resulted in what I have labeled the eight "Key Success Traits." Only the positive causal influences of greatness will be addressed. These have been cited as: *birth order, self-employed fathers, early transiency, parental doting, books and fantasy heroes as mentors, education, game playing, abstract problem solving,* and *crises.*

The eight traits cross virtually all professions and disciplines and the subjects represent a cross-section of the arts, business, humanities, politics, science, and sports who have reached the very pinnacle of their professions. One chapter is dedicated to each of these key traits with various subjects used to validate that particular quality. Ten of these subjects—Einstein, Marx, Darwin, Mao Tse-tung, Freud, Napoleon, Hitler, Mother Teresa, Martin Luther King Jr., and Edison—are considered the most influential people who ever lived by most ranking books. The other subjects were chosen based on the huge influence they had on their particular field of interest—Marie Curie as a female scientist, Dostoevsky as a psychological novelist, Bill Gates as the richest man in the world, and Babe Didrickson Zaharias as the world's preeminent female athlete. The subjects featured in each chapter were carefully selected to insure they were representative of a wide range of disciplines, eras, genders, races, and ethnicities. For example, 30 percent (12) of the subjects were from the Arts, 20 percent (8) from business, 13 percent (5) from the humanities, 15 percent (6) from politics, 18 percent (7) from science/technology, and just two athletes (see appendix). The majority, thirty-one of the forty subjects, achieved their greatest success in the twentieth century. Twenty percent are contemporary subjects (after 1950) and are still alive or just recently deceased. Nine of the subjects are from the nineteenth century and only Catherine the Great is from the eighteenth century.

As mentioned, one chapter has been dedicated to each of the eight key traits and features subjects from various disciplines, genders, races, and ethnic areas to demonstrate the pervasiveness of the influence. For example, chapter 1 is dedicated to charisma or effective communications skills. Such notable communicators as Napoleon, Hitler, Mother Teresa, and Fred Smith are used to authenticate *charisma* as one of the keys to greatness. Chapter 5, "Intuition," uses Darwin, Einstein, Freud, Nikola Tesla, and Joseph Campbell to show how tapping into the right-brain vision can prove beneficial to success. Chapter 7, "Risk-Taking," features Marie Curie, Howard Hughes, Amelia Earhart, Ted Turner, and Berry Gordy Jr. to demonstrate how living on the edge can catapult you into fame and fortune. After chapters 1 through 8 validate the eight key traits, chapter 9 will delineate the intrinsic factors necessary to the acquisition of these eight traits. Chapter 10 summarizes the findings with detailed analysis on the impact of religion, politics, libido, socioeconomic and other factors.

The forty subjects are listed in table 3. You might be wondering the criteria under which they were selected. Nineteen were included in previous books by the author on creative genius and entrepreneurship, but twenty-one are subjects unique to this book. No subject was used unless he or she had an enormous influence on or changed his or her field in some dramatic way. All represent a broad cross-section of six interdisciplinary professions held in high esteem by most people: the visual and performing arts (Hemingway and Isadora Duncan); entrepreneurship (Howard Hughes and Bill Gates); humanities (Margaret Mead and Martin Luther King Jr.); politics (Karl Marx and Mao Tse-tung); science and technology (Einstein and Curie); and finally sports (Michael Jordan and Babe Didrickson Zaharias). Table 1 illustrates these disciplines relative to various demographic data.

Table 1
Demographic Analysis of Subjects by Discipline

Discipline or Domain	Females	Males	Non-Americans	Blacks	Totals
Visual and Performing Arts	4	8	2	1	12
Entrepreneurship	1	7	1	1	8
Humanities	4	1	2	1	5
Politics	2	4	5	0	6
Science/Technology	1	6	5	0	7
Athletics	1	1	0	1	2
Totals	13	27	15	4	40

Source of Subjects

The subjects who have not been featured in my previous books are Honoré de Balzac, Joseph Campbell, Catherine the Great, Agatha Christie, Marie Curie, Charles Darwin, Fyodor Dostoevsky, Thomas Edison, Albert Einstein, Sigmund Freud, Ernest Hemingway, Stephen King, Margaret Mead, James Michener, Mao Tse-tung, Karl Marx, Anne Rice, Mother Teresa, Mark Twain, and Mildred "Babe" Didrickson Zaharias. The other subjects included were researched for my previously published books: *Profiles of Genius* (1993), *Profiles of Female Genius* (1994), *Profiles of Power and Success* (1996), and *Profiles of Black Success* (1997).

Selection Criteria

It is important to revisit the selection criteria for the subjects in this work whether they were used in previous books or for this one. For a subject to be included in this book he or she must have made it to the very top of his or her profession and remained there for a minimum of ten years. The subject must have changed the world in some material way or altered his or her profession due to his or her own efforts. In other words, the subjects could not have married into or inherited their position of power. This stipulation eliminated many worthy subjects like Indira Gandhi, Katherine Graham, Donald Trump, Eleanor Roosevelt, or Princess Diana. Both Roosevelt and Graham were super-successful leaders but had many important doors opened for them due to propitious marriages to powerful men. Donald Trump inherited his real estate empire and the Gandhi name was crucial to Indira's rise to power.

It is important to point out that social, moral, ethical, or religious criteria were not used to screen out any of the subjects. Criteria like personal sexual preferences, political correctness, and moral or religious views were outside the purview of the selection process. Reaching the top of their profession was the criteria, not any moral or ethical standards, which is why insidious characters like Hitler, Mao, and Howard Hughes are included. If subjects reached the very top of their field and changed the world in some material way they were considered despite their political, religious, moral, or other ethical standards of behavior. Hitler, for instance, had an enormous influence on the world in the twentieth century even though his methodology was self-serving and his Master Race ideology was based on persecution and destruction. He is probably the most controversial subject in this work but even his most ardent critics would agree that he changed the world in many ways. Additionally, he is found on virtually everyone's Most Influential List for twentieth-century leaders. In many ways Catherine the Great, Mao Tse-tung, Napoleon, and Howard Hughes were equally as perverse, diabolical, and destructive. But this book is about people who made it to the very top and altered the world, and that and is why they have been included.

What is Genius, Greatness, and Success?

Webster defines *creative genius* as "someone who influences another for the good or bad" or "an extraordinary intellectual power especially manifested in creative activity." That book also defines genius in the quantitative sense that America has latched onto as the key to greatness, i.e., as "very high intelligence quotient" or the cognitive thinking ability that we know as IQ. I disdain that definition since it is based on doing well on a test regardless of what is achieved in the real world. MENSA limits membership to those sporting IQs above 140. Most of the eminent people in this book would not have qualified for this social society of the cognitive elite. The bottom line is that genius is not a number. It's a quality just as the world is qualitative not quantitative.

The first definition of *genius*, "to influence others for the good or bad," will be used here. I believe the quantitative definition is inappropriate in a qualitative world. There are countless examples that show a quantitative measure of intelligence is lacking. Howard Gardner, of Harvard University, makes a case for eight different intelligence types and has written a number of books on the subject. Robert Sternberg, a Yale University psychology professor, says it takes a "successful intelligence" to achieve in the world, and successful intelligence is not a quantitative measure. He writes, "The idea that intelligence can be measured by tests is a myth," and he goes on to say, "Intelligence and IQ are modifiable" (Sternberg 1996, 85). Sternberg agrees with my premise that "The true measure of your intelligence is not in a test score; it is in your willingness to develop your own talents" (150). Validation comes from Henri Poincaré, who took his friend Alfred Binet's IQ test twice and both times scored at the imbecile level—even though Einstein and others considered him to be the greatest mathematical genius in the world.

Therefore, the premise in this book is that greatness is something far different than a number. It is the ability to see the forest where others only see trees; to effectively communicate where others are insufficient to the task; to rise to the occasion when others give up the ghost. It is the self-confidence necessary to defy those experts who call you nuts. The ability to bet the farm on your dream when your family and friends predict your quick demise. The ability to be different and suffer the ridicule of ignoramuses, bureaucrats, and myopics. It is the ability to work hard and persevere when everything appears lost.

The eminent individuals not included in my earlier books have been researched with the same detail used in my previous endeavors. At least ten secondary bibliographical resources have been used for the research on each subject with three complete biographical or autobiographical books cited for each. In those instances where the material is controversial, such as the sexual proclivities of Catherine the Great, a minimum of three sources have been consulted. In the case of sensitive materials such as nervous breakdowns, hypomania, or bipolar illnesses experienced by Fyodor Dostoevsky, Marie Curie, Nikola Tesla, Howard Hughes, and Walt Disney, the same meticulous care for detail has been observed so as not to distort the image of these great individuals. Biographical and other data has also been obtained from psychology and organizational behavior textbooks and extensive research undertaken for my doctoral dissertation, as well as general reference works such as *Current Biography* and *Contemporary Authors*, which are updated annually. Full publication information for all references can be found in the bibliography at the end of the book.

The Eight Keys to Greatness

I am either audacious or deluded enough to believe I have found the secrets of entrepreneurial, creative, and innovative genius. Hopefully, the mountains of data on my subjects will validate the principles outlined in the book, although there are always exceptions to every rule and I have attempted to deal with those as necessary. The premise is that personality is the key to success and crosses gender, ethnic, educational, racial, and other domains. Those readers more inclined to look for the destination than enjoy the journey may turn immediately to the final chapter to find the conclusions. The traits and those subjects who best personify them are listed here to give the reader some ideas what to expect:

Table 2
Eight Keys to Greatness
(And Those Who Best Personify Them)

Trait	Methodology
Charisma Napoleon Bonaparte and Mother Teresa	Effective communications skills
Competitiveness Mao Tse-tung and Babe D. Zaharias	The need to win at any cost
Confidence Margaret Mead and Martin Luther King Jr.	Believe and the world will follow you—anywhere
Drive Fyodor Dostoevsky and Bill Gates	A manic need to succeed at any cost
Intuitive Vision Albert Einstein and Sigmund Freud	Saw the forest, not the trees
Rebellion Karl Marx and Anne Rice	Abnormal success comes from abnormal behavior
Risk-Taking Marie Curie and Ted Turner	No great wins exist without great risk-taking
Tenacity Walt Disney and James Michener	If you never quit, you seldom lose

The forty subjects used throughout this book to demonstrate how these eight key traits contribute to great success are listed in table 3 for those not already familiar with their achievements. For those readers with a specific interest in just one or more subjects, one personality trait, or the derivation of success may look to the list of tables or index to find the location of that particular data.

Table 3
Forty Superstars and What Made Them Great

Honoré de Balzac	A prolific novelist who was driven like few other men in history. He is recognized as the father of the modern novel and the man who documented nineteenth-century French society
Napoleon Bonaparte	The world's greatest military leader who used charismatic power to conquer Europe
Joseph Campbell	The father of modern mythology and true visionary who advised us to follow our bliss

Catherine the Great	Russia's longest reigning empress whose persistence led her to the top
Agatha Christie	The Madam of Mayhem published one mystery a year for fifty-seven straight years and wrote the longest running play in the history of London Theatre: *The Mousetrap*
Marie Curie	The fearless discoverer of radium and only female winner of two Nobel Prizes
Charles Darwin	An inquisitive innovator who defined evolution as a function of "Natural Selection"
Walt Disney	A persevering spirit who built an empire out of his inner fantasies of animals and fun
Isadora Duncan	The rebellious mother of modern dance made a difference by daring to be different
Fyodor Dostoevsky	Acknowledged as the father of the world's first, and arguably, greatest psychological novel—*Crime and Punishment* —and world's greatest novel—*The Brothers Karamazov*
Amelia Earhart	World famous aviatrix who dared go where no one else had gone
Thomas Edison	World's most prolific inventor whose workaholic nature paid enormous dividends
Albert Einstein	An intuitive visionary who defined space and time as a relative force in the world
Sigmund Freud	The father of psychoanalysis who made a profound impact on the world of psychology
Bill Gates	An unstoppable drive to make the personal computer a ubiquitous tool for mankind made him the world's richest man and the most influential force in computers
Berry Gordy Jr.	The founder of Motown Records married soul and pop to revolutionize music between 1960 and 1990
Ernest Hemingway	A consummate storyteller who used frenetic drive to master the art of the novel
Adolph Hitler	The megalomaniac who almost conquered the world through the power of speech
Soichiro Honda	A tenacious refusal to fail or lose allowed him to build a $30 billion automotive empire
Howard Hughes	Living on the edge elevated him to become the most powerful and richest man of his time
Michael Jordan	A competitive spirit who proved you can become great by refusing to be defeated
Stephen King	The king of terror and the occult and master of the macabre wrote seven of the top twenty-five selling books in the 1980s

Martin Luther King Jr.	His "I have a dream" mentality moved mountains because he truly believed in himself
Mao Tse-tung	This intellectual revolutionary was the first president of the Chinese Communist party and led his nation through a cultural revolution known as the Great Leap Forward
Karl Marx	An intellectual renegade who used his power of the pen to vent his rage against the establishment via the *Communist Manifesto* and *Das Kapital*
Margaret Mead	The world's first and foremost female anthropologist whose self-esteem made her great
James Michener	The prolific author of historical novels overcame adversity to rise to the top
Maria Montessori	This prophet of pedagogy revolutionized educational technique via self-confidence
Mother Teresa	A charismatic and dedicated woman who created the Sisters of Charity through tenacity
Ayn Rand	A Russian immigrant who wrote the great philosophic epic novel—*Atlas Shrugged*—spawned a new philosophy—Objectivism—and a new political party—Libertarianism
Anne Rice	Iconoclastic author who created vampires as a cathartic means of seeking immortality
Helena Rubinstein	The tyrannical tycoon of beauty who built an international empire via competitive drive
Paul Robeson	A Renaissance man who became America's greatest black singer and Shakespearean actor, losing it all attempting to use artistic power to alter a nation's prejudice
Fred Smith	Charismatic entrepreneur who revolutionized overnight package delivery with Federal Express
Nikola Tesla	An imaginative and intuitive genius who developed the systems that drive the engines of the industrial world
Margaret Thatcher	Britain's first female Prime Minister who refused to be defeated
Ted Turner	The godfather of cable who risked everything for CNN and thereby won the news wars
Mark Twain	The renegade father of American letters and documentor of nineteenth-century Americana
Frank Lloyd Wright	America's quintessential architect who married function and form with the environment
Mildred "Babe" Zaharias	America's greatest female athlete of the first half of the twentieth century and possibly the greatest athlete of all time—regardless of gender

introduction

"Creative genius is the hallmark of those who dare to be different!"

Great people are different but there is a pattern to their uniqueness. First of all, the majority of great people see the world through a different lens and their motivations and drives are different from the norm. For one thing, they never get lost. They often don't know where they are but that is not threatening to them—in fact it seems to energize them. Finding themselves in some unknown place, they feel unshackled and free to explore the new environment. Most people become afraid of what might happen when they lose their structure. The opposite happens with the great. They use the opportunity to forage for new experiences and thrive on the chance to be out in front of the pack.

Why are great people so inclined? Because they are not programmed to fear the unknown, they are programmed to enjoy the lack of structure. They seek new opportunities and the possibilities available in such environments. The experience is euphoric and empowering—the opposite of what the average person, even someone highly steeped in education and experience, feels. Visionaries find being lost thrilling while myopics find it threatening. Leaders use ambiguity as a chance to utilize their guile and imagination to blaze new trails. Followers become immobilized and stifled when they find themselves lost on the highway of life. They become frightened and terrified. Why? Because the average person has been programmed for safety and fear is a dominant component of their internal operating systems. Unfortunately, all breakthrough ideas, all great visionaries, and all innovation is to be found where everyone else is not. You must be lost to become great and that is where the great tend to hang out. That will be the focus of this book. How can being lost be an empowering experience? How can we be out in front of the pack and enjoy the experience?

Being Lost and Creativity

Creative and innovative personalities thrive on the unknown and the ambiguous since it allows them to be free of the shackles of the establishment. Those steeped in structure do not understand such people and label them losers. When so labeled one must be emotionally resilient and be armed with a strong self-esteem since even one's families and friends may question his or her sanity. This makes visionaries both renegades and arrogant—necessary ingredients for survival and ultimate greatness. Every great technological or artistic innovation of the past two hundred years has been the product of the fringe. Innovation is a product of those who have become lost in their discipline and the experience has been responsible for the new. Therefore the subjects in this work all qualify as visionary renegades with a touch of egomania. They had to be so to survive, since the constant derision from pre-programmed myopics would otherwise have been lethal.

Innovator personalities therefore have a prescient vision, strong self-esteem, and are rebellious. Examples are legion. The constituency seldom understood Catherine the Great, Mao Tse-tung, and Nelson Mandela, but they followed them. Why? Because these renegades had a map of the future and were optimistic and charismatic enough to convince the masses they knew the path to nirvana. The same was true of the followers of Maria Montessori and Mother Teresa, the disciples of Margaret Mead and Martin Luther King Jr., the employees of Rupert Murdoch and Ted Turner, and the teammates of Michael Jordan. These visionaries didn't always know where they were but never allowed fear to interfere with their journey. They used the unknown to blaze new trails into creative opportunities. The challenge was exhilarating to these eminent leaders. Fear is the driving force for the followers and opportunity for the leaders and it is never more apparent than when lost.

It is important to understand that followers tend to be left-brain dominant (i.e., highly structured and analytical)—85 percent of the Western world is—and are incapable of functioning in unknown environments. That is not bad, just different, but it makes them less capable of functioning effectively when outside of a structured system. Visionaries are the 15 percent who see the world holistically—right-brain dominant types who are able to integrate both the forest and trees. Such individuals are capable of great insight because they do not get locked into a single dimension. They are introverts who can extrovert, CPAs who can see new opportunities beyond the numbers. This makes them different from the establishment and more prone to create and lead. Creative types love the feeling of freedom to explore in foreign environments. They do not want too much programming. This is why Einstein hated school and was kicked out of high school. Shackles stifle the gifted while they give solace to the pack. One is debilitated, the other empowered, by the same experience. One prefers to be spoon-fed and programmed the other prefers to be free to explore and get lost.

Born or Bred?

This book was written for people who desire to be special but do not know the path. It is for people who were raised to believe that "special" demands some genetic predisposition for greatness. Many people, including myself, were raised to believe that success is a function of being born in that big house on the hill where doors are opened for you. I was raised to think that the super successful—presidents and prime ministers, best-selling authors and Nobel-winning scientists, TV and movie stars, airline pilots and corporate executives—were all endowed with some mythical attributes that made them rich and famous. It took a long time for me to discover the error in that logic. I agree with Ayn Rand and Stephen King, who both said "writers are made not born." I have also come to believe that *it is never too late to be great* in addition to *there is no genetic predisposition to greatness!*

Early Programming

It is a sad commentary of life that our well-intentioned parents and teachers want us to be great but in fact unconsciously program us for mediocrity. Schools often place us in a box of conformity that is politically correct but counterproductive to our ability to self-actualize. We are forced to conform to a bureaucratic model that is socially acceptable but antithetical to creativity or an innovative life—especially in a fast-paced world. Tradition is sacrosanct in a world attempting to be too orderly. Too much conformity is inconsistent with creativity or innovation, however. Even so, teachers persist in grooming children to become robots, afraid to rock any boats—but it is the boat rockers like Darwin, Freud, Einstein, Robeson, and Montessori who change the world. By indoctrinating our young to comply we are merely replicating the past and that will not be sufficient to develop visionary leaders for the twenty-first century. Why? Because there are no wins where fear and safety dominate. Such indoctrination only succeeds in developing self-serving cover-your-butt adults programmed to fit into a structured world where bureaucracy reigns supreme. That is fine in a static world where change doesn't exist, but that isn't the case in this dynamic world.

Find the Pack and Then Go Elsewhere!

All innovation is found on the fringe where the masses fear to go. There are no wins where the pack is located so grooming our children to fit in only teaches them to become followers, not leaders. Such a world is the province of those who would capitulate their *will* to the pack. The terrible truth of our educational system is that it puts us all in a box of ordinariness, of mediocrity, one guaranteed to program us to become a carbon copy of our role models. When those role models are negative influences it is no wonder we find our youth dropping out or following the lead of the Marshall Applewhites or David Koreshes, cult leaders who claim to know the truth, preaching a visionary gospel.

Once our children are programmed for mediocrity it is very difficult for us to change them into visionaries who are unafraid of being lost on the highway of life. Although they are not genetic traits, both mediocrity and greatness emanate from within. When internal vision is limited in any way it becomes a roadblock to future success. Once we believe in our limitations we spend the rest of our lives fulfilling such a destiny. Once a child's internal belief system is programmed to the *known* and the *safe* it is too late to save him or her from mediocrity. We must mold our children into a life of greatness.

I grew up believing those in power had some prescient knowledge, talents, or intellectual gifts. The truth is that the great people of the world do not have any preordained package to the top. They were trained in the same robotic bureau-system where restraint, mediocrity, and security are king. We grow up believing the great are somehow special. They are not. They do not possess some magic elixir. They don't even have any special rights, although I do believe that some people are just more equal than others, albeit more internally equal than externally equal.

Greatness Programming

How do we get trained for leadership, for excellence, creativity, innovation, and greatness? A self-assessment for greatness is located at the end of this book. It may give you some indication of your propensity for the same. There was a time when I believed that those kids who lived in the big house on the hill were truly special. After all, they traveled extensively to Europe and Asia, spoke French, and were able to attend the college of their choice. For many years I actually believed boardrooms and ballrooms were of genetic origin. It has taken me a lifetime to learn the truth—that superstars have no predisposition for greatness.

What do they have? An internal belief system that says *SPECIAL* in capital letters. Virtually all of the subjects in this book thought they were special quite early in life. They had no idea how, why, or what it meant, but they felt self-sufficient marching to their own drummer because they were special. All they knew was that they were more capable, more aware, more inquisitive, and more intensely interested in learning more about how to use their power.

Much research has led me to the secret of greatness and being special. I am now convinced that great people have been imprinted along the way with success imprints and the losers have been likewise imbued with failure imprints. I will discuss how my subjects were unknowingly imprinted with qualities of greatness and attempt to demonstrate how those qualities in turn contributed to their ultimate fame and fortune. This book is about learning to be great, the road the subjects took, the cost of the journey, and the rewards of the trip. First, let's talk about the genesis of this research.

Silicon Valley

I spent twenty years in Silicon Valley working with many creative, ingenious, and innovative entrepreneurs. Many of them were integral to the digital revolution that transformed that valley into the worldwide epicenter of the technological revolution of the twentieth century.

Silicon Valley is located approximately fifty miles south of San Francisco and its inhabitants somehow acquired the Gold Rush mentality. It was here that I happened to stumble on those creative geniuses who piqued my interest in the creative process. The valley is home to some of the most advanced technological wonders of the century. I was there during the period when integrated circuits were replacing electro-mechanical devices. At the same time Ampex and Memorex, inventors of quality sound recordings, were revolutionizing the world of audio reproduction. Video games, hand-held calculators, digital watches, personal computers, and CB radios were born out of the microprocessor chip. New firms emerged out of what had been a valley filled with orchards and people learned to program those chips to perform awesome tasks.

I watched as the founders of Hewlett-Packard, Fairchild, Tandem, Intel, Atari, National Semiconductor, Apple, and Sun Microsystems made their mark on the world. The entrepreneurial leaders of these firms were a strange breed who violated traditional business dogmas and succeeded in changing the existing world of business products. These men were renegades on a mission of destruction, the destruction of electro-mechanical devices like the hundred-year-old cash register, office calculators, bookkeeping machines, mechanical counters, punch-card systems, arcade games, phone systems, and the mechanical typewriter.

It soon became apparent that these entrepreneurs were a different breed than what I had seen in the Midwest and South. They thought differently, risked differently, and operated differently. At first I didn't recognize the close tie between their personalities and their creativity, innovation, and entrepreneurship. Only after I left Silicon Valley was I able to discern how truly different these individuals were from what I was taught and how others operated. (Clarity often comes from distancing oneself from the action.) This demarcation clearly demonstrated the incredible precocity and intellectual fury that had taken place in those former orchards in northern California and led me to write about the importance of personality to the creative process.

Silicon Valley Entrepreneurs

What drew such a huge number of creative and innovative entrepreneurs to that agrarian land? Was it the water? No! What caused such a diverse group to come together in the land of fruits and nuts? Why would a group of entrepreneurial wannabes suddenly appear on the scene and in the short span of two decades launch such an astonishing number of breakthrough electronic innovations?

One answer is that there seems to be some mysterious attraction that draws genius to genius. History reveals a number of similar events that defy explanation. What happened in Silicon Valley between 1965 and 1990 was not dissimilar to what had occurred twenty-five hundred years ago in the golden age of Greek civilization. Homer set the stage with *The Iliad* and *The Odyssey* (c. 750 B.C.E.). How did such intellectual titans come from one area and period? Socrates, Diogenes, Aeschylus, Plato, Sophocles, Alexander the Great, Hippocrates, and Aristotle walked the same turf while espousing a wisdom of the world that would be quoted for the next two millennia. This small group of change masters appeared on the scene and then disappeared two centuries later, opening the way for another group to the West that formed the Roman Empire. A similar intellectual revolution appeared again to end the dark ages in the fifteenth and sixteenth centuries—a period that would become known as the Renaissance. The creative and intellectual precocity of this era spawned the likes of Newton, Descartes, Shakespeare, Da Vinci, Galileo, Raphael, and Michelangelo.

The thirty-year period in Silicon Valley between 1965 and 1995 saw a similar pattern emerge that will go down in history as the golden age of information and communications technology led by the semiconductor and computer industries. This era spawned men like Bill Hewlett and David

Packard (the founders of Hewlett Packard), William Shockley (transistor), Robert Noyce (Intel), Linus Pauling (a Nobel Prize–winning chemist), Alexander Pontitoff (Ampex), Nolan Bushnell (Atari), Steve Wozniak and Steve Jobs (Apple Computer), and countless others. Most of these men were transplants from other places who happened on the scene at this fortuitous time and played a role in the communications revolution.

Most of these men were free spirits who scorned tradition and disregarded the self-preservation mentality so prevalent in the world of the Fortune 500 companies that existed back East. These visionaries opted for technology as the path to exotic new paradigms destined to push the window of opportunity. They ignored the nay-saying experts like IBM engineers who said the personal computer was a fad that had no future and other experts with a like attitude toward the new and different. They took extraordinary risks, developed new concepts, and persevered beyond the norm. Most were iconoclasts who would not have been accepted in the halls of ivy. They dressed differently than the typical businessman, were off-the-wall, and disregarded standard business acumen. These visionaries ignored the industry experts and pursued their internal vision of reality.

Psychologist Alfred Adler in *Superiority and Social Interest* gives us some idea of the above metamorphoses in his insightful statement "personality can never be totally removed from its social setting." The Silicon Valley visionaries happened to be about as predictable as the San Andreas Fault and often have been described with many negative adjectives—psychopathic, diabolical, demonic, reckless, and Machiavellian.

New businesses open and fail in the Valley like no where else. And for every one opened, thousands are attempted. Many have their genesis outside of research and development labs, such as the pet rock, which was spawned by a bored advertising executive in a bar during happy hour. Within eighteen months the pet rock was history, but during its brief lifespan the entrepreneur became a multimillionaire. Silicon Valley is a frenetic hotbed of similar creative production. One of the area's most appealing qualities is that it is intellectually stimulating. Such an environment can prove to be contagious, making the most conservative bookkeeper in the Valley someone who is more frivolous and likely to take risks than the wildest entrepreneur in the Midwest or East.

During the twenty years I lived in the Valley I was unaware of the symbiosis that existed between these entrepreneurial whiz kids and the truly eminent personalities of the world, since I, too, had gone through a similar metamorphosis. These visionaries were carbon copies of Edison, Picasso, Curie, Einstein, and Freud, not to mention their similarity to Napoleon, Marx, Mao Tse-tung, and Hitler. Their operating styles mimicked Howard Hughes, Mary Kay Ash, Rupert Murdoch, Berry Gordy Jr., and Ted Turner; with the drive of Nikola Tesla, Maria Montessori, Margaret Mead, and

Martin Luther King Jr. Most viewed business as war and operated as competitively as Michael Jordan and Babe Didrickson Zaharias.

Right-Brain Dominant Visionaries

These Silicon Valley visionaries violated all the tenets of graduate business school traditions by violating the rituals of budgeting, quantitative analysis, and conventional organizational structure. They operated more like philosophers than tacticians. They did not adhere to the business school dogma of budgeting, modeling, and standard reporting structures. One of the most glaring differences was in the way they planned. Most did their planning in a very methodical or quantitative style (i.e., digital) which contrasts the one area of business where it is deemed acceptable to use one's imagination. These visionaries preferred detail in planning and a qualitative or analog approach to operating, which is diametrically opposite what is taught. In school the maxim is "Operate by the numbers!" These successful leaders had found a different altar to worship at and it wasn't the altar of numbers. They planned quantitatively and operated qualitatively instead of the opposite. This approach proved right in a dynamic world where numbers change like the wind so the planning function is what needs to be quantified, not operations, which must remain fluid. Opportunity, not security, was their god. They were generalists with a penchant for specialization and were able to integrate both the left and right brains—unlike the majority of the population. An example is budgeting. It is used for planning capital and personnel needs, but then ignored in operating the businesses. This contrasts with those who make budgets godly by their inflexibility.

This operating style was different and separated the visionaries from the pack. Being different proved to be the key to success. By definition, being visionaries made them unique and they were often labeled renegades. To survive they had to be arrogant optimists, otherwise, they would be devoured by the establishment. Once they became visionaries it was an easy step to radical nonconformity. Most of the great visionaries in this book became nonconformists quite early in life and tended to thrive on their uniqueness rather than be debilitated by it. An excellent example of this is the mother of modern dance, Isadora Duncan, who, ironically, grew up just north of Silicon Valley, in San Francisco. She told the *New York Times*, "I'm a revolutionist. Every artist has to be one to make a mark in the world" (Desti 1929, 118). Such an internal vision was critical to her ability to deal with the world's skeptics. She gloried in her role as a rebel and it was instrumental in her innovations in dance. Without Duncan's confident attitude and adherence to a rebellious lifestyle she would never have changed the world of dance. Her iconoclastic mentality was a key factor in her rise to fame and fortune.

Renegades All

Why is abnormality a function of greatness? Because average success comes from an average person. Conversely, abnormal success is born of abnormality. The one constant in this study is that virtually every subject included qualified as a radical nonconformist. They were abnormal visionaries who defied the establishment and the traditions of their disciplines. Think about the success of Darwin, Einstein, Montessori, Picasso, Disney, or Turner. They were all nonconformists and in complete defiance of the traditional norms of their domains. That is what made them famous but was also the cause of most their heartaches. James Michener wrote, "I had been thrown out of every school I had ever attended. I am a loner to an extent that would frighten most men" (Michener 1992, 327). He had a lot of company: Einstein was also thrown out of high school and Ayn Rand was at war against virtually every known ideology. She hated religion (and was a vocal atheist), communism (virulent Capitalist), homosexuality (she saw it as "psychologically flawed"), mass education (it "molds mediocrity"), the Right ("Militant Mystics"), Left (called *National Review* the "most dangerous magazine in America"), conservatives ("root of tribalism"), feminism ("man is superior to women"), government (Libertarianism is her Objectivism philosophy), and welfarism ("the weak should perish").

After much research I have come to believe that to be great one must be different since so-called normal people produce merely average results. At takes an *abnormal* person, one who is abnormally competitive, confident, driven, and tenacious to create abnormal success. In other words, you had better get comfortable with being called a renegade if you are interested in changing the world. You must deal with ridicule and being called a maverick if you would be a great creator, innovator, or entrepreneur. It takes an iconoclast with extraordinary communications skills, work ethic, passion, and temerity to make it to the very top of any discipline. These subjects qualified.

It is important to mention that the job descriptions coming from nearly all human resource departments define the ideal top executive as one who conforms to the system—one who is conservative, god-fearing, traditional, nurturing, and willing to sublimate his or her personal identity to that of the organization. You would be hard pressed to find that executive in Silicon Valley. What then is the profile of the Valley visionary? I found them to have egos bigger than God, the charm of an evangelist, impatient and competitive to a fault, and off-the-wall renegades who refused to listen to any counsel but their own. They also had the risk-taking propensity of Evel Kneivel. But most important of all, they possessed holistic vision and had an insatiable need to pursue the opportunities and possibilities in life.

One interesting discovery in the research regards these individuals' fathers. Parental influence will be discussed in some detail later but it is pertinent to mention here that many had fathers who were con men. History has indicated the fathers of tycoons like John D. Rockefeller and many of the subjects in this work lived right on the edge of social acceptance. Thus, the greats grew up seeing life being lived on the fringe.

Why Didn't the Big Guys Lead the Way?

During that historic era why didn't General Electric, Westinghouse, Bally, or IBM produce the breakthrough products and innovations? After all, they were the ones with all the resources and technological know-how. One of the puzzling paradoxes of business is that those with all the knowledge, money, and even the patents seldom produce the innovative breakthrough products. Why are the industry leaders so inept at innovation? Why are those who should be leading in product innovation always last to grasp the concept? Why are the great innovations always left to the ingenuity of the young who have no money, expertise, or organizations? Because the big guys tend to worship at the altar of the quarterly report and are dedicated to protecting their asset base, that's why. And that is never consistent with betting on the new and innovative. Consequently, such tradition-bound firms are always last in accepting breakthrough technology.

Why didn't General Electric, with its thousands of electrical engineers, or Westinghouse, the world leader in power generation systems, lead the way in integrated circuitry? And why didn't Bally, the most dominant game manufacturer in the world in slot, arcade, and pinball games, develop the video game? And most bizarre of all, how could IBM, a firm with a stranglehold on the computer industry, allow a hippie from Silicon Valley (Steve Jobs) a four-year lead in personal computers? Some of these answers come directly out of the IBM engineering department, which told a reporter in 1980, "we knew this couldn't happen, and that it made no sense at all, the development came as a profound shock to us" (Landrum 1993).

What happens to large firms once they are dominant? They become caught up in their own myopia. They begin to believe they are infallible and once that happens they are the most fallible. Arrogance is at the heart of this myopic mentality as is allegiance to the short-term at the cost of the long. Those who sacrifice the future for a better present are destined to have no future. Instant gratification is the bane of the creative process. It makes you happy for the present but you pay a horrible price down the road. Protecting assets is the most important factor for most industry leaders. Security becomes sacrosanct, but where there are no risks there are no big wins. When quarterly earnings become more important than market share or the long-term success of a firm that firm is on its way to the trash can of history.

A quick survey of management textbooks will show that 85 percent of the top executives in America receive the majority of their compensation from bonuses that are tied to quarterly earnings, stock price, or price-earnings ratios. Such incentives tie their decisions to the short-term bottom-line, not to any long-term innovation. Numbers and results are their god and this is antithetical to all creative growth. Their incentive compensation causes these executives to mortgage the future for their own self-interested present. They are motivated to the short run at the expense of the long run and consequently they refuse to spend funds that have any long-term rewards if it is at the expense of short-term ones. Those decisions are disastrous in a dynamic world. Why? Because if you don't make your own products obsolete you can be assured someone else will. All product breakthroughs come from individuals who are not protecting something, who do not play "cover your ass" games, and are willing to sacrifice the present for a better future. Unfortunately, virtually all bureaucracies tend to sacrifice the unknown future for a sure present. But the cost is no future technological successes, and that is exactly why America has lost the consumer electronics products to Japan and the other future-oriented Asians. Such myopic and arrogant thinking leads inevitably to mediocrity and failure. Carl Jung was quite insightful in seeing this as early as 1935 when he wrote: "Any large company of wholly admirable persons has the morality and intelligence of an unwieldy, stupid, and violent animal. The bigger the organization, the more unavoidable is its morality and blind stupidity" (Jung 1971, 224).

Organizations and individuals that become too lazy and happy soon become indolent. They become afflicted with that famous corporate disease known as NIH—the not-invented-here syndrome. Such organizations become too protective and too smart for their own good. Their leaders have such a psychological investment in *what is* they are never able to see *what might be*. They become overly security conscious and refuse to take risks. What they don't understand is that there are no wins without risks in business. Risk and reward is a zero-sum game. Eliminating risk in any venture removes a like amount of reward. As you eliminate any risk you simultaneously eliminate potential, so it would be preferable to take some risks rather than allow yourself to die slowly by sitting on assets.

This precept is as appropriate in the arts, politics, sports, and the humanities as it is in business. Oprah Winfrey understands what most corporate executives do not. When asked why she is able to remain number one in TV talk show ratings, she told Larry King on his show, "I act as if I am number ten and that is why I'm number one. The minute I start thinking I am number one, I'll probably be number ten." Touché!

Why Not NBC, UPS, IBM, or Pizza Hut?

When I decided to look into what made the great tick I began looking at subjects outside Silicon Valley like Ted Turner, Fred Smith (Federal Express), Soichiro Honda, Tom Monaghan (Domino's Pizza), Bill Lear (Lear jet), and Bill Gates (Microsoft). Later I would look at Mary Kay Ash (Mary Kay Cosmetics), Frank Lloyd Wright, Howard Hughes, and Walt Disney. Let us look at the first group and see if there are any patterns in what they did and why the industry leaders were unable to see the opportunities which skyrocketed these men to power. What was the paradox of creativity that permitted neophyte entrepreneurs to accomplish what the industry leaders could not?

Ted Turner

The networks were in the best position to become the cable innovators. A former billboard salesman who didn't know one thing about starting or managing a twenty-four hour international news operation certainly wasn't. Thus, the networks and print media predicted Ted Turner's quick demise, calling his idea a "joke." Most wrote, "It can't be done." Turner admitted that he knew very little about television before he bet his whole empire on the CNN venture. He told a reporter, "I hadn't watched more than a hundred hours of news in my whole life!" (Whitemore 1990, 54). The Godfather of Cable bet his total net worth of $100 million on his dream. His empire at the time included the Atlanta Braves, Atlanta Hawks, and a cable station (TBS, the Superstation), all of which would have been lost if he failed. Ted won because he had the guts to bet his bucks on what he saw as a great need to create an electronic global village. The networks did not have his vision or the courage to pursue such a risky venture (see Landrum 1993).

Fred Smith

Fred Smith was a Vietnam vet still in his twenties when he bet his total inheritance on overnight package delivery. Why didn't the U.S. Post Office see this opportunity? Classic marketing myopia! United Parcel Service had been in operation for eighty years when they woke up one morning and saw this new firm—Federal Express—taking away many of their customers. Smith now runs an $8 billion dollar enterprise that would never have started had it been left to the vision of the industry leaders.

Bill Gates

There was no reason Bill Gates should have been able to own the operating system that drove IBM computers. But the leaders at IBM could not see the opportunity in offering licensing to PC clones and once they saw it were incapable of catching the driven Gates. The ineptitude and mistakes made by Apple Computer and Steve Jobs allowed Gates to become the richest man in the world. This is the most inspiring story since David slew Goliath. It is truly ironic that the stock value of Microsoft now exceeds that of IBM and this phenomenal growth has taken place in just over fifteen years. Gates validates that vision and temerity are the tickets to greatness.

Tom Monaghan

Pizza Hut woke up one morning in the 1980s and found they had lost out to an underfinanced, uneducated entrepreneur named Tom Monaghan. The Pizza Hut executives thought home-delivered pizza was just a fad and refused to acknowledge this part of the market that was far more difficult to control. Their 8,000 restaurants could have annihilated any competitor but their myopia allowed Monaghan to gain a foothold that he wouldn't lose. He had been perceptive in recognizing the change in lifestyle resulting in a dramatic change in the buying and eating habits of the traditional pizza customer. Monaghan used ingenuity and hard work to create Domino's Pizza, becoming the largest producer of pizzas in America. He did it by offering a product the two-career family wanted. Pizza Hut didn't see the change, or wouldn't accept it, until they were far behind in the race for home-delivered pizza.

The above success stories by small, underfinanced entrepreneurs from the fringe led me to study other domains such as politics, the arts, humanities, science, and sports. I researched top political leaders who had changed the world and found Napoleon, Golda Meir, Hitler, and Margaret Thatcher to compare against my data on great entrepreneurs. In the arts I looked at the careers of Isadora Duncan, Maria Callas, Oprah Winfrey, Madonna, and Michael Jackson. Maria Montessori, Amelia Earhart, and Margaret Mead gave me insight into the humanities and Einstein, Edison, and Nikola Tesla were used in the field of science. A total list of subjects can be found in tables 4 and 5.

The subjects are listed in alphabetical order according to nine key factors that appear to have been important to their development. Birth order is the first. It is an important factor, but not as much as some psychologists claim. My study indicates that order of births is as important as the way one is treated by his or her family. (Of course, being first-born does affect how a child is treated by both parents and siblings.) These influences will be discussed at length in chapter 9. According to my study, the father's profession is far more important in one's development. Ninety percent of these eminent subjects had a self-employed parent, almost all fathers, although Mary Kay Ash and Isadora Duncan had self-employed mothers as their key influence. Being a college graduate or having an extroverted personality were not

Table 4
Common Behavioral Traits of Female Visionaries

Subject	Birth Order	Self-Employed (Father)	Education	Extrovert/ Introvert	Personality Type	High-Risk Taker	Hypomania*	Religious	Death of Parent/Sibling
Catherine the Great	1st	Yes	H.S.	E+	A+	Yes++	H	No	Yes
Agatha Christie	1st	Yes	H.S.	I	B	No	M/D	Yes	Yes
Marie Curie	Last	Yes	Ph.D.	—	A+	Yes+	H	No	Yes
Isadora Duncan	Last	Yes	5th grade	E	A+	Yes+++	H	No	Yes
Amelia Earhart	1st	Yes	H.S.	E	A+	Yes+++	H	No	No
Margaret Mead	1st	Yes	Ph.D.	E+	A++	Yes+	H	Yes	Yes
Maria Montessori	1st	No	M.D.	Both	A++	Yes+	No	Yes	No
Ayn Rand	1st	Yes	B.A.	I—	B	Yes	H+	No	No
Anne Rice	2nd	No	M.A.	I	A+	No	H+	No	Yes
Helena Rubinstein	1st	Yes	H.S.	E	A++	Yes+	No	No	No
Margaret Thatcher	2nd	Yes	Law	E	B	Yes	H	Yes	No
Mother Teresa	Last	Yes	H.S.	I—	B	Yes	H++	Yes	Yes
Babe Zaharias	6th	Yes	H.S.	E	A++	Yes++	H+	No	No
Total Females (13)	7 54%	11 85%	6 46%	8 62%	9 69%	11 85%	11 85%	5 38%	7 54%
Male Subjects (27) (see next page)	18 59%	26 96%	13 48%	15 56%	23 85%	26 96%	24 89%	9 33%	23 85%
Totals: 40 100%	23 58%	37 93%	19 48%	21 53%	34 85%	37 93%	35 88%	14 35%	30 75%

*Hypomania: A mood disorder "characterized by optimism and a decreased need for sleep. A mania or euphoria" (American Psychological Association). An M/D in this column indicates Manic-Depressive. Plus and minus signs indicate the order of magnitude (degree) to which subjects adhere to various traits.
Source: *Profiles of Female Genius* (1994), *Profiles of Power and Success* (1996), *Profiles of Black Success* (1997)

Table 5
Common Behavioral Traits of Male Visionaries

Subject	Birth Order	Self-Employed (Father)	Education	Extrovert/Introvert	Personality Type	High-Risk Taker	Hypomania*	Religious	Death of Parent/Sibling
Honoré de Balzac	1st	Yes	B.A.	E+	A+++	Yes+	M/D	Yes	Yes
Napoleon Bonaparte	5th	Yes	B.S.	Both	A+++	Yes++	M/D	No	Yes
Joseph Campbell	1st	Yes	B.S.		B	No	No	Spiritual	Yes
Charles Darwin	5th	Yes	B.S.	—	B	Yes	No	No	Yes
Walt Disney	1st	Yes	H.S.	—	A+	Yes	M/D	No	Yes
Fyodor Dostoevsky	2nd	Yes	H.S.	—	A+++	Yes++	M/D	Yes	Yes
Thomas Edison	1st	Yes	3 Mo.	E	A+++	Yes++	M/D	No	No
Albert Einstein	1st	Yes	Ph.D.	—	B	Yes	No	No	Yes
Sigmund Freud	1st	Yes	M.D.	E	A	Yes+	H	No	Yes
Bill Gates	2nd	Yes	H.S.	—	A++	Yes+	H++	No	No
Berry Gordy Jr.	7th	Yes	H.S.	E+	A+++	Yes+++	H+++	No	Yes
Ernest Hemingway	2nd	Yes	H.S.	Both	A+++	Yes+++	M/D	Yes	Yes
Adolf Hitler	1st	No	11th grade	I—	A	Yes+++	H++	No	No
Soichiro Honda	1st	Yes	8th grade	E+	A++	Yes+++	M/D	No	Yes
Howard Hughes	1st	Yes	11th grade	I—	A+++	Yes+++	M/D	No	Yes
Michael Jordan	4th	No	B.A.	Both	A+++	Yes+++	H++	Yes	Yes
Stephen King	1st	Yes	B.A.	—	A+	Yes+	H+++	Yes	Yes
Martin Luther King Jr.	1st	Yes	Ph.D.	I—	A+++	Yes+	H+++	Yes	Yes
Mao Tse-tung	1st	Yes	H.S.	—	A+++	Yes+++	M/D	No	Yes
Karl Marx	2nd	Yes	Ph.D.	—	A	Yes+	H	Yes	Yes
James Michener	1st	Yes	M.A.	—	B	Yes+	H	No	Yes
Paul Robeson	8th	Yes	Law	E	A++	Yes+++	H	No	Yes
Fred Smith	1st	Yes	B.S.	E	A+	Yes+++	H	No	Yes
Nikola Tesla	3rd	Yes	H.S.	—	A+++	Yes+++	M/D	No	Yes
Ted Turner	1st	Yes	H.S.	Both	A+++	Yes+++	M/D	No	Yes
Mark Twain	Last	Yes	3rd grade	E+	A+++	Yes+++	M/D	No	Yes
Frank Lloyd Wright	1st	Yes	11th grade	E	A+	Yes+++	H+	Yes	No
Totals: 27	16	26	13	15	23	26	24 M/D–12	9	23
100%	59%	96%	48%	56%	85%	96%	89%	33%	85%

*Hypomania: A mood disorder "characterized by optimism and a decreased need for sleep. A mania or euphoria" (American Psychological Association). An M/D in this column indicates Manic-Depressive. Plus and minus signs indicate the order of magnitude (degree) to which subjects adhere to various traits.
Source: Profiles of Power and Success (1996), Profiles of Black Success (1997)

important based on this data. Being a Type A personality (84 percent), risk-taker (96 percent), and having a manic personality (90 percent) appear to be important factors based on the high percentage of these visionaries who were so inclined. In contrast, religion wasn't important since only 38 percent had adopted one church that they attended regularly. Experiencing a life crisis, in contrast, was very important. More than 70 percent had a sibling or parent die prior to the subject's twenty-first birthday. This traumatic experience appears to have had huge influence on personality. All of these factors are discussed at length in the book and specifically in chapter 9.

Personality—The Key to Creative Genius

Carl Jung wrote, "My life has been permeated by one idea, the secret of personality." He went on to say that the "contents of the personal unconscious are acquired." He believed "tycoons, entrepreneurs, speculators, stockbrokers, and politicians are extroverted-intuitives" (Jung 1971, 224). It is important to understand that extroversion is not a key element in creativity. Males tended to be slightly introverted and females more extroverted but that is to be expected since women often have to crash through those glass ceilings. In a male-dominated world females are often forced to talk their way out of the kitchen into the boardroom.

The majority of the subjects in this book were more inclined to see the forest, the whole picture, than the trees, individual obstacles, which Jung described as the way of seeing the world—sensing (trees) versus intuiting (forest). This is the dimension of seeing life through a digital (micro) filter in comparison to seeing it in a more analog (macro) way. People who are sensors see life more in a left-brain or small way while intuitors tend to be right-brain dominant with a big picture view.

Jung's other personality groupings include how one makes decisions—thinking (rational) or feeling (emotional)—and how one prefers to operate—perceiving (spontaneous) or judging (structured). The majority of my subjects were thinkers and judgers. Putting all of these factors together we find that the vast majority of the subjects (84 percent) were more inclined to Intuitive-Thinking. Psychologists have labeled such a temperament *Promethean* after the Greek god who defied Zeus and stole fire from the heavens to give to mankind. He is the symbol of noble defiance and the metaphor for creative vision.

Promethean Personalities

These subjects were titans who defied the establishment to gain freedom to explore and create. They are defiant symbols of technological freedom, but they paid a horrible price for their nonconformity—just as Prometheus did. (He was chained to a rock and an eagle gnawed on his liver for his crime.) These leaders were ridiculed and mocked by the traditionalists and they became rebels in order to survive.

The Promethean temperament is characterized by an innate need to seek knowledge and competence. Such people are constantly pursuing the opportunities and possibilities in life with logic and ingenuity. They represent about 12 percent of the general population, although some defining factors would reduce the number to as little as 1 percent. The Prometheans' weakness lies in their insensitivity to others and their careless handling of details. Frank Lloyd Wright is a prime example. He designed utopian buildings of extraordinary scope such as the Guggenheim Museum in New York City and Fallingwater—probably America's most architecturally famous home—in the Pennsylvania mountains, but their roofs leaked and the plumbing did not work. Wright was the classic visionary personality and never sweated the details of any new creation, fully expecting others to follow behind and pick up the mundane pieces. Most visionaries have a similar propensity. Bill Gates saw this tendency in himself early and hired others to worry about the details while he took care of the future. Promethean personalities are famous, or infamous, for building wonderful castles in the sky, and when finished not moving in. They prefer to move on to another creation that can inspire them, leaving the "final touches" on previous projects for others to complete.

Why Is Personality Important?

Knowing your strengths allows you to set yourself up to succeed. When you don't know your strengths or weaknesses, you may place yourself in a position to fail and subsequently may start believing you are inept or worse. Not knowing your needs for interacting with the world can lead you to take a job simply because it pays well or for some other "peripheral" reason. It is imperative you place yourself in the best position to succeed and that can only be accomplished by knowing how you best interact with others. Most people are inclined to take a well-paying job even though they shouldn't and end up hating it or getting fired. Knowing your personality and being true to it will help avoid these and similar pitfalls.

Let's say you are just out of school and are offered a job as the concierge in a fashionable hotel. If you happen to be an introvert and prefer to deal with things rather than people, you shouldn't spend eight hours a day with people. If you take the job you are guaranteed to do poorly and in the process will become afflicted with severe anxiety and stress. Why? Because repressed aggression and stress build-up will slowly destroy you from the inside. In essence, you will have set yourself up to fail.

Introverts cannot be extroverted all day without severe consequences. Introverts need positions where they interact with computer terminals, for example. The reverse is also true. Putting an extrovert on a computer terminal will elicit the same frustration. A person who scores in the seventy-fifth percentile on the extroversion scale is best suited to a position where three-fourths of the time is spent interacting with people. An introvert with a similar score regarding introversion is best served by taking a position where 75 percent of the time is spent with things rather than people. This is how you set yourself up to succeed using a very simple example.

This example is self-evident to most people. What isn't quite as obvious is accepting a position that demands the use of the right-brain when you are left-brain dominant (85 percent of the Western world tests as left-brain dominant). For some inexplicable reason executives constantly place MBA types with a penchant for controlling everything quantitatively—"analysis paralysis" is the operative term—in positions where they can control the expenditure of marketing dollars or as product or brand managers with responsibility for releasing new products. There are many examples of huge firms not releasing technologically superior products due to financially motivated executives who don't see the market potential. The most poignant example of this was the Parc Labs' refusal to release the Macintosh to the market in the mid-1970s. They had developed this breakthrough personal computer years ahead of the industry and lost billions because they assigned the responsibility to a number-crunching executive who had to be shown there was a market for the product before he would begin manufacturing and selling it. Because Xerox (which controlled Parc Labs) had a misplaced executive, who may have been very talented in one area but was an inept entrepreneur, they lost out on a billion-dollar coup.

Similar debacles occur every day and many individuals do the same to themselves. The secret is putting the right person in the right slot; number-crunchers should crunch numbers and visionaries should pursue life's opportunities. This does not take a nuclear scientist to figure out, but for some reason businesses are often inept at assigning the right person to the right job. Assigning the responsibility for new product introductions to a financially oriented executive appears to be a mistake that any neophyte could identify but it is seldom seen in the executive suites. How could the key executives at Xerox not see that research and development product releases should not be the province of a number-cruncher? In the Xerox example, the board of directors made a disastrous decision because they allowed financial security to get in the way of logic. Would a visionary-type executive placed in that same position have released some products that would have failed? Probably! But the loss of this billion-dollar industry was a far more disastrous loss than those caused by a few mistakes. The only people who don't make mistakes are those who don't try anything new, and that is often the trend in older, myopic corporations. The irony of this example is that most boards of directors immediately recognize the foolishness of placing an inventor-type in charge of corporate budgeting but are seldom perceptive enough to notice when the opposite error is made, placing a conservative executive in charge of innovations. They never notice what is lost due to the lack of guts, only what is lost because of some aggressive decision-making.

Setting Yourself Up to Succeed!

The important message here is to refuse to allow yourself to be set up to fail. You can do so by setting yourself up to succeed. How? By recognizing that most people have been molded to feel more comfortable dealing with the details, "trees," or the big picture, "forest." There is no right or wrong in having such a predilection. It just happens that one type tends to be more security conscious and the other tends to thrive on the unknown. One allows fear to be more dominant in their decision-making process, the other allows the excitement to guide their decisions. One is best suited for structured environments, the other for unstructured ones. Placing yourself where you are best suited is critical to your success.

Another dimension of this is decision-making. Some of us prefer to make decisions rationally. Others are more comfortable with making emotionally based decisions. Again, there is no right or wrong here, only a preference for one or the other, although research shows that those who see the forest and make their decisions rationally are better suited to innovative pursuits. Those who see the trees and prefer to make emotional or feeling type decisions tend to be more suited to structured environments and often find themselves in the government, hospitals, ministries, or other bureaucratic type positions. Horace Walpole felt strongly about this. He said, "Those who feel see life as a tragedy and those who think see life as a comedy."

You need to find out if you prefer to live a structured or an unstructured life. Are you a cautious or capricious risk-taker? Do you prefer the known or the possibilities offered by the unknown? Do you prefer to make emotional or rational decisions? Until you know your preferences in these areas placing yourself in the best position to succeed will prove difficult. In other words, it is imperative for you to place yourself in a position best suited to your personality type. It is important for you to clearly understand your strengths and weaknesses, motivations and failings, and most importantly of all, how you prefer to deal with the world around you. If you are inept at spatial concepts then a job as an air traffic controller is not your thing. If you cannot stand the uncertainty of whether you will have a paycheck then you shouldn't be an entrepreneur, but if you cannot stand doing the same thing every day of your life then you had better do something that offers a lot of variety. If you are a visionary then do not allow yourself to become a desk-jockey whose success or failure depends on shuffling papers. You are only setting yourself up to fail even though the money and power may be appealing. Life is far too short to prostitute yourself for short-term expediencies.

Are You Capable of Greatness?

You are certainly capable of greatness, as long as you have a slightly above average ability to grasp new concepts and have the internal will to pursue your dreams. Charles Darwin is considered one of the great creative geniuses in history, yet he was notoriously average according to his teachers. Darwin was quite introspective and admitted in his autobiography that he was just average, saying, "I have no great quickness of apprehension or wit, which is so remarkable in some clever men" (Darwin 1958, 140). Darwin viewed this as an advantage. He believed the smartest people "seldom make the most important discoveries," which is what we have discovered with these subjects.

Even though Darwin was educated to become a minister, he ended up using his inquisitiveness and workaholic nature to revolutionize biological thought. In no way was he "gifted," in that he utilized diligence, intuitive vision and hard work, none of which are inherited, to change the world. The father of evolution was a rebellious personality willing to risk ridicule by his family and friends and expulsion from the church for his work. His innate inquisitiveness first led him to the ship *Beagle* and then to the Galapagos Islands. His observations there of finches then led him to concoct the theories of natural selection.

Thomas Edison and Walt Disney were even "more average" than Darwin. Edison had but three months of formal education and some people even suggest that he had less than an average IQ. But the "Wizard of Menlo Park," as Edison was known, was tenacious and driven and took it upon himself to discover the truths of life and technology. When he took on any new project he would attempt to read everything ever written on the subject. Diligence alone made him into the most prolific inventor in history. He was self-made in every sense of the term. He told the media, "I didn't read books. I read the library" (Josephson 1992, 33). "Uncle Walt" Disney is another example of a self-educated man. Disney didn't graduate from high school and after one week on the job as a cartoonist he was fired for incompetence. Consequently, Disney refused to allow the word "art" to be used at Disney Studios. Why? Because he knew better than the experts that he was not in the "art" business. Disney was in the entertainment business, specifically, fantasy entertainment for children and adults trying to escape into a happier place. Both Disney and Edison were creative geniuses who altered the way the world operates.

Isadora Duncan would not have appeared to have a genetic predisposition for greatness, but she was about to change the world of dance even though she never had a dance lesson and had only attained a fifth-grade education. When August Rodin, the sculptor of *The Thinker* and one of the world's artistic geniuses met Duncan, he told the media "Isadora is the greatest woman the world has ever known." What motivated such a genius to make such a claim about a woman with little education and no socioeconomic pedigree? Easy! Duncan spent every waking hour in museums and libraries studying the arts, Greek classics, philosophy, and music. She was a self-taught amazon of learning who could converse with anyone on virtually any subject. That is what made her great.

Duncan had made her way to Europe at age nineteen on a cattleship where she actually slept with the cattle, ate little, slept less, and arrived in London "smelling like a bovine." She had an insatiable need to learn from the masters. She mimicked them and used them as role models. By selecting such larger-than-life mentors, she programmed herself to have few limits to achievement. That is what Rodin saw when she performed her "dance of freedom" which simply captivated him. It was her mastery of the knowledge of his art, Nietzschean philosophy, and the Aphrodite imagery that got his attention. She choreographed the Greek classics into a dance of Promethean creation and it swept him off his feet. How did she become so smart so quickly? By hanging out in the cultural centers of the world. Her first stop in every city she visited was the art museum or library. She knew these by heart in Chicago, New York, London, Paris, Berlin, Rome, and Athens. She taught herself to speak a number of languages including French, German, Hungarian, Russian, and Italian. Thus she grew into one of the best read women of the early twentieth century.

Duncan made her way to Athens and impulsively decided to establish her first school of dance on a hill overlooking the Acropolis, calling it her Temple of Dance. When in France, the "Mother of Modern Dance" spent countless hours at the Louvre studying the human body in an attempt to understand the nature of kinetic energy. Later she opened dance schools in Berlin, London, New York, and St. Petersburg, Russia. Dancing barefoot in a free-flowing white gown was her signature and it is easy to see how Rodin was captivated. Duncan didn't have to have doors opened for her, she kicked them open with her elegant bare feet, making her a defining example of how one can learn to be great.

What Price Glory?

The price of glory can be high, as these wunderkinds discovered. They dared to be different and it led them to the top, but the price for taking a divergent path was often greater than they had bargained for. Was the price worth the win? Few would think so, but the people discussed here were so driven they never questioned it. Napoleon, Balzac, Hitler, Hemingway, and Martin Luther King Jr. paid the ultimate price, as did Amelia Earhart and Babe Zaharias—all died long before their time. The British purportedly poisoned Napoleon when he was fifty-one and Balzac burned himself out by age fifty. Hitler committed suicide, as did Hemingway. Martin Luther King Jr. was murdered in his prime at age thirty-eight. Amelia Earhart died at age thirty-nine while making a valiant attempt to go where no one else had been. Babe Zaharias died at forty-four from too much of everything. Karl Marx died a man without a country. Michael Jordan is such an icon he cannot eat a meal without being mobbed and he often spent Thanksgiving or Christmas day alone in a hotel room when on the road. Many suffered from their excesses although the trauma was not readily apparent. Charles Darwin suffered most of his life from deep anxiety because of the guilt of his theories on evolution, which contradicted his early training as a minister. Think of the misery of living with a religious woman who abhors your life's work. Walt Disney suffered eight nervous breakdowns, and many of the other subjects discussed also had more than one. Almost half the subjects attempted suicide during some point in their frenetic life. Does this sound like the life of someone who has conquered the world? Hardly!

Most of the subjects lived a life of quiet horror and loneliness. Who would want to be a man without a country like Karl Marx, who was expelled from Germany, Belgium, and France and was forced to live in exile while creating his masterpiece *Das Kapital*. Who would have put up with the loneliness of Hughes, Tesla, and Robeson, or the vagabond existence of Maria Montessori, who was forced to live in India to escape from Mussolini and Hitler? Not many of us would want to move every five years for most of our lives like the globe-hopping James Michener. Such is the cost of being the very best and being labeled "great" and "genius."

Formal Education by Era

As strange as it may seem, subjects from the last century were far more educated than those of recent vintage. Two-thirds of the subjects from the twentieth century did not graduate from college while two-thirds of those educated in the nineteenth century did. Today we link college education with success or at least as necessary to open important doors that may lead to success. It is important to point out that the contemporary subjects made their mark in business, the arts, humanities, or entertainment without the benefit of much education. (Formal education isn't quite so critical to success in those fields.)

Although this is but a limited study, it is still very interesting to see that you can make it to the very top without the benefit of a college degree. But there is one constant. No matter how much or how little formal education, knowledge in a given discipline was critical to the success of the subjects. Even those without formal education were able to make it in a very competitive world. How did they do it? In every case they knew more than anyone else about their given field. Darwin and Agatha Christie were extremely observant and used that to conquer their worlds. Honda knew engines inside and out, Wright taught his own brand of architecture, Hughes designed airplanes, Disney invented full-length animated cartoons, and Turner has revolutionized satellite cable systems. All this proves is that a sheepskin pedigree isn't critical to the process—a lot of insight and knowledge is. Bill Gates is the definitive argument in this as he is arguably the most knowledgeable person in the world of computer science, yet only spent one semester in college.

It is interesting that there is a definite trend to this. Even the subjects from the first half of the twentieth century were more educated than those who attended school after 1950. That isn't too surprising based on the fields in which they succeeded. Of the twenty-seven subjects educated during the twentieth century, two-thirds did not graduate from college, some didn't even graduate from high school. Those include Mao Tse-tung, Agatha Christie, Frank Lloyd Wright, Isadora Duncan, Honda, Howard Hughes, and Walt Disney. Of the twentieth-century subjects who did graduate from college half held doctorates or law degrees including Einstein, Marie Curie, Paul Robeson, Margaret Mead, Margaret Thatcher, and Martin Luther King Jr.

The eleven subjects from the nineteenth century were far more formally educated. Freud, Marx, and Maria Montessori earned doctorates. Both Freud and Montessori had medical degrees but made their contributions in disciplines outside medicine—psychology and education, respectively. Darwin had a degree from Christ's Church College at Cambridge, preparing him for the pulpit, a far cry from his work in biology and his revolutionary work in evolution. Paul Robeson had a law degree from Columbia University but it was of little help in his becoming America's greatest Shakespearian actor.

Strangely, the two technological wizards of the nineteenth century, Thomas Edison and Nikola Tesla, did not graduate from college—Edison only completed three months of formal schooling. Both were inveterate readers who were largely self-taught. Edison claims to have read the whole library and Tesla would spend all night reading until his father took away his candle. The young inventor then made his own light and read through the night to find the secrets of energy. Edison told reporters, "Do you think I would have amounted to anything if I went to school? University-trained scientists only see what they are trained to look for and thus miss the great secrets of nature" (Josephson 1992, 412).

Paradoxes of Success

Most of these subjects were considered quite average during their teen years. Few were expected to have made the enormous contributions they made. No one could have predicted that Ted Turner, a billboard salesman, could have outfoxed ABC, CBS, and NBC. Every network predicted the early demise of CNN. Fred Smith's overnight package delivery system was even more shocking. No one believed it made any sense, because if it had, the U.S. Postal Service or United Parcel Service would surely have done it. Who would have believed a young Vietnam vet could revolutionize package delivery systems?

The theories of evolution, incandescent lighting, and psychoanalysis were all equally bizarre. Who would have believed such remarkable innovations would come from the fringe? These surely should have come from the minds of some astute university-trained scientist, not from observant visionaries who were not trained in the areas of their incredible breakthroughs. Other paradoxes found in this work are listed in table 6.

Table 6
Paradoxes of Innovation

Catherine the Great, Napoleon, and Hitler became rulers of world powers on the basis of nationalism yet were of a different nationality than those they ruled.

A man of the cloth concocted the theory of evolution—the most pernicious argument against the Church's most fundamental dogmas.

A medical doctor who denied her own child became the Messiah of Education.

A man who couldn't hear invented the phonograph and first sound movie camera.

A Russian immigrant with no philosophical background wrote the greatest epic philosophical novel—*Atlas Shrugged*.

A peasant farmer rose to the status of god and implemented China's Cultural Revolution.

A man kicked out of high school derived the theory of relativity, became an avid pacifist, and then advised the U.S. president to develop the atom bomb.

A man who hated art and would not hire an artist or allow the word "art" to be used at work, created Mickey Mouse, Pluto, Donald Duck, and Goofy.

A woman became the Mother of Modern Dance without ever taking a dance lesson.

A man who feared the common housefly became a daredevil test pilot.

The woman known as the Duchess of Death never met a criminal.

Nikola Tesla, a pathological recluse, was a mesmerizing speaker who could captivate hundreds for hours.

The man who claimed sex was the motive behind all behavior did not have sex after age forty.

An eighth grade dropout solved the technological mysteries of the catalytic engine.

An average-sized female outdrove 80 percent of the world's professional male golfers.

A man who claimed he couldn't write became one of the most successful authors in the 1980s.

The Keys to Greatness

Luck, personal attributes, freaky experiences, timing, and myriad other things can contribute to reaching the very top. Therefore, it is surely pompous for anyone to imply he or she has the key to such success. Deluded or not, I am convinced these subjects represent a reasonable sample of what it takes to make it through the morass and reach the top of any discipline. Studying hundreds of biographies and autobiographies was enlightening, and patterns kept emerging that demanded explanation. Many behavioral similarities that were obviously more than mere coincidence appeared. Reading about the early lives of Mao Tse-tung, Charles Darwin, Sigmund Freud, Agatha Christie, Ted Turner, and Stephen King showed that too many factors were the same to be ignored. It was not a coincidence that Napoleon, Balzac, Darwin, Tesla, Montessori, Thatcher, Murdoch, Fred Smith, Tom Monaghan, and Ted Turner were educated in boarding schools they hated. Even though they all detested the time spent in these institutions, and were lonely and anxious while there, it is important to see how they were forced to cope with an unknown environment at an early age. The experience helped mold their temperaments and the adversarial atmosphere forced these future visionaries to escape into books and other diversions. Many sought fantasy heroes to cope with their unhappy life.

Hero worship—*mythical success syndrome*—was at work here. These subjects escaped into heroes who were larger-than-life. At first I wasn't quite sure what all these coincidences meant. After more research I came across other similar coincidences. Bill Gates found a fantasy hero in Da Vinci, as did Joseph Campbell. Tom Monaghan and James Michener were caught up in the technological fantasies of Tom Swift, Isadora Duncan came to believe she was Aphrodite, and Karl Marx became so enamored of the Promethean myth he used it to begin his doctoral thesis. One of the more dramatic instances of these fantasy hero mentors comes from Stephen King, who "lived and died with *Dr. Jekyll and Mr. Hyde*, *Weird Science*, *Tales from the Crypt*, and horror movies" (Beahm 1992, 25). Anne Rice found the same inspiration from Dickens's supernatural classic *A Christmas Carol*, which she read hundreds of times.

Fantasy Hero Mentors

It was becoming increasingly obvious that something important was at work in the minds and souls of these subjects. Then I discovered Joseph Campbell and it all came together like magic. Campbell spent his life exploring myths and their impact on man. By marrying Campbell's mythological research with my findings it became obvious that something happened in the lives of young people who escaped into the fantasy world of great heroes. It appeared that these subjects identified with their heroes to such a degree that they were able to remove all limits to their own success. They were growing up to become limitless adults in the image of their mythical heroes. This will be discussed at great length in chapter 5 but suffice it to say that it has led to many of my conclusions on greatness. Campbell says it best: "All myths make heroes out of those who heed them. They are models for under-standing our life" (Moyers 1987). He had identified what I had suspected.

Frank Lloyd Wright validates many of Campbell's hypotheses. Wright was actually raised to believe he was the reincarnation of the Welsh God Taliesin. This wasn't some idle mother's rapture over an idolized son. She told him he was god and he began to believe his mother was correct. His penchant for naming his estates "Taliesin" evidences this. Wright's favorite aphorism was, "Early in life I had to choose between honest arrogance and hypocritical humility. I chose arrogance." That gives some idea what he thought of himself. His childhood included a hero worship of Aladdin and his magic lamp, but his mythical mentor was always Taliesin. It is easy to envision how he saw himself in the image of each as he made his way through life. Both fantasy images became ingrained in his psyche and he came to believe he was so special that he could live outside the bounds of ordinary men. He dressed in sartorial splendor and led the life of a man-god.

The most emotional hero worship in my research came from the founder of Motown, Berry Gordy Jr. Gordy wrote an autobiography in 1994 in which he gave credit to Joe Louis for his success. Gordy spoke of the day when he was only eight years old when Louis won the heavyweight championship of the world. Gordy describes that moment as his metamorphosis from an average person into someone special. If Louis could reach such heights, then Gordy, too, could reach them. He described that moment as inspirational and "At that moment a fire started deep inside me, a burning desire to be special."

It may help to summarize the uniqueness of these subjects prior to delving into their behavioral characteristics. A quick summary of what made them tick can be found in table 7.

Proscription for Greatness

In keeping with the great people of the world this book will define the char-acteristics of personality in the beginning rather than at the end. Frank Lloyd Wright began with the answer in marrying architecture to the envi-ronment and Einstein befuddled traditional scientists by starting with the conclusion on the theories of relativity rather than the proofs. Tesla did the same by creating the power systems that drive the engines of the world.

Table 7
Common Characteristics of the Supergreat

- All were intensely inquisitive
- Most were loners—not team players
- Most had short attention spans
- They did not get ulcers, but they gave them
- All were self-starters and prodigiously productive
- All had a philosophically motivated internal mission
- They generalized about life, but specialized the journey
- Impatience, impulsiveness, and intolerance defined them
- Every one reached the very top, but few enjoyed the journey
- Most lived in an imaginary world where fantasy ruled all decisions
- The majority believed they were special and not subject to societal rules
- All of them viewed life as a game with fame and fortune the spoils of victory
- Employees, family, and friends saw them as ticking time bombs ready to blow
- They were loved by their disciples, feared by their peers, and hated by the aristocracy

Maria Montessori reversed the process and revolutionized educational teaching methodologies by defining the system and forcing the teaching to adhere to the needs of the students.

The findings on these subjects would suggest that personality is a key factor in how successful one can become. These individuals saw the world through a unique filter and that uniqueness appears to be critical to the process. They were iconoclasts whose concepts led them to fame and fortune. Here are ten key differences between them and the so-called average person.

Attack Your Weaknesses

Many of these subjects took on their worst fears and once those were defeated everything else was a piece of cake. Our latent strengths tend to take care of themselves. It is our weaknesses we must overcome to become truly great. If you hate accounting take a class in it and become an expert— if only on paper.

Simplify the Complex

The secret of complex personalities—the nature of the creative beast—is to simplify things others see as difficult and in that way you will be seen as a guru. No one ever accused Einstein, Freud, Margaret Mead, or even Bill Gates of being simple. Their complexity proved to be their strength. And they were able to reduce the most obscure concepts into easily understood words or systems.

Syzygy Yourself!

Creative and entrepreneurial geniuses are able to successfully tap into their opposite gender, which Carl Jung labeled the syzygy—the conjunction of the male and female in the unconscious. Compassionate and intuitive women like Catherine the Great, Isadora Duncan, and Margaret Thatcher were able to become assertive risk-takers when the occasion demanded such behavior but never lost their female qualities. Conversely, risk-taking macho men like Napoleon, Ernest Hemingway, and Walt Disney were highly sensitive and intuitive.

Fear and Insecurities Should Be Motivating, Not Debilitating

The unknown and traumatic become catalysts for further achievement to the creative personality. The great thrive on not knowing and are intolerant of useless conformity. Tell them they can't and it drives them to succeed, as in the case of an aging Michael Jordan, who refused to lose in the 1998 NBA finals. Great people are not intimidated by fear, they are inspired by it.

Integrated Brain Types— Using Both Right and Left Hemispheres Simultaneously

Visionaries are able to collect data in a very deductive approach to problem resolution and then suddenly opt for a gut or intuitive solution that is quite inductive. Darwin is the consummate example of this approach in his development of the theory of natural selection in evolution as documented in his *Origin of the Species*. Freud did the same, as did Ted Turner, Marie Curie, and Maria Montessori. These people seemed to generalize about life but specialized the journey.

Childlike Inquisitiveness Bordering on Fantasy

Einstein said that he never had another truly original idea after his teen years. The ability to regress to that age where we can use our imagination without feelings of remorse is the magic of creativeness. The bizarre and arcane is the land of the innovative. We must be willing to find the pack and then go elsewhere if we are to become visionary geniuses. Pursue your professional fantasies and allow those inner myths a home.

Adaptable Personality

The eminent have an ability to change and adapt to the situation. Introverts like Ted Turner are capable of functioning as either extrovert or introvert as the situation demands. Great people seem to be more empathetic and adaptable to the needs of the moment and capable of exhibiting both traits simultaneously. No one ever did this better than the reclusive introvert Howard Hughes, who appeared before Congress to defend his Spruce Goose airplane and later came out of seclusion to challenge salacious biography by Clifford Irving.

Successful People Are in a Hurry

Many people are double-parked on the road of life—too rushed to find a parking space—but the most successful people eat, walk, talk, and think faster than most. They tend to be polyphasic—keeping many balls in the air simultaneously—they are not enervated by the pressure of managing many things at once but seem to be empowered by it. In fact, many subjects in this book were able to read a book while simultaneously listening to a conversation and a radio or TV.

Creative People Are Passionate

Enthusiasm and emotion are contagious for those around you. Passionate people attract followers even when they are deluded, such as Napoleon, Mao Tse-tung, and Hitler. Don't be afraid to express yourself even to the extreme. Great people are excessive.

The Eminent Follow Their Bliss

The great allow free expression to those inner dreams. For them all pursuits are a labor of love. If the task isn't interesting it will not light the spark within which is the source of success in any venue. You may lose everything else but if you are able to pursue your dream then you will know that you gave it your best shot when you get to the end of the trail.

CHAPTER 1

Charisma

THE GIFT OF DIVINE GRACE

"Charismatic leaders are effective because they arouse power motivation in their followers."

Jay Conger, *Charismatic Leadership* (1989)

Charismatic Power

All successful people have style, magnetism, and charm. Seductive appeal is one of their most important characteristics since it arms them with the tools for effective communications. Many would argue that charismatic power is the overriding factor in anyone's rise to fame and fortune. It certainly can open many doors, and it was the key in the ascent of both John F. Kennedy and Bill Clinton to the oval office. It was also a critical factor in the lives of the subjects studied here. Those who used their charisma most effectively were Napoleon, Hitler, Mother Teresa, and Fred Smith. In addition, this chapter will provide anecdotes on Catherine the Great, Mary Kay Ash, Oprah Winfrey, Maria Montessori, and Babe Didrickson Zaharias. Without the ability to communicate effectively one cannot sell his or her ideas, dreams, or programs.

Charisma is the weapon used by politicians to get votes, salespeople to get orders, entrepreneurs to get money, authors to get published, scientists to get grants, and entertainers to get applause. It was the basis on which Edison and Tesla received the funding to pursue their inventions. You cannot sell your ideas without it. Presidents cannot get elected or remain in office and nations are unable to enact change without it. Charisma enables religious leaders to motivate their flock. It is the methodology of all great leaders in attracting disciples to a common cause.

Examples of this power come from Picasso and others who drew great people to their side. Voltaire and Potemkin were passionately drawn to Catherine the Great and became patrons of her court. Frank Lloyd Wright and Joseph Campbell both attracted the intellectual elite. Wright entertained human consciousness guru Georgi Gurdjieff for many months and they hosted a salon for the enlightened in America. Ayn Rand wrote *The Fountainhead* as a testimony to Wright's iconoclastic genius. Campbell was friends with human consciousness guru Krishnamurti and lectured on human consciousness at Esalen (Big Sur, California) with Abraham Maslow, visited with Carl Jung in Switzerland, and socialized with John Steinbeck and Adele Davis, a health faddist. Picasso was always in the company of the intellectual elite of Europe and spent great amounts of time with Gertrude Stein, Jean Cocteau, French poet Paul Eluard, Jean-Paul Sartre, and Coco Channel. Channel claims "I was swept up by a passion for him and trembled when near him." Cocteau had a similar experience: "Picasso has a magnetic radiance and nothing seems beyond him." Stein told the media, "He has an inner fire that I am unable to resist" (Landrum 1995).

Effective Communicators

More than any other success factor, across all the disciplines, effective communication is the most important. Those unable to sell their dreams to the important people in their field are destined to fail. If you are an entrepreneur you must be able to convince the investment banking community to back you or you will never be able to launch your venture. Scientists must get university support or outside grants or they will fail. Artists must use their communications skills to gain a following for their work and sell it to the influential patrons of art. Authors must get published, and politicians must get elected or neither has a chance at the brass ring. And one only had to watch Michael Jordan in the 1998 NBA finals to see his influence on his teammates.

Interpersonal communications have always been the secret of success in the humanitarian, political, and religious fields. Martin Luther King Jr. and Mother Teresa used their charisma to open important doors without which they would have remained followers rather than the great leaders they became. Neither would have won the Nobel Peace Prize without this power. The same talents were at the bottom of the power of Jesus, Mohammed, Buddha, and Gandhi. They attracted millions of faithful disciples through the art of communication.

Magnetic charm was the internal power behind the influence of leaders Joan of Arc, Winston Churchill, and Billy Graham, as it was for their antitheses, cultists Charles Manson, Jim Jones, David Koresh, and Marshall

Applewhite. It was the power used by Mary Kay Ash to overcome male chauvinism; Fred Smith to revolutionize overnight package delivery; and is the reason Saddam Hussein still holds power in Iraq. It was the secret weapon used by Nelson Mandela to destroy Apartheid in South Africa. Charismatic power was the energy that created the business empires of Howard Hughes and Berry Gordy Jr.; and was used by authors Honoré de Balzac and Fyodor Dostoevsky to stay out of debtor's prison. Charm allowed Maria Montessori to sell her educational system around the world and without Golda Meir's charisma, Israel would now be an Arab state.

Political leaders must communicate effectively. They will remain unknowns if they are unable to effectively articulate their ideology to those who will back them and help them get votes. Without his seductive appeal Napoleon would never have been able to motivate his troops to fight against insurmountable odds, which is what ultimately led him to take over power in France. Without his allure Hitler would never have risen to the top of the Nazi party, and without her special aura Mother Teresa could never have convinced the Roman Catholic Church to establish a new religious order in some remote, non-Catholic land. Motivation via the spoken word was a weapon these people used often and well. Oprah Winfrey is a more recent example of this power at work. She is so effective that the National Cattlemen's Beef Association filed a $10 million dollar lawsuit against her in early 1998 because people stopped eating beef after one of her programs exposed the abuses committed by the meat-packing industry. She was not demeaning beef but discussing the topical subject of the potential for disease, but her power is such that she impacted the beef industry. If Oprah invites an author to be on her show or designates a book to be an Oprah's Book Club™ pick, the sales jump, averaging 150,000 books. The average book only sells around 4,000 copies without such media exposure (Cohen 1990).

What is Charisma?

Charisma is the ability to persuade, influence, and inspire through personal interaction—usually through the spoken word. Some cult leaders have gone to extremes using sex, drugs, and other devices, but the subjects included here got to the top through effective articulation of their dreams. Charisma is not just words, although they are often the most obvious demonstration of this quality. Hitler very carefully selected psychologically powerful words to fit his brand of fire and brimstone rhetoric. A great deal of the magic of the charismatic lies in the marriage of body language, powerful words, facial expression, and emotionally generated enthusiasm. True charismatics find their power internally not externally. They are able to combine their ideology with passion, style, confidence, and an enthusiastic delivery. Verbalizing isn't always necessary when the audience is small. Effective use of eyes, facial expressions, and other kinds of body language can communicate your ideas.

One definition of charisma is "spiritual gift," but that definition has now been overthrown since charisma isn't necessarily innate. Psychologists now know that you can learn to be charismatic. Hitler is the best example in this book of someone who was manic but not effective until Dietrich Eckart, a highly educated anti-Semitic German, took it upon himself to make him into a charismatic speaker.

Many of great people were very effective speakers but they weren't necessarily aware of the derivation of their power. They knew they had it, but didn't know it emanated from their internal drive and passionate interest that communicated extreme self-confidence to their followers. Quotes from Isadora Duncan indicate how closely she tied her inner self with her external expression of that power. The "Barefoot Contessa" described her inner vision as an emotional appeal that expressed itself externally in her dance:

> When dancing I feel the presence of a mighty power within me which listens to music and then reaches out through all my body, trying to find an outlet for this listening. Sometimes this power grew furious, sometimes it raged and shook me until my heart nearly burst with passion. . . . This is the Spiritual Vision, not the brain's mirror, but the soul's, and from this vision I could express dance. (Duncan 1927, 224)

Joseph Campbell labeled this internal feeling an "Inner Vision of One" or "Life Energy." He said, "Myths are reflections of the inner being and necessary for optimum external expression." He believed our internal visions or myths would lead us to the sublime or toward an "epiphany state of emotional exultation" (Moyers 1995). Mother Teresa had this inner power that she believed came from God.

Those who have *it* know they do and take advantage of their special power to attract followers to their cause. They immediately move to center stage in any venue or they leave. The awesome ego needed to fuel the charismatic makes him appear arrogant but the manifestation appears different relative to the discipline. Mother Teresa's power was spiritual, but for Maria Callas it was an on-stage persona and for Fred Smith it was the glory of Federal Express. For Golda Meir it was Zionism as a life goal. And for Mary Kay Ash it was being a part of a "woman's-way company."

A friend said of Margaret Mead, "The sex appeal of that mind of hers was absolutely captivating." What was she saying? That she was enthralled and energized by person capable of articulating her special kind of charismatic power. Mead's second husband described her as "life force incarnate." When a highly talented young man of thirty met her in 1973 he said "If she had pointed at me and said, YOU! You're the one I choose! Come off with me. I would have gone with her. Anywhere" (Howard 1984).

Psychic Energy

People like Margaret Mead emit an aura that comes from the psychic energy of an omnipotent inner-belief system. They have presence and an inner knowledge that transcends the pack. They believe they have some special endowment that allows them to live outside societal rules. When you come in contact with such a person that air of omnipotence is transmitted as a force field of energy. Charismatic people have presence! They know it, and you know it. The knowledge transmits a message, "I *know* the path or way, and that inner confidence empowers the listener.

The charismatic has enormous energy and that in itself proves contagious. When they speak others listen because their words and body language both imply "*speak to me and I will empower you*." Such inner confidence borders on overconfidence and sometimes turns disciples. Those drawn closer, however, into that inner web are often in search of an omniscient role model or mentor to lead them out of some personal morass. Personal magnetism attracts the weak and indigent as well as masses of followers looking for a strong leader to emulate. The followers are energized since they suddenly feel good, have a leader and a purpose to pursue, and a dream to contemplate. It gives them a reason for being in addition to a passion for living.

Omniscience or Egomania

In psychological terms, charisma is the external manifestation of an omnipotent internal belief system. Those who have it are capable of transcending normal barriers because they believe they have been endowed with a special calling or knowledge, even when that belief is deluded. They believe to such a degree that disciples will follow them anywhere, even to their deaths. Consider the nine hundred People's Temple followers who drank cyanide-laced Kool-Aid in Guyana because Jim Jones gave the order, or the Branch Davidians in Waco, Texas, who burned alive because David Koresh told them it was the only way to salvation. That debacle was soon followed by the Heaven's Gate tragedy in San Diego. In this case, a terminally ill charismatic leader, Marshall Applewhite, convinced thirty-nine young, healthy computer techies to join him in suicide.

Impassioned charismatics, like military leaders, often become carried away with their power. Many are megalomaniacs on a mission of personal aggrandizement or egomania. Both Napoleon and Hitler are examples of men who used personal charm to gain power with the intent of feeding their own egos and pursuing their own selfish ends. Napoleon loved to say, "power is my mistress." What was he really saying? That he needed the power for ego gratification and not to achieve noble goals.

Both Napoleon and Hitler were intent on gratifying their internal needs. Their constituency was a distant second to their own need for glory. Both men deftly hid their true motives until they were about to go down in flames. Napoleon finally admitted, "If I lose my throne, I will bury the world beneath my ruins" (Hershman and Lieb 1994, 177). Hitler had a similar motive, as demonstrated by the insidious statement, "I have to gain immortality, even if the whole German nation perishes" (Hershman and Lieb 1994). These diabolical men accomplished the impossible through charismatic power and conquered major powers on the basis of nationalism even though neither was of that nationality (Napoleon was descended from an Italian family living on the island of Corsica, a French department; Hitler was Austrian). How is that for the power of speech?

How did these two dictators achieve such success? Charisma was both men's strength but both men adroitly adopted a platform for the masses to endorse. Napoleon preceded Machiavelli in saying that he had to beat the Prussians and British or they would take over France. Hitler's task was easier. He told the people he would end the out-of-control inflation caused by the Great Depression, and stop the Red Menace from the East. He did what he said but failed to tell the people that he would accomplish these goals through a military build-up. Creating a common enemy to hate is the standard ploy of cultists and dictators. They must invent someone or something to hate in order to ally the masses with their cause. Once the masses buy into their fearmongering, the charismatic postures himself as the savior. Hitler told the German people, "I will fight to the death to defend the fatherland against this menace [Communism]" (Landrum 1995).

Both Napoleon and Hitler began as antisocial loners and ended as psychopaths. Both believed that destiny had sent them as omniscient messiahs to save the French and German people, respectively, from a common enemy. Both men were manic-depressives, but both were passionate in their rhetoric and were hard to deny. Napoleon wrote, "I am not like other men; the laws of morality and decorum are not for me." Hitler was even more egotistic declaring, "I never make a mistake. . . . I am superhuman, more godlike than human." (Hershman and Lieb 1994, 184) Further testimony to his egomania, Hitler forced all German youths to sign a pledge that stated, "I consecrate my life to Hitler; I am ready to die for Hitler, my savior" (Hershman and Lieb 1994, 184)." Alfred Rosenberg, a German supporter, said, "Hitler had a fanatical belief in his own mission which became incomprehensible." (Landrum 1995).

These two megalomaniacs convinced themselves they were gods and above the conduct of ordinary men. Their dementia, when packaged in emotional dialogue, attracted disciples by the droves. Passion was their weapon and they used fear and scare tactics to gain support, frightening the masses with the loss of their freedoms in order to control them. The irony is that both men ruled with an iron fist once in control and the people who gave them power to insure their freedom actually lost it. Napoleon's domination led to the Napoleonic Code and Hitler's to the Final Solution. Both men had a unique talent for attracting the masses and most would follow them blindly—many did, to their death. Most of their opposition came from above and their support from below.

Passion Sells

The power of charisma emanates from the energy of a driven personality. A number of the charismatic subjects in this book were manic-depressive, including Napoleon, Hitler, Tesla, Hemingway, and Picasso. Even those not bipolar were hyperactive, including Mark Twain, Dostoevsky, Isadora Duncan, Margaret Mead, and Mother Teresa. When up these people were ebullient and often euphoric in their communications. Grandiosity, expansiveness, and expanded self-esteem are all features of the hypomanic personality. No wonder these people were able to motivate and excite others.

Charismatics paint vivid word pictures that tend to raise the adrenaline in their followers. Enthusiasm and passion is their forte. They inspire others to take action and their delivery is electric. Most have a unique ability to select just the right words and deliver them eloquently and in a timely fashion.

Hitler found that passionate words could move audiences more than indifferent ones. He selected simple but powerful words to communicate his message, words like "force," "hatred," "ruthless," "smash," and "drive." A German worker hearing him speak told a biographer, "I felt I had come face to face with God. . . . The intense will of the man seemed to flow from him into me." Rudolph Hess, Hitler's confidant and ghost writer of *Mein Kampf*, told the British, "Hitler held the masses and me under a hypnotic spell." Hitler was a master of imagery and worked a crowd like a show business veteran, telling stories with metaphors and emotional endings. The characteristics embodied in Hitler and other charismatics are listed in table 8.

Table 8
Characteristics of a Charismatic

- Awesome self-esteem and self confidence
- Indomitable will and conviction of the rightness of their ideas
- Superman-type energy and enthusiasm
- Hyper-expressive
- Highly articulate
- Image-conscious egomaniacs

How Do You Get it?

You can't get charisma if you don't get charisma. Sounds like a play on words, but it is not. It is a fact that all people who have charisma have a cause or some great mission in life that so energizes them they cannot stifle their enthusiasm. And enthusiasm usually leads to articulate communication. If you don't have something to be excited about then it is difficult to get excited. You must find something you believe in more than anything in the world and then work at gaining expertise in that product, service, or idea. When you start communicating with some stranger about that product or idea you will find you are an extremely effective communicator, in fact, far better than average. Think about when you get mad. Angry people communicate very effectively and with passion. The internal energy when one is mad is that same energy found in a charismatic leader. It must come from within and you must believe to the point of delusion. People who believe are convincing and exciting to be around even if you don't agree with their take on life. If nothing else, they can be very entertaining. Vast amounts of data in drive theory show that "arousal" enhances effectiveness in all venues up to a certain point after which effectiveness drops off.

The result is a deep-seated ardor that energizes your whole system. You can see it in the eyes, muscles, and body language, and hear it in the voice. Anyone who has ever seen a movie clip of Hitler making one of his impassioned speeches will see that he believed in what he was saying, and even though he was deluded, he was awe-inspiring. I used to watch a brilliant engineer speak who was extremely charismatic. He was known for his mesmerizing delivery. When he spoke on a subject that I knew nothing about I sat in wonderment and rapture and soaked up every word. Others in the audience were equally impressed. When this electronics expert spoke on a subject of which I was an expert, and I knew he was mistaken in his claims, I would look around and see people with their mouths open listening to his eloquent delivery. That is when I discovered the secret of the cult leaders and evangelists famous for indoctrinating people in order to take advantage of them via propaganda.

In the past twenty years psychologists have demonstrated that charisma can be learned and that a person can be groomed to become a charismatic leader. Dr. Laura Rose, an Atlanta psychologist, writes, "It is that individual quality that allows an individual to empower themselves [sic] and others. . . . I think it exists in all people to some extent." She says everyone has the innate power to attract, motivate, and inspire others and that it is present in most people, but not acted upon. (Buffington 1990, 103).

Nikola Tesla had a similar affect on people. Julian Hawthorne, son of Nathaniel Hawthorne, wrote in the *New York Times*, "When this titan spoke one could grasp the future in his face. His psychic energy was awesome. He was ethereal brilliance." Elise Barrett said of her mentor, Maria Montessori, "When she was around there was nothing else in the room. To us she was God" (Landrum 1995, 165).

Mother Teresa believed her awesome attraction was a gift from god. This saintly woman was able to walk into a room of strangers and command complete silence merely by her presence. She was armed with that internal power of belief which she believed had been given to her by Christ, who had told her to go out among the poor and do God's work. Testimony to this woman's extraordinary powers of persuasion came in early 1950 when she convinced the pope to authorize a special religious order to be known as the Sisters of Charity, which ultimately became the Missionaries of Charity. It is truly amazing she was able to convince the pope to establish her "Pontifical Congregation" reporting directly to the Holy Father in Rome because the Roman Catholic Church changes very slowly. This diminutive powerhouse had stepped into a phone booth in the habit of Sister Agnes Bejaxhiu and came out in sari and sandals as Mother Teresa, a woman in charge of her own destiny. Her mesmerizing and charismatic nature emanates from within in what she calls a lack of "rage" and "indignation," both of which cause one to become immersed in the moment and removed from the essence. Essence is the battleground of charisma and Mother Teresa was the living testimony of someone with no power possessing absolute power.

Self-Esteem & Charismatic Power

Self-confidence is critical to the charismatic. And of course self-confidence is a function of self-esteem—a personal belief that you are worthy of great things. A strong sense of self is critically important to charisma. No one will follow you unless you know where you are going (or at least act as if you do) and believe in your own destiny. An intractable and intransigent belief system is critical to the process. Latch onto that one dream for which you are willing to sacrifice everything and then you will have mastered the first step of charisma. If you believe the world will follow you anywhere so it is imperative that you remove all doubt and begin your conquest of self before you strike out in a conquest of others. No one can be charismatic without being passionate and passion is born of belief and knowledge. That belief then transforms you and enthusiasm follows. Soon after you will find disciples buying into your dream.

Introspection & Charisma

Charisma emanates from within the personal unconscious of each of us. That is why such an inner force is necessary for each of us to tap into our natural passion for life. In other words, charisma cannot be externalized without having first been internalized. We must have an inner knowing before we can lead others or tap into our charismatic power. We must become self-confident and self-actualized or at least appear to be. All charismatics appear to have their act together even if they don't, which is why the old adage, "fake it until you make it" is an appropriate methodology for becoming charismatic. An indomitable internal belief system is critical to the process.

Believing oneself to be omnipotent is only an externalized view of an internal belief system. The great charismatics of the world, even when deluded, never doubted their right to lead. Conning oneself can often become a catalyst for self-transformation. For example, Oprah emulated Barbara Walters in those early years when she had no confidence in her own ability. Now that she has overcome her inner doubts she doesn't have to emulate anyone, but until she had confidence, the self-delusion was critical to her success. The same thing happened in a different way to Estée Lauder. She refused to admit to her true heritage—that she was born in a Queens ghetto and was not of royal lineage—and lied about it in her autobiography. The beautiful thing about it is that she actually became the person she portrayed to the world.

We live out our internal self-images and therefore, to become a visionary leader, one must see the vision internally before he or she can inspire others to pursue that same vision. We must first believe and then that belief can be realized. In other words, becoming is a function of believing. That is why introspection is so critical to becoming charismatic. If you aren't sure you should be captaining your ship, no one is going to buy a ticket. Convince yourself first and only then will you be able to convince others.

What is that internal energy that is so obvious in the charismatic? It is what Carl Jung labeled psychic energy. He believed psychic energy to be a powerful inner force that manifested itself as our persona. Charismatic leaders are capable of tapping into that inner energy and using it to move mountains. They are masters of their fate because they are masters of their own inner self. The world's followers "lack" this ability.

Most of these preeminent overachievers had a strong inner drive that allowed them to motivate and inspire others. They were self-actualized and never allowed anything or anyone to interfere with their goals. In researching Mother Teresa I spoke to a Florida schoolteacher, Jeanne Nealon, who had met the great lady in Cleveland, Ohio. Nealon brushed against Mother Teresa's habit and experienced what she described as a "scintillating sensation that shook me to my soul." Nealon described the experience as ethereal and metaphysical. When the great woman walked into the room Nealon said, "I froze and felt a tingling sensation in my body. I went into a kind of trance-like state. It scared me."

Public Relations Gurus

The great people in this book were marketing experts who had some intuitive sense of self-promotion that is often lost on bureaucratic leaders. *Life*
magazine wrote in mid-century that "Helena Rubinstein's greatest promotion is undoubtedly herself." The "First Lady of Beauty" knew that image was
everything and the media was the vehicle to gain that all-important image.
You can create the greatest painting, write the best book, build the best
product, or have the best credentials for president, but if you are unable to
communicate those qualities to your target audience you will fail. Early in
his career Balzac said, "There is no point in knowing how to write without
knowing how to talk and talk at great length, talk volumes, in a word, in
order to attract a buyer" (Robb 1994, 108). He then went out and acquired
a printing and publishing company. He constantly badgered the newspapers
to serialize his books, and was the first writer to exploit this medium. He was
clearly ahead of his time but was right on target which these other subjects
would learn.

The subjects in this book were great promoters, one reason they became
rich and famous. Creating a great concept and not getting recognition is tan-
tamount to having not made the breakthrough at all. These subjects recognized they had to promote or perish and publicity was usually their vehicle
to the masses. Samuel Clemens became Mark Twain because of this. He was
writing such caustic material he was afraid of getting shot and took the pseudonym that he ultimately made famous. Later he would write articles under
assumed names and submit them to the media in order to get coverage for
his books. One article he wrote as a hoax was picked up and reprinted on his
book *Innocents Abroad* (1870). He referred to "The insolence, the impertinence, the presumption, the mendacity, the majestic ignorance of the
author," hoping that the papers would only print the good material. They
printed it all and it cost him dearly since the article was syndicated and
Twain had to spend huge sums attempting to prove it was a farce.

Thomas Edison probably was the most skilled at using the press as his
personal messenger. He was extremely adept at fueling the media's need for
sensational new material. The Wizard of Menlo Park would get a new idea
and call a press conference and announce he was close to solving the mystery of this great new technological breakthrough. The truth was he hadn't
even begun to think about it, but his strategy succeeded in two important
things: It attracted venture capital and forced him to work diligently or
appear incompetent to the media. The result is Edison became the best
known scientist in history before Einstein. The reclusive Nikola Tesla did
not promote himself nearly so well and died in anonymity while the ebullient Edison became a legend because he was constantly on the front page of
the *New York Times*.

Amelia Earhart was made into a living icon in much the same way. Much of her notoriety arose from the greed of her publicist husband. Every major air record she attempted to break was preplanned, with a book or other news story in the works. Without George Putnam, who made a living off hyping her every move, Earhart would have been just another adventuresome daredevil living ahead of her time. Putnam urged her, and at times forced her, to attempt to break a record because her image was on the wane.

Howard Hughes was a dashing charismatic who was also a master at controlling the press to fit his own vision of reality and to protect his image. He learned early that image was everything in the fantasyland of Hollywood. He had money and that was power to influence the press. Numerous sources, most recently the FBI, indicate that he paid off senators, FDR's son, Nixon's brother and that he was actually instrumental in the Bay of Pigs operation in Kennedy's administration, hiring the key individuals and financing the operation (see Landrum 1995). Hughes's most notorious publicity move came after Hollywood censored his movie *The Outlaw*, starring Jane Russell. The movie had been banned in many cities for a blatant display of cleavage from a bra Hughes had personally designed to be provocative. Hughes ignored the censorship set up a media circus including balloonists and billboards, and he put the film in lights in defiance of the law. The hype and controversy made the film more successful than it would have been otherwise. His ploy worked since the box office success caused a San Francisco, California, judge to rule "there is nothing wrong with breasts."

Hughes carefully protected his eccentric lifestyle by buying off the gossip columnists. He made sure Louella Parsons and Hedda Hopper flew first class anywhere in the world on TWA, which he owned. Even if there wasn't a plane available he made one available for them and they never paid. Most people were mesmerized by his Spruce Goose—the plywood plane that was, and still is, the largest ever built. Even his own executives weren't aware that he saw it as nothing but a gigantic publicity stunt to get the Air Force to award Hughes Aircraft contracts. It worked and his company became the leader in satellite electronic component production for many years. Hughes was able to manipulate the media to his own ends and often the product turned out to be himself.

Author Leonard J. Leff wrote a 1998 biography on Ernest Hemingway with the subtitle "The Marketing of Hemingway." Leff concluded, "without all the publicity surrounding the man and his literature, he might have been just another obscure author." Singer Madonna has the same penchant for using the press to promote. She self-published her book *Sex* and the movie *Truth & Dare* as a tongue-in-cheek publicity stunt. The Material Girl knew perversity and provocative behavior sells and used the media in a very intelligent way to poke fun at what she considered to be a society stuck on archaic Victorian standards.

No one in recent times has had the market influence of athlete Michael Jordan. He was a marketer's dream, virtually creating the sports video market. His movie *Space Jam* grossed $230 million but his status as the $10 billion dollar man as reported by *Fortune* (June 22, 1998) is mind boggling. The magazine estimated that Jordan's presence as an NBA icon had pumped $10 billion into the 1998 economy. The 1998 TV ratings were the highest in history due to his spectacular play with game six of the NBA playoffs against the Utah Jazz viewed by 65 million people—the most for any college or pro basketball game in history.

Historical Examples of Charismatic Power

Jay Conger wrote in *Charismatic Leadership* (1989), "Charismatic leaders have always personified the forces of change, unconventionality, vision, and an entrepreneurial spirit." That statement was never truer than in the lives of world's great leaders. Let's review some of the ways the subjects selected here changed the world through the art of charismatic power.

The majority of the subjects were charming and could open doors through their presence. For example, Nelson Mandela was described by his friend Bishop Desmond Tutu as "regal and quite simply a giant of a man." His biographer Mary Benson says, "He is electrifying, a passionate man with a great zest for life."

In contrast, Babe Didrickson Zaharias wasn't described as elegantly charismatic, but she had that special sense of the moment. When she was playing a major golf tournament with a large gallery and her drive would slice into the rough, she would smile, look at the crowd and say, "There must be some scotch in those woods."

Napoleon Bonaparte

The Little Corsican was an enigma, a diminutive man who was five feet, two inches tall but had a huge ego. He was able to mesmerize friend or foe. After he had been captured and interned on the island of Elba he showed the charismatic power that defined his rise from obscurity to the most powerful man in the world. He had been on the island for ninety days when he became bored and decided to regain his throne. On March 1, 1815, Napoleon returned to France with one thousand of the men who had also been imprisoned on the island. The force had commandeered a ship in Elba's harbor and made their way to Paris. The intrepid warrior landed at Antibe, in southern France, with virtually no chance of success. Although the French army had remained loyal to Napoleon, and many Frenchmen also thought they'd be better off under his rule, he faced the forces of King Louis

XVIII, who was backed by every European nation—including Britain and Prussia.

Alarmed at Napoleon's audacity, the French king chose General Ney, one of Napoleon's archenemies, to stop him. Ney had served under Napoleon in the infamous Russian campaign (1812). Ney left Paris with a regiment with instructions to take Napoleon prisoner or kill him. The two met at Grenoble. Napoleon knew that force could not win this battle so he walked, unarmed, into Ney's encampment, shouted with grandiosity, "Kill your emperor if you wish or follow me to Paris." Ney was shocked at the impertinence of this man who had nothing but courage and pluck, and ordered him to surrender immediately. Napoleon refused and began walking among Ney's armed troops imploring them to join him on his march to Paris. Ney told the soldiers to take him prisoner. No one moved and Napoleon didn't stop acting as if he were in charge. Then the soldiers burst out "Vive L'Empereur!" and joined Napoleon in his impetuous march on Paris to reclaim his throne. Later, in exile in St. Helena, Napoleon would write, "Before Grenoble I was an adventurer; at Grenoble I was a reigning prince." Balzac would later write of the episode, "Before him did ever a man gain an empire simply by showing his hat?" (Landrum 1995, 132).

Napoleon was a notorious optimist who rose to power through sheer force of will. He was a Corsican who had risen quickly due to the loss of military leaders after the French Revolution. He was a manic-depressive who, when up, had "superhuman energy." His valet said "He had the energy of a whirlwind," and one anecdote describes how he rode across Europe in a mad dash that killed five horses—not stopping to eat or sleep and not even showing any ill effects. It was not uncommon for him to dictate to five secretaries on different subjects at the same time. But his most important trait was his ability to motivate his men to Herculean effort. This was never so apparent as in 1796 at the battle of Lodi (Italy) when he was twenty-four. The Austrians and Italians had a combined force of 70,000 men against his 30,000. Napoleon was a titan that day and urged his men to follow him as he won the day. That was the day that transformed him into a person destined for greatness. He went back to his tent after the resounding victory and wrote, "I am a great being and will one day be great" (Landrum 1995, 128). Within four years he was First Consul of France and within six he was crowned emperor after having conquered most of Europe and Egypt.

Adolph Hitler

One of Adolf Hitler's biographers wrote, "When he spoke men groaned and hissed; women sobbed involuntarily caught up in the spell of powerful emotions" (Landrum 1995). A young German who attended one of Hitler's speeches even though he disagreed with Hitler's political ideology wrote:

I forgot everything but the man, then glancing around, I saw that his magnetism was holding thousands as I. Of course I was ripe for this experience . . . weary of disillusionment, a wanderer seeking a cause, a patriot without a channel for his patriotism, a yearner after the heroic without a hero. The intense will of the man, the passion of his sincerity seemed to flow from him into me. I experienced an exultation that could be likened only to a religious conversion. . . . I knew my search was ended. I had found myself, my leader, my cause. (Hershman and Lieb 1994, 149)

Hitler had promised to stop the terrible inflation that had beset Germany and to improve the economy, which, like the rest of Europe, was experiencing the Great Depression, which he blamed on the Jews. Then he found, another even more appealing scapegoat—the Red Menace of Communism from the East. He used these two—communism and the Depression—as enemies of the German Republic to rally the people to his cause. During those early days many people forget Hitler was seen as a potential savior and was the *Time* magazine Man of the Year in the mid-1930s. He had solved Germany's unemployment, inflation, and basic insecurities. He had a good plan, a willing electorate, and the power of charisma and that catapulted him to the leadership of a major nation.

Hitler had never held a legitimate job until he took over the National Socialist party. How did he make such a transformation in just a few years? A German intellectual by the name of Dietrich Eckart became his mentor. Eckart decided to teach Hitler to be charismatic and spent four years grooming him to become a great orator. Eckart was a German mystic and intellectual who knew he was dying and latched onto Hitler as a protégé with the despotic potential to perpetuate his influence. Eckart taught Hitler to speak with passion and to incite people through the spoken word. Eckart headed a human potential movement known as Thulism that used mind-control techniques to motivate and incite racist-oriented followers. Thulists believed in a Master Race that had been destroyed along with the lost continent of Atlantis. Eckart was determined to revive it through Aryan supremacy in a Third Reich in Germany. This mystical movement bordered on black magic and appealed to Hitler's anti-Semitism. Four years later, in 1923, Eckart wrote to a friend, "Follow Hitler! He will dance, but it will be to my tune. We have given him the means of maintaining contact with them (the Masters). Don't grieve for me. I have influenced history more than any other German" (Scwarzwaller 1989).

Hitler biographer George Stein wrote, "He had the magnetism of a hypnotist" (1968, 568) and a German socialite who recalled meeting Hitler exclaimed, "I simply melted away in his presence. . . . I would have done anything for him" (Stein 1968, 58). Most people agreed, and as a result forty million people who didn't fit Hitler's ideal perished.

Mother Teresa

The magnetic power of Mother Teresa, a tiny, stooped woman, was contagious. She was diminutive physically but a titan spiritually. When she spoke audiences listened and when she entered a room everyone and everything stopped. She possessed a kind of mystical power that commanded attention of even nonbelievers. Jim Castle, a forty-five-year-old management consultant, in 1981 boarded a plane in Cincinnati and wondered what was happening when total silence occurred amidst the normally frenetic boarding process. He looked up to see Mother Teresa and another nun about to become his seat companions. He said, "I finally understood the term 'aura.' " As she looked at him he said, "I felt a sense of peace as if it were a warm summer breeze."

Mother Teresa founded the Sisters of Charity religious order in September 1948 after having received an inspiration on a train on September 10, 1946. She said, "The message was quite clear. I was to leave the convent and work with the poor while living among them" (*Current Biography* 1973, 404). In 1950 Pope Pius XII allowed her to set up her own mission for the poor, and named her a special envoy of the Church reporting only to the pope himself.

The woman known as the "saint of the gutters" was one of the truly inspirational women in history. She lived and worked in th poorest sections of Calcutta, India, where millions of people live their life on the streets, never knowing the luxury of a bathroom or a cover under which to sleep. In this environment Mother Teresa was able to use her charismatic powers to raise millions of dollars from the rich to feed, clothe, and house the poor, including the terminally ill, who were normally left to die in the streets. She chose anonymity and a low profile but was constantly elevated into international celebrity for her daring work—the *coup de grace* being her 1979 Nobel Peace Prize. When she died on September 8, 1997, at eighty-seven, the world mourned. In acclamation the media and national leaders asked that she be granted instant sainthood, although it was refused by the Vatican. The woman who disdained power had more than anyone could imagine. She flew the world like a diplomat without so much as a bag, ate little, asked for nothing and yet had everything. That is power.

Mary Kay Ash

Mary Kay Ash built an empire on personal charisma, dash, and daring. She was the impetus behind the business, constantly motivating her sales ladies to perform beyond the call of duty. Her favorite aphorism was, "If you think you can, you can. If you think you can't, you can't." During one of Mary Kay Cosmetic's annual sales conferences in Dallas, Texas, one of the sales leaders for the cosmetics line came on stage to receive an award and became emotional just watching Mary Kay walk on stage. When the entrepreneur came close enough the woman said, "I touched her and got chills."

Mary Kay likes to say, "we fail forward to success." Her sales ladies referred to her as the "Moses" of selling due to her motivational techniques. The pink Cadillacs which top cosmetics salespeople can win became an institution within the industry. Mary Kay was once asked by a stockholder to stop frivolously giving away those Cadillacs. She decided that no stockholder was going to tell her how to run her company, and so she bought back all of the stock, making the company a private venture. What chutzpah! One of her most famous lines involves asking, "How are you?" and being told "Fine." "No," Mary Kay answers, "You're great! Fake it till you make it." Many of her sales agents strive to emulate her in speech, dress, and action.

Fred Smith

Fred Smith is the visionary entrepreneur who founded Federal Express. He is the acknowledged father of overnight package delivery, a highly complex networking matrix system that has revolutionized the parts world. Smith has been called a business evangelist. The head of the human resources department at Federal Express was quoted as saying, "If Fred Smith lined up all 13,000 Federal Express employees on the de Soto bridge in Memphis and said 'jump!' 99.9% would jump into the swift Mississippi River" (Landrum 1993, 87). Such is the emotion and power conveyed by charismatic people. They elicit passion in their followers and give them a reason to believe and a path to follow.

Smith's story is quite inspirational. He was born with a congenital bone disorder called Calve/Perthes disease. He walked on crutches for the early part of his life. His father died when he was just four but he left his son an inspirational letter imploring him to use his inheritance to further society and to avoid becoming part of the idle rich.

Smith spent his life doing just that but, after betting his total inheritance on overnight package delivery, he was close to bankruptcy for five years. Once he went to Las Vegas and bet everything he had at the time and won $36,000 to make his payroll (Landrum 1993, 91). In those dark days in the 1970s he urged his executives and employees to stay on even thought he couldn't pay them. Smith convinced many employees to work for stock and a number actually sold their watches and jewelry to help the company make payroll—quite a testimony to Smith's charisma, as well as to his employees' loyalty. One biographer said, "Federal Express is a miracle. It is one of the great entrepreneurial sagas of the twentieth century." Ex-president Art Bass says the firm's success was a direct result of Smith's "resilience and charismatic leadership" (Landrum 1993, 87).

Oprah Winfrey

The queen of daytime talk shows, Oprah Winfrey, is about as charismatic as you can get. Her special abilities have usurped race, creed, generation, and all ethnic bounds. She has that special ability to win over the most hardened criminals, rapists, machismo males, and racists. The *Washington Post* gave credence to her charismatic power when they wrote, "This phenomenon can't be reduced simply into terms like *charisma* or *star quality*. Something much more profound is going on!" However, it is her charismatic power that has made her the preeminent talk show host of the last ten years. One media projection has her becoming the first black billionaire, male or female.

Testimony to Oprah's power of speech is the 1998 court case between her and the American Beef Industry. She so influenced the purchase of meat that a group of Texas beef producers filed a major lawsuit against her. In April 1996, Oprah aired a show that focussed on the possible existence of Mad Cow Disease in the American beef supply, and said, "It has just stopped me cold from eating another burger." The sales of beef nationwide dropped off significantly as a result. Now that is power.

Oprah has had a similar influence on book sales. By naming a title as a pick of the Oprah Book Club™, book sales can jump as many as 300,000 copies in just a short period. To put that in perspective, the average book published in the United States sells about 3,000 to 5,000 copies. The media has proclaimed her as "the greatest saleswoman in television history" (Landrum 1994).

The Dark Side of Charisma—Evangelists & Cults

The dark side of charisma may have become famous due to many unscrupulous nineteenth-century evangelists and traveling snake-oil salesmen who often personified "fast talk." The prevalence of television during the late twentieth century provided a new and broader audience for such preachers. Many TV evangelists found that they could weave their web on the airwaves and collect money through the mail. Jim Bakker, Jimmy Swaggart, and Robert Tilton all abused their power by swindling millions of unsuspecting faithful out of their hard-earned money.

Many of these "negative charismatics" have appeared since the late 1960s. Televangelists can be considered tame in comparison to the likes of Charles Manson, Jim Jones, David Koresh, and Marshall Applewhite. These men employed some of the same devices to lead and destroy that others, such as Mother Teresa, used for positive ends. Manson, Jones, Koresh, and Applewhite all used spiritualism and "god" to achieve their divisive ends. There was no limit to their hypocrisy and duplicity. They preached doom and gloom, offering salvation to their followers. In each case they characterized themselves as supernatural messiahs, attempting to lure their victims by promising some mystical experience or deliverance to the Promised Land. All of the men named were responsible for the deaths of others, either their followers (many of whom committed suicide at the urging of the charismatic) or those who were murdered by the charismatic's followers.

The difference between these cultists and other extraordinary leaders lies in goals and ethics. Eminent charismatic leaders like Catherine the Great, Mother Teresa, and Martin Luther King Jr. had noble goals and ethical objectives. They used their communications skills and charisma to build and enhance, not to destroy or for personal gain.

Cultists always place personal agendas above those of their flock. Jim Jones misled his disciples into believing he was supernatural. He created an intricate spy network to con his disciples. All new candidates at his People's Temple would be hypnotized; their homes were broken into, all to validate Jones supernatural powers. He would order his henchmen to find something of a highly personal nature and bring it immediately to him so that he could shock them with his omnipotent knowledge of their personal lives. In his first meeting with a follower he would casually drop some bit of information about them in a sermon or in face-to-face conversation and they became instant converts.

Cultists typically resort to duplicity and unethical tactics to sell their programs to an unsuspecting group of weak and needy followers. They used hate tactics and brainwashing to mold their flock. Sexual encounters called interpersonal therapies are often prevalent, as is isolation, subjugation, fear, lack of food and sleep, and the threat (or promise) of Armageddon.

The motive of the cultist is to gain control of the minds, bodies, souls, and often fortunes, of their followers. One of the major themes used is to establish a common enemy whom can be hated and whom the leader can promise to destroy. The objective is always to incite followers with fear and hatred directed at someone outside the cult. Sometimes history provides that enemy. In Hitler's case it was easy. The Communist revolution was threatening to take over Europe. Russia had fallen and Italy appeared to be on the verge. The German people were not educated enough to know of his deception and voted him into power since they wanted no part of communism and desperately wanted an end to inflation and to create a better economy. Hitler's early success was an economic wonder to the people, reinforcing their patronage. What they didn't realize was that the economy had improved and jobs were created through a build-up of arms that violated the treaty that had ended World War I and set the stage for World War II. Many people around the world began to see him as a messiah or economic genius, and they were not prepared to challenge him when he began his "Final Solution" to ensure Germany's perpetual world domination.

Who follows cultists? The weak and disenfranchised, people in transition, the recently divorced, lonely students away from home, and those in trauma or in need of affiliation. In other words, the cultist seldom attracts the strong, the thinking, or self-assured individual. Cultists purposely pursue the weak and promise them membership in a group with a common identity. They promise security, camaraderie, and future happiness. These can be strong enticements for insecure people looking for nirvana or attempting to resolve some major life crisis. Freud believed followers "are striving to resolve a conflict between who they are and what they wish to become." Cultists feed on this.

The late Carl Sagan wrote in *Parade* (December 4, 1994), "All of us long for a competent, uncorrupt, charismatic leader. We will leap at the opportunity to support, to believe, to feel good. Once you give such a charlatan power over you, you almost never get it back." The allure of the charismatic is knowledge. The charismatics are seen as knowing the way to enlightenment. That is power. Manson, Jones, Koresh, and Applewhite represent the negative side of this power. The positive side is found in great leaders such as Fred Smith, Mother Teresa, and Oprah Winfrey.

The Positive Aspects of Charisma

Charisma allows people to gain converts. Mother Teresa is a prime example of someone with a noble goal who was able to convince others to join her. So is Catherine the Great, who helped finance the first encyclopedia, among other noteworthy cultural improvements. Great leaders with noble goals— those with ethical agendas—are capable of changing the world for the better. They become the transformational leaders in dynamic societies and these leaders are very important in dynamic societies.

Motivational scientist Amitai Etzioni says, "all *personal powers* like charisma are motivated by *love*." In contrast, *positional powers*—like getting elected to office as president or prime minister—are driven by *fear*, a concept to be explained shortly. Charisma is therefore a concept that has been used for personal and self-serving purposes, but is fundamentally a positive force. It is an ideal method of leading, motivating, and influencing.

Many political leaders opt for a Machiavellian approach to gaining power. They live by the philosophy, "Get them before they get you." Charismatic business, entertainment, and humanistic leaders almost always use positive methods to win. Those selling spiritualism ironically opt for a more negative use of their charismatic powers. Ethical givers use the carrot while self-serving takers opt for the stick as a motivational tool. High-Mach leaders—who believe the *ends* justify the *means*—almost always turn to fear to motivate. Low-Mach leaders utilize opportunity to motivate. The High-

Mach religious and political zealots are one of the sad commentaries on today's world.

David McClelland, in his book, *Power: The Inner Experience,* wrote, "Charismatic leaders are effective because they arouse power motivation in their followers" (1978, 7). He found that leaders desirous of influencing others must first empower them individually, make them feel better, personally empowered, prior to their becoming a powerful leader. It is apparent people prefer to follow an ethical but driven leader, which is why the aforementioned cultists and evangelists have been forced to disguise their true natures in order to maintain control.

Gender Implications of Charismatic Power

Are males or females more inclined to be charismatic? Recent research indicates women have a higher propensity for verbal acuity than men. They certainly seem to have an edge in turning heads when walking into a room with powerful men wilting when they focus on them. Margaret Mead personified this. Biographer Jane Howard (1984) said of her, "The sex appeal of that mind of hers was absolutely captivating." A very successful male thirty years her junior met her at a social gathering and commented, "If she had pointed to me and said 'YOU! You're the one I choose,' I would have gone with her. Anywhere" (Howard 1984).

Both genders have demonstrated a propensity for charismatic power both in this work and throughout history. But it was apparent to me that the men had to work harder than the women to become effective communicators. There are always exceptions to anything and both Napoleon and Hitler are in this case, but their manic tendencies seem to have contributed to their effectiveness in communicating. When in that euphoric state they were mesmerizing. But aside from these notable exceptions, the females in this work were more charismatic than the males. Why? One reason is that women learn early in life to fight verbally rather than physically. They use speech to succeed and at times to survive. Their verbalization skills probably stem from their greater use of words to persuade and to communicate. Recent studies have shown that women speak four times more words each day than males. Women on average score higher on verbal tests than males. Sharon Begley, in *Newsweek* article, explained, "Women tend to have better language skills and better intuition" (48).

Other researchers believe women are just more adept at conversation. Norman Geschwind was working on gender differences in brain hemisphere in 1987 when he discovered that testosterone in fetal environments was a key factor in why females test superior to males verbally and why men test superior on spatial relationships (See Hutchinson 1990, 179–80).

In hundreds of speeches around the United States it has become apparent that women tend to be more verbal and more comfortable with extemporaneous expression. Why is this? Because women have spent centuries talking as a survival technique while men resorted to their fists. Consequently, women became more adept at linguistic warfare while men became more proficient at physical combat. As in all things there are exceptions, as can be seen in this book in Napoleon, Mark Twain, Hitler, Joseph Campbell, and Fred Smith.

Cultural Nuances of Charisma

The best known of charismatics are often evangelists and cultists who are a by-product of the Judeo-Christian belief systems which hold that a messiah will save the world. The mysticism surrounding such a metaphysical system is fertile ground for enterprising leaders to pose as the new messiah. Asian cultures like China do not have such a prophet-oriented system. Mao Tse-tung is about the only charismatic in all of China's long history. Mao was worshiped by hundreds of millions Chinese, not as a man or an emperor, but as a god. The masses wished him a life of 10,000 years as a daily ritual.

Japan, too, has few charismatics. The Zen religion of that country seeks to attain nirvana, and in such a system charisma is not admired or pursued. In contrast, in India, charisma is associated with a religious, almost supernatural state. Mahatma Gandhi is an example of a charismatic leader.

Summary

Charismatic power is the stuff of geniuses. It made Napoleon great and allowed Hitler to alter the path of the world. It is an internally generated power lies dormant in most people, although all can access it if they learn how. It can help political leaders like Napoleon and Hitler to rise to power, artists like Picasso to sell their works, entrepreneurs like Mary Kay Ash and Fred Smith to fund their enterprises, humanitarians like Mother Teresa to open their missions, and entertainers like Oprah Winfrey to attract sponsors. All are able to draw a wide following of disciples.

Charismatics are able to open doors closed to others. They are armed with a unique power that can be used either positively or negatively. Many use it for both. Napoleon did, so did Catherine the Great and Picasso. Some, like Howard Hughes and Berry Gordy Jr., used their power to seduce. Hitler used his power for self-serving aims. Mother Teresa used her power to encourage people to help care for the poor. Psychotics like Charles Manson and Jim Jones used their magnetic charm to maim and kill. Evangelists like

Jim Bakker and Jimmy Swaggart used their communication skills to achieve mercenary objectives. David Koresh and Marshall Applewhite were misguided souls who thought they were messiahs and they used their charm to encourage mass suicide. Fred Smith used his power to revolutionize an industry while Maria Montessori, Mary Kay Ash, and Oprah Winfrey used their allure to improve the world. The only axiom in all this is that charisma is a powerful tool that can move people toward their dreams. Be sure to use it with care and diligence.

CHAPTER 2

Competitiveness

THE NEED TO WIN
AT ALL COSTS

"Chairman Mao was merciless and would destroy anyone and anything blocking his ambition."

Dr. Li Zhisui, Mao's physician (1994)

Superstars Have an Obsessive Need to Win

Thomas Edison's son spoke of his obsessively driven father as being "intensely competitive." It was obvious the son saw his competitive drive as a key element in his father's success. Research indicates that Edison was extremely well read, but not close to being an intellectual giant in concert with his title as the world's most prolific inventor (Simonton 1994). It appears he was marginally bright with an IQ ranging between 110 and 120. He certainly didn't come from money and had only three months' formal education. What was it, then, that made Edison such a successful inventor? He did not have anyone opening any doors for him and he was virtually deaf since age eleven. The Wizard of Menlo Park had two choices: compete or accept mediocrity. One hint of Edison's combative spirit comes to us from his lab notes, in which he wrote, "If there are no factories to make my inventions, I will build them. The issue is factory or death" (Josephson 1992).

Many other examples tend to validate competitive drive as an antecedent success. Olympic gold medallist and world-class athlete Mildred "Babe" Didrickson Zaharias was so competitive she once went out and bought a big fish to win a bet with her best friend. Why would a woman who had won it all have to prove herself in such a silly thing as catching the biggest fish? Whether it was fishing, bowling, or softball Babe had to win. Even playing cards for fun she had to win. She wrote in her autobiography that when playing cards with friends she had a compulsion to cheat and did so by using her opponent's eyeglasses to see the reflection of the playing cards. Now that is competitive.

Napoleon was another successful leader who was compelled to cheat rather than lose at cards or chess. The Little Corsican wrote in his memoirs from St. Helena, "From the very beginning I could not bear to be anything but first in the class." Napoleon approached life and war as a game and was unable to bear losing at anything. His wife, Josephine, confirms his obsession with winning saying, "He was unable to accept losing so much as a chess game" (Landrum 1996).

Catherine the Great had a similar compulsion and wrote in her memoirs, "I was sustained by ambition alone." It is pertinent that she was responsible for engaging war to the south in order to expand the territory of Mother Russia. She attacked the Ottoman Empire to secure a warm water outlet, one that would remain unfrozen during the long Russian winter, via the Black Sea. Crimea became the spoils won in the Russo-Ottoman war. Catherine was indomitable and it proved to be a key element in her greatness.

Others with an obsessive need to win were Karl Marx, Chairman Mao Tse-tung, and Sigmund Freud. It is a little known fact that six of Freud's protégés committed suicide due to the competitive intransigence of the father of psychoanalysis (Storr 1989). Karl Marx made his mark in the world by defying the establishment. In one introspective moment he told his wife, Jenny, "Happiness is to fight" (Berlin 1978). His fight was not physical, but was undertaken through his prosaic pen, and he was at war with a capitalistic world that had denied him the right to earn a living as a teacher because he had become a member of the radical group, the Young Hegelians. When he found a job writing for a newspaper, the establishment saw fit to have him fired. These events made him into a life-long competitive radical with the need to fight his mortal enemies with words. He wrote articles criticizing those in power and he spent his life using his only weapon—intellectual warfare—against an insidious system. The result was a new political ideology delineated in *The Communist Manifesto*.

Chairman Mao Tse-tung's physician was the first who dared tell of the competitive nature of the long-time leader of Communist China. Dr. Li Zhisui wrote a best-selling biography on the man the Chinese had worshiped for half a century as a messiah but he removed the emperor's clothes, saying, "His quixotic crusades may have killed more people than the mass exterminations of Hitler and Stalin combined" (1994, 284). Zhisui went on to speak of the 20 million souls Mao sacrificed in his Great Leap Forward during the 1959–1961 famine. The Machiavellian leader ruled 500 million people like an omniscient potentate and always justified his moves as necessary "for the people." His most memorable quote from his *Little Red Book* of communist philosophy gives some indication of his competitive nature: "Out of the end of gun comes political power." Mao's ideological view of life is testimony to his competitive spirit—he took no prisoners (Zhisui 1994, 284).

"Competitive" is not an adjective expected to be heard in any description of Pablo Picasso, but it is in fact the most accurate way to describe this combative fireball. Picasso was never content with just winning; he had to annihilate anyone in his path including his wives and mistresses. His love of bullfights was second only to his love of women and he attended to both with the same hostile fury. Biographer Arianna Huffington (1988) described the father of cubism as "worshipping strength" and "despising weakness." Picasso once described the optimal life as "fighting every day and fornicating every night." Huffington wrote, "Picasso saw his role as a painter as fashioning weapons of combat against every emotion, against nature, human nature, and God" (quoted in Landrum 1996, 170–72).

Margaret Mead was another creative genius who was competitive to a fault. Her husband, Gregory Bateson, said, "She was goal-oriented when there wasn't even a goal." He said, "She wouldn't stop and I couldn't keep up," in explaining the cause of their breakup after a volatile marriage of eight years (Howard 1984). Even the gentle Mother Teresa was competitive. Biographer Malcolm Muggeridge (1971) wrote, "I never met anyone less sentimental." Margaret Thatcher was fiercely competitive and loved to compete via verbal warfare. She earned her name "The Iron Lady" from her competitive nature. Biographer Hugo Young (1989) described her as "approaching every issue as if it were a game to be played out on a battlefield." Even the placid Oprah Winfrey told Larry King, "I am far more competitive than I ever thought I was."

When entrepreneur Rupert Murdoch was picked 1994's Most Fascinating Person by Barbara Walters, he told her, "Combat is good for the soul, and business is like war." Murdoch may be the most competitive person in this book and is certainly the most competitive businessman. Biographer William Shawcross wrote, "Murdoch always played tennis as if the future of the world hung on his winning. His life has been an endless assault on the world . . . incessantly moving, questing, searching, striving, fighting, cajoling, bullying, demanding, charming, pushing, always for more—newspapers, TV, space, power" (1993, 4). Murdoch's competitive streak is epitomized in his professional sports empire. He acquired the Los Angeles Dodgers in 1998 and immediately went after the Los Angeles Lakers and the Los Angeles Kings to show his nemesis Ted Turner that he was ready for combat even though he was approaching seventy. He was emulating his mortal enemy by vertically integrating into highly visible prime time broadcasting.

Bill Gates, Ted Turner, and Nikola Tesla have all been described as intensely competitive, and Tom Monaghan, the founder of Domino's Pizza, told me his success was a function of his "competitiveness." He wrote in his autobiography "I am determined to win, to outstrip our company's best performance and beat the competition." Business writers Tom Peters and Robert Waterman gave credence to Monaghan's competitive nature in their book *In Search of Excellence* (1982). They said, "If there were 500 Tom Monaghan's to run the Fortune 500, America's *competitive* woes would be over."

Competition—Good or Bad?

Competition makes everyone better. To a point it is a real asset, but beyond a certain level it can prove detrimental. Why does it make us better? Because without the drive to act caused by competitors we become too complacent and content. The only way to optimize any performance is to be pushed by someone. That is how we can become more than we are, to strive to be better, to reach out and improve. Unfortunately, competition is a double-edged sword. It can help us conquer the opposition but when taken too seriously it can destroy us from within. To the truly competitive spirit everything else is secondary to winning, even personal relationships—including marriage. Super-competitive individuals often destroy valued relationships rather than lose.

Research indicates we are far less effective, in any discipline, if we are not faced with some kind of opposition or adversity. Burton Klein, a Harvard professor, analyzed business as a function of competition and published his findings in *Dynamic Economics* (1977). He said "the rate of advance in an industry will depend upon the degree of competitive interaction. . . . All progress is a function of competitive rivalry and when a firm no longer faces genuine challenges it has a very small chance of remaining dynamic" (quoted in Landrum 1997a).

It has long been known that competitive games and sports relieve pent-up anxiety and aggression. Ernest Hemingway and Nelson Mandela took up boxing as a hobby to do just that and became quite proficient. Mandela wrote in his memoirs, "Boxing is egalitarian. In the ring, rank, age, color, and wealth are irrelevant" (quoted in Landrum 1997a). Berry Gordy Jr. chose boxing as a profession prior to founding Motown Records. He was competitive to a fault and fought as a professional welterweight winning ten of fifteen professional fights. When he saw the toll the ring was taking on his body, however, he abruptly quit. In the early years of Motown he turned to competition to evaluate the talent of his entertainers. He formed what he labeled "Creative Commando Teams" and pitted them against each other in The Battle of the Bands. The Supremes battled the Velvettes and then the Marvelettes competed against Martha and the Vanellas. In this way Gordy was able to judge each group and discern which ones had the most audience appeal.

Without a contest most people flounder. Competency is a function of opposition because looking over your shoulder forces you to try harder than you would if you were allowed to compete alone. Competition forces us to try harder and releases some inner energy that spurs us on to superior effort. Even problems can be motivational—without them we would not be nearly so skilled in any endeavor. Psychologists have shown that we cannot enter the "zone" or "flow" of superlative performance without intense competition. In fact, they have found that the closer the competition the better chance of optimum success. Most athletes have discovered that they get the optimum workout only when there is an optimal opponent—one that is almost identical in skill level. If the difference in skill level is too great—the opponent is either too good or too bad—then the amount of effort expended is compromised and the workout suffers. This is true in all one-on-one sports such as tennis, track and field events, racquetball, and ice-skating.

Michael Jordan has a quiet demeanor but inside he was not one to challenge. Speaking to his ability to rise up and strike down an opponent after reading some disparaging remark in a newspaper article, Jordan told a reporter during the 1998 NBA playoffs, "Unless I'm challenged you don't see that mean streak in me." Jim Croce described him best in his lyrics to "Don't Mess Around with Jim": "You don't tug on Superman's cape, you don't spit into the wind, and you never pick against Michael Jordan." USA Today writer John Feinstein defined him as "Like no other athlete we have ever seen" due to his internal drive (June 3, 1998). Why would a man exhaust himself after having won it all in the playoffs? Not only did Jordan's team win, but his earnings in 1998 were over $75 million and he surpassed Kareem Abdul Jabbar as the all-time scorer in the history of the NBA playoffs. He certainly isn't driven by the money, or the need to win more accolades. It is that competitive spirit that seems to drive Michael Jordan and all the greats, no matter the discipline.

Michael Jordan seems to epitomize the admonition of not waking the docile dragon. The smarter NBA coaches have learned not to comment on his "losing it" or getting old as that only seems to result in greater effort by Jordan. But some coaches could not resist goading him and paid the price. For example, New York Knicks coach Jeff Van Gundy told the press that Jordan was befriending his players in order to take advantage of them on the court. This so incensed Michael he buried the Knicks under a fifty-three-point barrage—twenty or so points above his average per game. The lesson: Don't mess with Superman.

No matter what you think about competition, personally or professionally, it is what makes the products you purchase better, cheaper, and easier to buy. Without Burger King or Wendy's, a McDonald's Big Mac might cost $10 and it would not be nearly as tasty. Without fare wars a flight across the United States would cost a fortune. The heated competition between American and United Airlines gave us frequent flyer programs and more flights at lower prices. We owe low prices on gasoline to competition among Shell,

Exxon, and Mobil. Without the keen rivalry in the communications industry the cost of a long distance phone call could be far more than it is. The struggle for market share among Sprint, MCI, and AT&T gives the consumer a better product at a lower price and forces the companies to give better service. If they don't, customers will turn elsewhere and the companies will bite the dust.

The Drive/Arousal Theory

"Drive" is synonymous to "arousal"—an emotionally charged state that results from a competitive nature. The quality of performance in business or sports is a direct function of the degree of arousal up to a given point, after which performance declines. This results in what sports psychologists label an inverted U-curve. What the U-curve demonstrates is that performance increases with increased arousal or drive. When that internal energy continues to increase beyond what is necessary for optimum performance it becomes counterproductive and performance declines rapidly. Why? Because the extra drive—or arousal—interferes with performance. This concept demonstrates how closely aligned the mind, body, and emotional system are. Therefore, one can argue that all Olympic medals and Pulitzer Prizes are a direct function of an optimum state of arousal. These subjects found themselves in this state of emotional, mental, and physical euphoria more often than most. They didn't stay there for long periods, since no one does, but they appeared to be able to get into this zone far more often than the average person.

In this transcendental state you find yourself optimally situated between euphoria and depression, boredom and excitement, and relaxation and anxiety. When you get there you know it and we would all like to package it and store it away for future access, but that isn't possible. Relaxation, transcendental meditation, and other mind-altering mood devices seem to help but no one has yet found the exact formula for entering and/or controlling access to that transcendent mental, physical, and mental state.

Michael Jordan is in this "zone" when he floats through the air with such ease and then dunks the ball to the roar of the crowd. It is a state of euphoria and Jordan cannot miss when he finds himself there. It is that same state you are in when you can try to hit very difficult tennis backhands or serves and they fly off your racket like you were a pro. They also occur when you are asked to make a presentation and you stand up and deliver a heart-rending speech that you hardly know happened. It is that "flow" or "zone" where you are on top of the world and feel that nothing is beyond you. Drug addicts find themselves elevated into this euphoric state, which is why they pay such a high price financially and physically for mind-altering stimulants. Mihaly Csikszentmihalyi wrote a book called *Flow* (1990) describing this state. He said, "Flow is a highly focused state of relaxed concentration that obliterates all else out of consciousness. It is the state of self-actualization or transcendental behavior that is euphoric." Athletes say they are in the "zone," religious mystics refer to it as being in "ecstasy," and artists and musicians call it "aesthetic rapture."

Competitive drive is anxiety-inducing, therefore many people have a hard time seeing optimal performance during states of anxiety. Most motivational psychologists, especially sports psychologists, agree that winning teams have the highest testosterone levels compared to losers, and tend to be far more emotionally charged. Anxiety up to a certain point is key to the process, which is why tests used to study such behavior are called "trait-anxiety" questionnaires. The preponderance of individuals in this book were Type A personalities and highly manic and therefore anxiety prone. These individuals were highly competitive and the anxiety created due to that competitive state contributed to their emotional euphoria as well as to superior performance. For them, the negative (manic) behavior was worth the benefits of winning over less-driven foes. Thelma Horn describes this in her textbook, *Advances in Sports Psychology* (1992, 131). She says a fine line exists between being "psyched-up" and "psyched-out" and that optimal performance occurs right in the middle of these two extreme states. When psyched-up she says a "positive psychic energy" is at work and when psyched-out a "negative psychic energy" is at work. The secret is for a person to operate somewhere in the middle. Horn concludes, "Drive is considered synonymous with arousal. . . . A moderate degree of tension offers the greatest advantages." A maximum potential for achievement is reached when a subject performs under "moderately stressful situations" (125).

It is important to get into this state in order to compete with someone equal in ability. If you don't, it is far harder to reach up and turn on those internal juices that make you better. Numerous studies have demonstrated that playing tennis (or any other sport) against someone much less accomplished does not make you better; instead you tend to play down to the level of your competitor. The optimal experience occurs only when you are perfectly matched against someone equally as proficient. If the competitor is too good or too bad nothing good happens mentally, emotionally, or physically. Playing against someone too accomplished is counter-motivational and you tend to give up. True competitive juices flow best when close competition exists in sports, business, the arts, or any other discipline. When competition ceases, anxiety or boredom is the result. When opponents are perfectly matched, the optimal flow of energy occurs and everyone benefits.

This state of relaxed but intense concentration is the source of all competitive success. It lies somewhere between high and low arousal and high and low stress and when you get there you feel like King Kong. When you feel it, that is the time you must throw caution to the winds and go for it, because you are capable of amazing things of which you may not ordinarily be capable. Why move with haste? Because the one truth is that flow is fleeting and will disappear as quickly as it came.

Aggressive and Machiavellian Personalities

High Machs, as Machiavellian personalities are called in the world of psychology, are people determined to defeat you before you can beat them. Any means justifies the ends in their eyes. They are the consummate competitors in business and politics. Studies have shown that High-Mach types tend to be very competitive and low-machs tend to be more submissive. High-Machs also are often Type A personalities, those with a propensity for aggressive behavior since they confuse personal worth with winning. A research study found that entrepreneurs were "competitive to a fault" and had a "killer instinct" either at work or play. One of their subjects described his feelings when competing. "It doesn't matter whom I play with. I always win. I play to win, and when the game's over it's kind of a letdown to give back the paper money" (cited in Landrum 1993).

Certain disciplines seem to attract Machiavellian types. There seem to be many politicians who have read Machiavelli's *The Prince* and lived their professional lives by its tenets ("get them before they get you"). So often they put on that holy-than-thou persona to get elected and then vote their personal safety and survival rather than follow any platform that got them elected. Type A's often fall prey to Machiavellian tendencies because they are programmed to win at all costs since they feel their self-worth depends on winning or losing.

Polyphasia: Keeping Many Balls in the Air at Once

Creative geniuses have an unusual propensity to handle many tasks simultaneously. They appear to function more effectively when overworked or when juggling many things at the same time. In computer parlance this is known as multi-tasking since such a computer can perform numerous tasks simultaneously. Psychologists refer to such behavior as being polyphasic. Regardless the label, those who have it seem to be overachievers.

Research on the subjects included here showed an unusual pattern that was consistent across disciplines. Honoré de Balzac, Agatha Christie, Mark Twain, Fyodor Dostoevsky, and Ernest Hemingway all had many books underway at the same time and they managed not to allow the multiplicity of concepts to interfere with the success of any one. Agatha Christie told one author she had seventeen plots in her head that would ultimately become books and this was at a time when she was in her sixties. She broke a record by having three plays running simultaneously in the London theatre during the mid-1950s—*Spider's Web*, *Witness for the Prosecution*, and *Mousetrap*.

Meryle Secrest called Frank Lloyd Wright a "champion juggler" who was able to "keep many balls up in the air simultaneously." Napoleon was famous for dictating to six secretaries at the same time, confusing them more than himself. Maria Montessori carried on a medical practice at night while functioning as Director of the Orthophrenic School in Rome during the day as well as lecturing and teaching. Helena Rubinstein and Rupert Murdoch functioned as CEOs of many different companies, running their many organizations autocratically, making virtually every decision. The freneticism that would bury most people seemed to energize these wunderkinds.

One typical characteristic of the aggressive superstars was the ability to watch TV, read a magazine, and hold a conversation simultaneously. Another characteristic was the insistence on scheduling far more work than was possible to complete. Thomas Edison told the media he was close to solutions to technological advances when he had just conceived the idea. These great people were impatient with associates who could not keep up and the majority were intolerant of mediocrity as well as impulsive.

Competitively Driven Subjects

The combative subjects discussed here will be Maya Angelou, Ernest Hemingway, Michael Jordan, Mao Tse-tung, Tom Monaghan, Helena Rubinstein, and Babe Didrickson Zaharias. Others in this work were equally as competitive but space considerations limit us to these examples.

Paul Robeson spent most of his life competing. He competed in athletics while in school and then he competed against bigotry and politicians for the rest of his turbulent life. Finally he came to say, "my song as my weapon," to show how he planned to fight back. Robeson worked his way through Columbia Law School playing pro football in the days when there were no facemasks and other safety equipment like today. His competitiveness came to the fore one day when his team won a game in Chicago Field against Jim Thorpe's Chicago team. Infuriated that they had lost to a team with a black man, Thorpe's players decided to teach the impertinent Robeson a lesson. Robeson's teammates left him alone on the field to fight eleven burly white football players set on revenge. Robeson had no choice but to fight for his life against the whole team. It was fortunate that *Chicago Tribune* sportswriter Grantland Rice was in the stands to witness the fight (Landrum 1997a, 328). Afterward, Rice attempted to back Robeson in a fight against Jack Dempsey, the reigning world heavyweight champion. Robeson politely declined, saying he was in school to become a lawyer.

Ernest Hemingway

John Cardinal O'Hara called Ernest Hemingway the "greatest writer since Shakespeare." The Nobel committee lauded him as the master of narration when they awarded him the Nobel Prize for Literature in 1954 after the publication of *The Old Man and the Sea*. Hemingway's story was befitting of his combative style. The author had a preoccupation with the human predicament and how to deal with it morally. He was obsessed with the life and death struggle between man's ineptitude and his quest for survival, saying "Everything kills everything else in some way." Aggression, death, and survival permeated his work, which frequently employed big guns, courageous heroes, lions, tigers, big game hunting, bullfights, and other macho imagery.

Fighting pervaded Hemingway's personal and professional life. His books and short stories focus on the hero against an adversarial world. Some were about war: *A Farewell to Arms* (1929), which described surviving in World War I; *The Fifth Column* (1937), about the Spanish Civil War; and *For Whom the Bell Tolls* (1940), about Spanish loyalists fighting for survival. In other novels, Hemingway used bullfighting as a metaphor to explore his unconscious fear of death and women: *The Sun Also Rises* (1926) and *Death in the Afternoon* (1932). Hemingway's other obsession was big game hunting and surviving against the elements in treacherous seas or jungles. This theme was pursued in his three best known short stories, *The Short Happy Life of Francis Macomber* (1935), *The Green Hills of Africa* (1935), and *The Snows of Kilimanjaro* (1936), as well as his prize-winning novel *The Old Man and the Sea* (1953).

Hemingway was a manic-depressive high testosterone personality and consequently was characterized by his competitiveness, risk-taking, high sex drive, and creativity. He began boxing in high school and used it as a release of some deep-seated need to strike out in a socially acceptable manner. At age seventeen he took on the whole football team in a boxing contest. Later he would become notorious for drunken bar fights. He also exorcised some of his competitive drives by the annual running with the bulls in Pamplona, Spain. While Hemingway was in Cuba he became a high-roller gambler, with racehorses and boxing matches his favorites. Big game hunting, boxing, competitive tennis, and alpine skiing were pursuits in which he participated because they were aggressive and exciting. He loved his assignments during both the Spanish Civil war and World War II, as they allowed him to play "Mach man" and live on the edge. A telling line from *The Old Man and the Sea* reads, "Man can be destroyed, but not defeated." The master of the short novel and short story was competitive from an early age and his drive didn't wane as he aged.

Hemingway's need to live on the edge caused him to be seriously wounded in the war, and led to near-death experiences on the sea, in auto and shooting accidents, and plane crashes. Ultimately his competitiveness proved to be his undoing. Hemingway was incapable of being less than his internal image of himself, and when he felt he was not living up to this expectation, he was incapable of dealing with it and so committed suicide.

Mao Tse-tung

Historians have labeled Chairman Mao Tse-tung of China an intellectual revolutionary due to his rapture with military theory and prosaic pen. The co-founder of Chinese Communism and the Father People's Republic of China was a combative personality who would rather destroy an enemy than capitulate. His personal physician and biographer, Dr. Li Zhisui wrote, "Mao was devoid of human feeling, and incapable of love, friendship, or warmth" (1994, 80). Li described Mao's behavior as that of a hypomanic personality who could stay awake for twenty-four to forty-eight hours at a stretch. Li said of Mao, "He was a man of tremendous energy who was happiest when he had several young women simultaneously sharing his bed" (1994). Conquest was his style in both politics and in his personal life.

Testimony to Mao's aggressiveness and need to win was the Long March that began in 1934. (The Long March was not a march at all, but was a retreat from Chiang Kai-Shek's Nationalist government and later from the Japanese invasion.) The march was not what he made it to be but it was the first sign of Mao's true tenacity. He led 30,000 young men, mostly under twenty-four, when he was in his forties, across the hinterlands of China in a 6,000-mile retreat that ended in Yenan, a remote Chinese province. It was an exercise in pillage, death, rape, and mayhem in the name of political independence. Mao wrote in his *Little Red Book* that "To rebel is justified," and the march proved him to be a man of his word.

After the war Mao led the Red Army in a takeover coup that ended in the formation of the People's Republic of China, of which he became president. After consolidating his power through force, Mao proclaimed the Great Proletarian Cultural Revolution (1966–1969), an exercise that cost his nation 20 million lives. Mao always downplayed the costs of his adventures and conquests saying, "a small number were killed" when the number may have been as high as 70,000 for a particular event. (He may have been correct in a relative sense since he headed a nation of 500 million, whom he ruled with an iron fist.)

This self-educated peasant had always turned to his mythical hero worship and vision to win the day. He was an avid swimmer and when some of his more timid companions panicked in the water he advised, "Maybe you're afraid of sinking. Don't think about it. If you don't think about it you won't sink. If you do, you will." Such a philosophical approach to life is what made him a great leader, and it was the reason he was able to survive over insurmountable odds and defeat his lifelong nemesis Chiang Kai-shek.

Mao's philosophic approach to battle and politics was borne of reading. He was a voracious reader throughout his turbulent life. At age twenty he spent six months in a library devouring book after book on the lives of great heroes from Napoleon to Peter the Great and Catherine the Great, Rousseau to Marx and Darwin. He applied his theories to a pragmatic military ideology aimed at conquest and control of the masses. The masses saw him as one of their own who had made it to the top through intellectual insight. They became faithful disciples since he was able to read and write and knew the answers to their questions. The young Mao grew into a messiah figure, a kind of cult leader, whose followers had deified him by the time he took over in 1949 as their self-appointed savior.

Helena Rubinstein

Helena Rubinstein, a dominant force in the cosmetics industry during the first half of the twentieth century, was a "tyrannical holocaust," a term coined by *Life* magazine and endorsed by her live-in lover and assistant Patrick O'Higgins. He said, "the impact of her personality was smothering. She played power games." The First Lady of Beauty described herself in much the same way, writing in her memoirs, "I drove myself relentlessly for most of my life. I am very difficult to please." O'Higgins described her as "ruling imperially, dictatorially, and making every decision" (cited in Landrum 1995, 306).

In 1938 *Vogue* called her a "four-foot ten bundle of monstrous vitality deviating from established routes." Rubinstein was the richest woman in America at mid-century and probably the richest self-made woman in the world. Her combative reputation was earned by beating enormous odds. She sold her burgeoning beauty empire in the late 1920s to Lehman Brothers, a powerful Wall Street investment banking firm. After a few months she came to dislike the way they were managing the business and began to undermine it. She became a competitive nightmare to the new owners and when she knew she was getting to them she made them an offer to buy back the firm. This uneducated, diminutive matron coerced a Wall Street firm to sell her back the business, making $7.5 million profit on the one-year transaction. This high school dropout had outmaneuvered the smartest financial men of the era through pure supreme self-confidence and drive.

Artist Salvador Dali immortalized Rubinstein in a 1943 painting that captured her essence by depicting her as a female Prometheus chained to a rock by her glittering emerald robes. What insight! The *Saturday Review* characterized her as a "human whirlwind" and voted her as one of the Ten Richest Self-Made Women in the World (Landrum 1995, 305). In 1940 *Life* magazine called her "the world's most successful businesswoman."

The competitive vitality of this woman reached its zenith when she was ninety-two. Two young thugs broke into her Manhattan penthouse intent on robbing her. It was widely known that she kept millions in jewels and paintings in her penthouse suite. The two men accosted her in her bedroom and threatened to kill her if she didn't give them the keys to her safe where, in fact, millions in jewels were stored. The old woman dropped to her knees pretending to pray giving her the time to figure out how to outfox them. Looking at her they said, "What are you doing?" "I'm praying for you," she responded while slipping the keys to the safe down her ample cleavage. "I'm an old woman," she told them, "You can kill me, but I'm not going to allow you to rob me. Now get out." Frustrated, the robbers emptied her purse, which contained $100 in cash and her diamond earrings worth $40,000, among other incidentals, on the bed. They began a frantic search of the room for the hidden safe key. In their desperation they ignored the earrings that had fallen from her purse. Then her secretary appeared in the door and fainted. Alarmed, the men took only the $100 cash and ran out, leaving millions in art and jewels. Once again Rubinstein's temerity had won out.

Maya Angelou

This self-made woman, a prize-winning poet, was aggressive and assertive to a fault. She survived because she dared to. She wrote, "You may encounter many defeats, but you must not be defeated." Angelou was the epitome of the self-made woman. She was a mother without a husband, an actress without credentials, a singer and dancer who had never had a lesson, a writer who couldn't type, and a tenured college professor who had never been in a college class until the one she taught. Now that takes some doing.

Angelou was honored to recite a poem at Bill Clinton's 1993 inauguration. She has been the recipient of the prestigious Horatio Alger Award for her rags-to-riches life. In addition, she has twelve published books, hundreds of published poems, an Emmy nomination for her role in *Roots*, fifty honorary degrees, and is fluent in six foreign languages including Arabic. She performed *Porgy & Bess* on a world tour and has written screenplays, been an actress, dancer, singer, author, and college professor.

This spirited woman is a survivor. She told the media just prior to her recitation of the inaugural poem "On the Pulse of the Morning," "You cannot cripple my spirit. It is not yours to cripple. I have nothing but my spirit and I will not allow anyone to trample on it" (Gillespie 1992). How did she acquire such resilience? She wrote, "I challenged myself to do whatever job assigned to me with intense commitment." Angelou says she owes her inner power to her mother and grandmother who taught her to "never back down to a bully."

Angelou was able to face that bully once in Harlem during the turbulent 1960s. Angelou was a single mother who had just moved to Harlem from Los Angeles. Her son Guy was a teenager and had innocently asked a girl named

Susie for a date. Susie just happened to be the girlfriend of Jerry, a notorious leader of a gang named the Savages. Jerry put out a contract on Guy for his innocent action. Angelou became alarmed when she learned that Jerry was noted for his brutality and had killed numerous innocent people. She managed to get the address of Jerry's girlfriend from Guy. She boldly walked in on the couple and walked right over to Jerry. She stared at him and pulled a pistol from her purse, engaged the hammer, and screamed at him in her deep voice. "If the Savages so much as touch my son, I will come over here and shoot Susie's grandmother first, then her mother, then I'll blow away that sweet little baby," looking directly at Susie. "You understand? I will then find your house and kill everything that moves, including the rats and cockroaches" (Angelou 1981, 74). The young hoodlum was taken aback, and looked at this fiery woman and said, "O.K. I understand. But for a mother, I must say you're one mean motherfucker."

Where did Angelou learn her fearlessness? She says from her mother, Vivian. One time they met in a "whites only" motel in the violent 1960s at the height of the race wars. Her mother insisted they go inside where they were sure to meet some terrible end. Walking into the lobby Vivian pulled a gun from her purse and dared anyone to stop them (Landrum 1997a, 116). No one did and the success imprint took on Angelou. She now attributes her success to the competitive lessons learned from her mom and her grandmother who had raised her in Arkansas.

Mildred "Babe" Didrickson Zaharias

At mid century sports journalists voted Mildred "Babe" Didrickson Zaharias the greatest female athlete of the first half of the twentieth century. "The Golden Cyclone" dominated basketball, track and field, baseball, and golf. While playing tennis socially, she beat ranking champions. Her exploits earned her the nickname "Babe" after Babe Ruth, but it also derives from her status as the baby of a large family of roughneck boys. Zaharias often attributed her success in sports to early competitions with boys, saying "I am what I am today because I had three brothers who were pretty tough" (Cayleff 1996, 39). A high school friend once said, "She could outdo all the boys." And Zaharias would only compete against boys. When she competed against girls she beat them too easily. In her thirties, a golfing friend described their social life as "making bets on everything. Competition always came in . . . and once she went out and bought a big fish rather than lose the bet." Golf pro Betty Hicks, a long-time adversary of Zaharias, said, "She ate little girls on the golf tour," giving praise to Zaharias's ability to consistently drive a golf ball over 250 yards—a feat unheard of in that era with that golf equipment. Grantland Rice, the legendary sportswriter for the *Chicago Tribune*, called Zaharias the greatest athlete of her era, male or female. He wrote, "You are looking at the most flawless section of muscle harmony of complete mental and physical coordination the world of sport has ever known." After she had set the lowest golf score ever recorded—a 258 in Tampa in 1951—a sportswriter said, "She is capable of winning everything except the Kentucky Derby" (Cayleff 1996, 62).

Competitive drive dominated Zaharias's life. It was her strength and the main ingredient in her being selected as the greatest female athlete in the first half of the century. I am convinced she is the greatest female athlete in history. Zaharias dominated every sport she ever attempted, from marbles to basketball, track and field, baseball, softball, tennis, golf, and bowling. Nothing seemed beyond her. She once hit thirteen home runs in a double-header. In golf, Zaharias holds a record that will never be broken: In the 1940s she won thirteen consecutive professional women's golf tournaments. When she contracted cancer and the doctor gave her one year to live, she left the hospital determined to beat it and won her very first golf tournament six weeks after having a colostomy. Sportswriter Tony Scurlock wrote, "She is the just the athletic marvel of this age."

When a sportswriter asked Zaharias, "Which sport do you do best?" she responded without hesitating, "I do everything best." When challenged she was incapable of backing off. A high school football player challenged her to a boxing match and she knocked him out despite her 5′ 5″ height and 120 pounds. Once at a party a macho male guest who had too much to drink began bragging that no one could throw him. Without thinking Babe grabbed the 6′ 4″, 250 pound man and threw him to the floor in one try. She was embarrassed by her instinctive action and apologized profusely afterward.

Her combative attitude made Zaharias few friends on the golf tour. She infuriated her opponents because of her obsessive need to win any athletic event she entered. Zaharias was an all-American basketball player at nineteen and an Olympic gold medalist at twenty-one. She once held six world records in track and field (javelin, high jump, high hurdles, and various sprints) and as testimony to her competitiveness once beat the field (all other competitors and teams) in a track and field meet. Babe walked into the locker room at the 1932 Amateur Athletic Union Olympic trials track meet and announced, "I'm gonna lick you all single-handed." She had asked her coach to leave her teammates home so she could take on the other teams alone, and he did. That meant she would have to compete in two sprint events, the long jump, high jump, javelin, and shot-put, among others. She lived up to her brazen prediction and won eight gold medals and set four world records. Zaharias easily defeated all the other teams with an average of twenty athletes competing against her.

Babe was a world-class athlete in twelve sports and every win was based on competitive war. She said, "It's not enough for me to play a game, I must win even at fishing or gin rummy." In 1948, when Zaharias walked into the

U.S. Open clubhouse for the first time she said, "They may as well give me the cup now, cause I'm gonna to take it," and went out and destroyed the field. Competitive drive made her hit golf balls until her hands bled. An antagonistic sports writer, Paul Gallico, wrote of her exploits, "She can do anything athletically. . . . [She is] the very paragon of Muscle Moll, but she is the greatest woman athlete in the world."

Tom Monaghan

In his autobiography, *Pizza Tiger* (1986), Tom Monaghan, the founder of Domino's Pizza, attributed his success to his competitive nature. He said, "I was the best jigsaw puzzle solver, the best ping-pong player, the best marble shooter. I stood out in every sport."

Testimony to his integrity and competitive spirit came in the early years when he lost control of Domino's after defaulting on a bank loan. He said of the time, "I had become a 'reverse millionaire.' " Tom found himself millions in debt and the bank took over his company. When they were unable to find anyone with his knowledge and talent to run the company they retained him. A year and a half later they gave the company back to him with some disclaimers since they fully expected him to file bankruptcy. He refused to be defeated and contacted every creditor and spent the next eight years paying them off. When Monaghan returned to Domino's in 1990 he told the media "I am returning to the pizza wars." One of Monaghan's aphorisms for success is "competition makes us sharper, keeps us looking for new answers and prevents us from getting complacent and thinking we know it all." To Monaghan, repaying his debts was a challenge to his integrity and it is truly fitting that within ten years he turned the company around and was able to realize a childhood dream and acquire the Detroit Tigers. Ten years after that he was a billionaire.

Another example of Monaghan's competitiveness is his exercise regimen. He is a man in his fifties, but six days a week he does forty-five minutes of floor exercises—including 150 pushups—and then he runs the six miles to his office. He then works out on the Nautilus machines for another hour before showering and beginning a day of work. Such a competitive nature is what made him great and it is still the driving force that keeps Domino's the second largest pizza chain in America.

Michael Jordan

"His Airness," Michael Jordan, is Mr. All-Universe as an athlete and is universally acclaimed by sports writers and his peers as the greatest basketball player who ever laced up sneakers. Even those outside the sport like political columnist Albert Hunt of the *Wall Street Journal* sing his praises. On May 7,

1998, Hunt wrote, "He is unsurpassed as a hard working, intense competitor and the century's greatest athlete." Hunt goes on to describe Jordan as a combination of Babe Ruth, Jim Thorpe, and Muhammad Ali, describing how he had not missed a game in five years, has not fouled out of a contest in seven, and didn't miss scoring in double figures in over twelve years. Jordan holds the highest scoring average in a season—over thirty points per game—and in the playoffs—over thirty-four points per game.

Michael Jordan is pushed to win by a competitive drive that defies description. New Jersey Nets coach John Calipari lost to the Bulls in 1998 and spoke of playing against Michael as "playing blackjack against the dealer. He ain't losing." Jordan is aware of his intense inner drive and says, "If you're not going to compete, I'm going to dominate you."

Jordan is the personification of the competitive spirit that refuses to be beaten and that mentality has made him one of the world's truly great athletes. His late father told *Newsweek*, "Michael has competition problem," just after Michael's "$2 million loss" to a golf hustler had made sports page headlines. He had actually lost $250,000 on one hole and the amount increased due to pressing (doubling the bet)—the consummate sign of a competitive spirit. Michael didn't apologize for his losses, which he could easily afford, saying, "I love to compete and it isn't the money. I just love competition. I like the challenge. If I'm going to play then I'm going to play to win" (Landrum 1997a, 230).

Competition is what makes Jordan tick. It has allowed him to win an unprecedented ten NBA scoring titles, as well as the MVP award three times for league play, twice for the playoffs, and once for the annual all-star game. Jordan has won it all and for 1997 and 1998 he was the highest paid athlete in the world with a $33 million salary plus endorsements of $45 million. That total of $78 million seems like an awesome amount of money for playing a game you love, but most of his peers in the NBA admit that he is worth every cent due to his charismatic drawing power and positive force for a game some believe beset by druggies and thugs. In June 1998 *Fortune* did a study on Jordan's influence on the economy and found that he had a $10 billion-dollar impact with $5.2 billion emanating from his Nike sneaker deal. Other products endorsed by Jordan were valued at $408 million.

Chicago Bulls owner Jerry Reinsdorf sums up the mystique of Michael Jordan: "I used to think that Michael Jordan was the Babe Ruth of basketball. I have now come to believe that Babe Ruth was the Michael Jordan of baseball." The fans have validated Jordan's approval rating by honoring him with the most all-star team votes nine times. His closest rival is Julius "Dr. J." Erving who received the most votes only three times. When Madonna was spotted at a Bulls game she was asked about her favorite players and responded, "M. J. is an amazing human. A god. If I could come back as another person, it'd be as him." NBA Commissioner David Stern told the media in mid-1998, "No one player will ever replace Michael Jordan. He is the most famous athlete of his time, and perhaps of all time." Even his mortal enemy in a basketball uniform, Isaiah Thomas, told a TV audience "He's a messiah in a red uniform." How did Jordan become so revered during his life-time? By living his dream and competing in every facet of it.

How competitive is Jordan? When a new player joins the Bulls the first thing the coaches do is take the new player aside and tell him, "Don't play cards with Michael." Most players also soon learn not to shoot hoops with him after practice. He likes to shoot from half court for $1,000 a shot. Michael told *Ebony*, "I prefer anything with competition involved. I don't care what it is—playing ping-pong, golf, cards, shooting pool, or playing bas-ketball." What caused him to be so competitive? One argument says it is because he was cut from his high school basketball team. The trauma was so devastating to him he promised himself never to go through another similar experience. Ever since that time he has hated to lose and that internal drive has made him into the greatest ever at his profession.

The Down Side of Being too Competitive

Pushy behavior can be harmful to your health according to medical research. Dominant or highly competitive individuals, those who interrupt conversa-tions and feel compelled to be the center of attention, are more prone to heart disease than others. A twenty-two-year study at Duke University looked into "social dominance" as a risk factor to health. They found those with the dominant traits associated with competitiveness were 60 percent more likely to die of all causes, particularly of heart disease.

Competitive people are intimidating to those not so driven causing them to have few friends other than other aggressive types like themselves. Michael Jordan's best friend, Charles Barkley, says, "M. J. is the only person I've ever met who is more competitive than me." Magic Johnson told ESPN in April 1998, "I thought I was the most aggressive person alive until I met Michael. If you ever beat him you better be prepared for a war. M. J. takes no prisoners." Babe Didrickson Zaharias was even more competitive than Jordan and consequently had few close friends and most of those were males. An intimate said, "she ate up little girls on the pro golf tour" because they were intimidated by her aggressive style. Zaharias was unable to turn it off and most of the pros actually rooted against her due to her arrogance.

There is a lot of data that indicates Type A behavior and competitive-ness are highly correlated. Both tend to elicit a similar response in others and not much of it is positive. Both tend to achieve at a high level but leave many bodies in their wake. Most of these subjects who were Type A+ tended to destroy any chance of happiness and lived lonely lives, dying without many friends. Examples include Napoleon, Tesla, Picasso, Zaharias, Hughes,

Hitler, Rand, and Mao. If these people were unable to control something they were inclined to destroy it and that does not make for attracting a lot of friends. Picasso was the worst offender of this insidious behavior. He said, "Every time I change wives I should burn the last one. I'd rather see a woman die any day than see her happy with someone else." That is taking competitive drive too far.

Gender Implications of Aggressiveness

Females are less likely to be competitive than men according to most studies including the Duke study mentioned above. Psychologist Mihaly Csikszentmihalyi found that "Women artists and scientists tend to be more acquisitive, self-confident and openly aggressive than other women" (1996, 71). The Duke University study found women more likely to collaborate than compete although the super successful did not behave like the typical female. Csikszentmihalyi wrote in *Psychology Today* (July 1996), "Creative and talented girls are more dominant and tough than other girls, and creative boys are more sensitive and less aggressive than their male peers."

Men and women play games differently whether it is the game of life, chess, bridge, or the club tennis championship. Men are driven to win at all costs since they view games as a contest and a test of their manhood. Consequently, men will destroy a valued relationship in order to win. In contrast, women would rather quit the game rather than jeopardize a valued relationship. To most women the game is merely part of socializing, not a war to be won or lost. That is why women seldom enjoy playing highly competitive games.

There are some notable exceptions to this generalization. Helena Rubinstein, Babe Didrickson Zaharias, and Madonna were more competitive than 90 percent of the males included in this book and probably more competitive than 99 percent of males in general. These three women were also guilty of destroying virtually every valued relationship in their life in their trek to the top. Each left hundreds of bodies in her wake. Helena Rubinstein's second husband died when she was in Europe sitting for a portrait by Picasso. She would not stop her project to return for his funeral, saying "It's too late now. What can I do?" She remained in Europe allowing others to bury him. When her son died in a car accident two years later she was again in Europe, this time on business, and repeated the same cold-hearted act once again.

Babe Zaharias always placed winning above everything else in her life including family, husband, and friends. Betty Hicks, a golf buddy, said "she would do anything to win, causing her teammates to despise her." One example of her intense need to win occurred when she was cast in a cameo role as a golfer in the movie *Pat and Mike*, starring Katharine Hepburn and

Spencer Tracy. The script called for her to lose a golf match to the leading lady. Zaharias adamantly refused to lose even in the movies, forcing the writers to rewrite the script. Such refusal to lose cost her personally even thought it carried her to the very top of the sports world. Such openly hostile aggression at sports destroyed virtually all her chances of having a long-term relationship. The sad truth was apparent when only a handful of people showed up at her funeral.

Zaharias's golf success was a direct result of her aggression. A Beaumont, Texas, sportswriter described her success on the golf tour as a function of "her aggressive, dramatic style, hitting down sharply and crisply on her iron shots like a man." Zaharias confirmed this assessment in her autobiography writing, "I played with boys rather than girls. . . . I am what I am today because I had three brothers who were pretty tough." Her biographer Susan Cayleff (1996) wrote, "the degree to which she internalized masculine traits was shocking."

Madonna had a similar predilection, but in the entertainment field. Ex-manager Camille Barbonne told the media "She seduces men like men seduce women." The Material Girl's aggressiveness led her to use and discard many managers on her way to the top. She admits that she isn't easy to work with and says, "I'm not interested in anyone I can't compete with." Needless to say she doesn't have many female friends. Virtually all of the females in this book, with the notable exception of Mary Kay Ash, Maya Angelou, and Oprah Winfrey had more male friends than females. They seemed more comfortable around men than women. A few went so far as to say that they felt they had more in common with men than with women.

Few people were as competitive or as aggressive as those profiled in this chapter. These women refused to capitulate to anyone of any gender. When Helena Rubinstein's ombudsman, Patrick O'Higgins, met the First Lady of Beauty for the first time, a European friend warned him about her aggressiveness. He took O'Higgins aside and told him, "You eat what she eats; otherwise she eats you." One of Rubenstein's most memorable acts occurred when she was trying to buy a penthouse apartment in Manhattan. When the realtor didn't respond to her offer she called and asked the reason. Embarrassed, the realtor finally admitted that the building was off limits to Jews so she was looking around to find her another penthouse apartment. The combative Rubinstein bought the building, fired the bigoted management, and moved into her penthouse.

Cultural Nuances of Competitiveness

According to the 1996 *World Competitiveness Yearbook*, the United States is the most competitive nation in the world and had been for the two years prior. The study was based on 230 different criteria including economic strength, technology, financial services, trade, government policies, management, and educational skills. Forty-six nations were compared and the United States came out on top. Asian powerhouses Singapore, Hong Kong, and Japan were the next most competitive. Switzerland and Germany ranked ninth and tenth respectively, and Britain and France nineteenth and twentieth. Russia ranked last in the study. Japan had been the most competitive nation for a number of years but was finally replaced by America in the mid-1990s. It is currently ranked fourth.

Summary

Competitive people catch the brass ring but the price they pay is sometimes horrific. The subjects highlighted here often sacrificed their friends, mates, and their own personal health to reach the pinnacle of success. Marie Curie paid a price of radiation poisoning. Howard Hughes became a drugged-out zombie after daring to push the limits in an airplane and crashing. Napoleon and Helena Rubinstein both died friendless and scorned by their families because winning was not only important to them, it was the only thing. When Rupert Murdoch was in his late seventies, his wife left him because she could no longer tolerate his need to win it all. Such is the price these eminent superstars paid to be the very best.

Ambition and the competitive drive from within usually win the war over close relationships although that is truer of men than women. Agatha Christie and Maria Montessori valued the family more than the other females in this book but even they often chose the professional over the personal. Most of the rest put their need for success first. Catherine the Great had a number of abortions and relegated her son to a position that would not interfere with or challenge her power. Ayn Rand and Margaret Mead refused to take their husbands' names and then both had blatant affairs aimed at enhancing their careers. Isadora Duncan refused to marry any of her lovers, the fathers of her children, so as not to constrain her from roaming the world. Helena Rubinstein is the most ignoble of these examples. She was so competitive she refused to return to America from Europe to attend the funerals of her husband or son.

We all become better when challenged by a strong competitor. That is the one truth that we should remember. Attempting to find someone less capable does not improve our own ability. The only way to improve is to fight the tough battles and not avoid those who would attempt to defeat you either personally and professionally. As discussed, the only way to get into the "zone" or "flow" state is to find the best competition. That will optimally program your psyche for the best performance and can occasionally elevate you to that euphoric state of transcendence to which we all aspire.

The competitive personality is often hyperaggressive, very Machiavellian, polyphasic, and the province of loners. The most competitive personalities in this work are authors Hemingway and Angelou, entrepreneurs Rubinstein and Monaghan, and athletes Zaharias and Jordan. Others in the book were equally as competitive at times but did not allow this trait to become such a dominating influence. Greatness is difficult to attain without being competitive, but one must ask, what price success?

CHAPTER 3

Confidence & Self-Esteem

BELIEVE AND THE WORLD WILL FOLLOW YOU!

"Self Esteem—high or low—tends to be a generator of self-fulfilling prophesies."

Nathaniel Branden, *Six Pillars of Self Esteem* (1994)

Great People Have an Awesome Self-image

Successful people believe. They believe in themselves and their ideas with an optimism that borders on arrogance. Researchers have found that optimistic Olympic athletes are empowered by their losses and tend to win the next event while pessimists are destroyed by a loss and typically lose the next event. Psychologist Martin Seligman found, "Optimism leads to higher achievement than pessimism. . . . Optimistic professional baseball and basketball teams do better after they are defeated than pessimistic teams" (cited in Goleman 1995, 88).

I have found confidence and self-esteem to be critical to the successful and great. All eminent people have one thing in common: They have an intransigent belief system that is crucial to their greatness. Martin Luther King Jr., Margaret Mead, Maria Montessori, Ayn Rand, and Frank Lloyd Wright will be the subjects reviewed in this chapter in addition to anecdotal reference to others including the ever-confident Catherine the Great, Picasso, Thurgood Marshall, and the egoist Napoleon. Without a powerful self-image none of these subjects would have achieved greatness or been able to overcome the attacks on their work and persons. Each of them faced constant ridicule and derision by family, friends, and industry experts, to say

96

nothing about their enemies. This is the reason all successful people must be armed with a resilient, if not impenetrable, self-esteem. Without an iron will and strong sense of self, these great people would have failed miserably.

Those reaching the top in business, the arts, politics, and the humanities must be convinced they will achieve their goals despite what the experts say. Obstacles must become motivators rather than roadblocks. That is what these visionaries were able to do in their heads. They viewed obstacles as opportunities to overcome, instead of some eerie predictor of their inadequacy. The roadblocks were merely hurdles and temporary deterrents to validating their dreams.

One of the interesting facets of successful people is their mindset. Successful people *think* differently than losers. In fact, one of their secrets to success is removing the mind once under way. Active thought stops and "gut reactions" take over. In sports, business, politics, the arts, or science not much separates winners and losers. Winners have the ability to focus without thinking. The only thing dividing Olympic gold medalists or Wimbledon champions from the rest of the field is what is in their heart and head. There is virtually no difference in athletic ability. That same thing is true in virtually everything in life. Winners focus on how to win while most of the rest of us concentrate on how not to lose. Losers in life spend entirely too much energy trying not to lose instead of concentrating on how to win. And it isn't a coincidence that losers always seem to be unlucky. They see themselves as unlucky and they habitually complain about how lucky their opponents are. Lucky people make their luck, and do so in their heads and hearts. Unlucky people are their own worst enemy for the same reason.

Losers like to whine and seem to have some kind of dark cloud permanently hovering above their heads. Skid row is filled with talented losers who look for reasons to justify their ineptitude and failures. Winners need no such validation for their successes since it has already been validated beforehand in their inner confidence. Optimism pervades the muscles and minds of the winners before they hit a tennis ball, decide on a business strategy, or select a political ally. All of these decisions are permeated with a positive energy that causes winners to end up on top and losers to end up on the scrap heap of life. Where does that optimism come from? It emanates from the self-image that has been preordained for success because of a strong self-esteem.

Lady Luck Smiles on the Optimists

Luck and success are highly correlated. All of the adversaries of Bill Gates called him lucky. Margaret Thatcher's political foes did the same. There is no question that timing assisted them in their drive to the pinnacle of their disciplines, but they exploited the opportunities that arose while others only watched from the sidelines. Success and luck are inextricably tied together. Michael Jordan is really lucky that he can make shots that win games at the buzzer and Frank Lloyd Wright was lucky to have ignored traditional building concepts, thereby making his name as an architect. Wright lived through the suburbanization of America and revolutionized architecture by daring to be different, and that is what contributed to his luck. Maria Montessori was lucky that she was given idiot children to teach since the male power elite refused to allow her to practice traditional medicine. Had she been one of the fortunate she would never have been "lucky" enough to revolutionize education.

Linda Erikson Denning wrote, "Study after study has shown that children with superior intelligence but low self-esteem do poorly in school while children of average intelligence, but high self-esteem, can be unusually successful" (1992, 11E). Mark Rosenzweig, a Berkeley research scientist, went even further saying, "Positive experience alters brain size, IQ, and learning ability." Ayn Rand is one of the overachieving women in this book. She based a philosophical movement on what she termed "Egoism as enlightened self-interest."

What is Optimism?

Optimists never allow negatives to enter their life. They are energized by the positive and turned off by the negative. In researching these eminent people I found extreme overconfidence pervading everything they touched. Most ignored any negative that came into their life and refused to acknowledge defeat even when it was staring them in the face. No pessimism was permitted to invade their heads. When someone told them they couldn't succeed they ignored the negative message and continued onward toward their goal. Margaret Thatcher was famous for asking all new party members, "Are you with us?" This was her reference to what was known as Thatcherism, a laissez-faire ideology. If they equivocated in any way they were rejected and the party would look for someone who would support the cause. Thatcher was on a mission and refused to spend one minute with nonbelievers. If nothing else, the Iron Lady was an "indomitable optimist."

Never was optimism so critical to success than in the life of the late Viktor Frankl, a Jewish psychiatrist who survived the degradation of Auschwitz and Treblinka to create a whole new movement in psychology known as logotherapy. He lost his pregnant wife, brother, mother, and father in the concentration camps. He had lost everything but his will to live, which he described so poignantly in his famous work *In Search of Meaning* (1959). He wrote, "The search for value and meaning in the circumstances of one's life was the key to psychological well-being. . . . For success like happiness, cannot be pursued, it must ensue as the unintended side-affect of one's personal dedication to a course greater than oneself."

Supreme Court Chief Justice Thurgood Marshall was labeled Mr. Civil Rights because he was "overly optimistic" according to his most ardent supporters. No one ever accused him of humility, but that self-confidence is what made him great. He believed he could win no matter the odds and his confidence armed him to win. He said, "I have to keep believing because I know our cause is right." Friends referred to Thurgood Marshall as "confidence freak." During his battle on the historical *Brown* v. *Board of Education* trial a newspaper reporter wrote, "I left Marshall that fall day of 1953 thinking that he believed in himself and his cause so much that it was impossible for me and others not to believe in him."

When Catherine the Great was a teenager in Germany her father took her to meet King Frederick the Great. Witnessing her behavior, the king told her father, "She is impertinent!" Catherine married the imbecile grandson of Peter the Great at age fourteen and was destined to a life of loneliness and subservience as a Russian housewife. Her confidence interceded and led her to become Catherine the Great. Optimism was the main reason for her becoming the Empress of all the Russias. Confirmation of her egoism comes from her memoirs: "I was arrogant. There was no woman bolder than I, and there was something within me which never allowed me to doubt for a single moment that I should one day succeed in becoming the Empress of Russia." Pretty strong words for a German girl who was only expected to mother the next king of Russia, not usurp his power and take over the throne.

Albert Einstein was also an arrogant young man. Professor Weber of the Zurich Polytechnique told him, "You have one fault: one can't tell you anything." Einstein's confidence, however, helped him overcome all the negative predictions people had of him to become one of the world's most famous scientists.

How Do You Become Self-Confident?

Self-confidence arises from "success imprints" that were acquired early in life or later through some kind of positive life-experience. It comes from within and is imprinted there through past successes. This book is rampant with those who bought into their *success imprints* and our prisons are full of those who bought into early *failure imprints*. Those fortunate people who were told by some important role model or mentor that they were bright, hard workers, or destined for success had that message imprinted onto their psyche, and most of the time have lived to fulfill that prophecy.

Anyone who has successfully achieved something that was thought to be difficult or impossible has experienced a success imprint. Accomplishing a difficult task provides us with the belief that we can repeat our achievement in the future. Failing to achieve has the reverse result. Failures are also imprinted on our psyches and we may live to fulfill those destinies as well. Penthouses are filled with those who have bought into their successes and skid row is filled with those who believe they are failures. Picasso once told a reporter, "I have the revelation of the inner voice." It was his testimony that he knew better than art critics what was right in art. His self-esteem bordered on arrogance but contributed to his becoming one of the world's most famous artists.

Hitting a perfect backhand in tennis imprints a positive message on our unconscious, making the next backhand much easier to hit. The same is true of hitting a difficult golf shot or skiing down a difficult slope. Constant reinforcement of positive experiences is critical to reshaping one's self-image, and will ultimately result in a stronger self-esteem. Once you believe, what was once difficult becomes routine. But until that happens, the task will remain a challenge. In other words, the positive begets the positive. No one could break the four-minute mile until Roger Bannister did it. Within six months runners all over the world were breaking the "impossible" barrier. To become great, we must work on rewriting negative internal scripts, turning them into positive ones and self-esteem will grow geometrically with each success. Successes are the building blocks of future successes and they ultimately become a fixed component of your inner belief system.

One of history's most revealing examples of this theory is the insurmountable odds Napoleon, a young general, faced at the Italian battle of Lodi. He was expected to lose since the enemy had two and half times as many men. When he won that battle he returned to his tent and decided, "I am a superior being destined for greatness." At St. Helena he wrote of his metamorphosis, "it was only on the evening after Lodi that I realized I was a superior being and conceived the ambition of performing great things."

Our successes in life are a function of our internal belief systems. Once we have achieved we start believing we can continue to do so. Unfortunately, failures have the same affect on us. Why does Michael Jordan always want to take the last shot in a basketball game? Because he *knows* he can make it. Why? When he was eighteen and a freshman at the University of North Carolina, with time running out, he found himself with the basketball and the NCAA title at stake. He sank that shot and it changed his life. Jordan says that one shot changed him from an average player to a superstar. He told a reporter, "After that shot my career started. . . . I was fearless."

Parents are the people most responsible for the internal images that are imprinted on children's unconscious minds. Those who did not get enough positive reinforcement to grow a strong self-esteem in childhood will have to change all those negative imprints into positive ones in adulthood. The above story about Napoleon is one example, but there are innumerable examples in this book. Isadora Duncan was fortunate to have gained her strong sense of self at a very young age. She said, "I was never subjected to the continual don'ts which it seems to me make children's lives a misery. . . . My brothers and I were free to follow our own vagabond impulses. . . . It is certainly to this wild untrammeled early life of my childhood that I owe the inspiration of the dance that I created."

Historical Examples of Self-Confidence at Work

Some examples of self-confidence in the super successful come from the infamous Marquis de Sade, who wrote, "Egoism is the primary law of nature." Hitler told his henchmen, "For me the impossible doesn't exist." A newspaper said of Nikola Tesla, "He has that supply of self-love and self-confidence that usually go with success." Gloria Steinem wrote, "Self-esteem isn't everything, it's just that there isn't anything without it." Those who best personify the high confidence needed to make it to the very top include Maria Montessori, Pablo Picasso, Margaret Mead, Frank Lloyd Wright, Ayn Rand, and Martin Luther King Jr.

Maria Montessori

Maria Montessori became the Prophet of Pedagogy by defying tradition. She entered the field of education only because she was never accepted as a medical doctor. Montessori had always been a renegade. She attended an all-boys school to study mathematics and then went to a technical college in Rome to become an engineer. She was set on avoiding becoming an educator because it was the only acceptable profession for women at the turn of the century. When she decided to become a medical doctor both her father and the head of Rome's Medical College said it was impossible. Undeterred, Montessori defiantly told the head of the medical school "I know I will become a doctor of medicine." Refusing to be denied, the ever-confident woman appealed to the pope, who interceded on her behalf. In 1896, Montessori became the first female in Italy with a medical degree from the University of Rome, but was not allowed to practice medicine on adults because she was a woman.

Instead, the future Messiah of Education was given "idiot" children for whom to care. These children had been deemed uneducable and were being fed by having food thrown into their room. They presented a challenge to the young doctor, who decided to improve their lot. In her assignment to provide total care for them, she was not constrained by teaching standards or guidelines, which was the reason for her amazing success. Montessori had these "idiots" reading and writing at normal levels within months. This experience was repeated several times until she founded the Orthophrenic School of Rome in 1899. Within a decade she had revolutionized teaching techniques and had opened the Children's House in 1907. Montessori preached an educational methodology based on "empirical pragmatism." She was one of the first educators to see the child as a whole, recognizing that hungry children, or those with severe physical, emotional, or other behavioral problems could not complete (or learn) effectively. This led her to a system of scientific positivism. Montessori documented her findings in *The Montessori Method* (1910) and went on to write many books and spread her gospel of "social engineering."

Montessori never allowed rules to interfere with her dreams, but it took a powerful self-esteem to overcome her father and the establishment. When her biographer E. M. Standing asked about the reasons for her success, Maria Montessori responded, "At that time I felt as if I could have done anything. . . . The more I was taunted and denied the more I decided *the higher I would go*" (emphasis added). She wrote, "Liberty and freedom is power," and turned to what she called her "inner-certitude" and "inner-drive" to succeed. That strong sense of self is what contributed to her development of the Montessori method, which would revolutionize education around the world.

Pablo Picasso

This iconoclast was determined to find truth through art and to destroy whatever he deemed stood in his path. He was seen as sadomasochistic artist with a penchant for the bizarre and surreal. He is credited with documenting the nihilism of the twentieth century through his masterpieces *Les Demoiselles d'Avignon* (1907) and *Guernica* (1937). These works were considered orgies of destruction and emotional cruelty.

Picasso was the father of the artistic movement known as cubism, but he became famous due to his egomania. Confidence was his trademark, as described by his friend Jean Cocteau, who said, "He radiated an almost cosmic and irresistible self-confidence. Nothing seemed beyond him." His biographer Arianna Huffington (1988) described him as having "supreme confidence." Where did he get it? He said, "I have the revelation of the inner voice, and am willing to sacrifice everything to my painting."

Picasso was card-carrying egomaniac who never listened to critics because he believed he was the person qualified to evaluate his work. One of his favorite sayings was "I do not seek, I find" which is a tribute to his resolute optimism. An example of his all-consuming self-confidence was the signature he used at age eighteen on a drawing he gave his parents as he left Barcelona for Paris: I the King!

Picasso was probably the most prolific painter in history. He created one new piece of art each day from the time he was twenty until his death at ninety-two. His contribution to the visual arts encompassed 50,000 works of art including 1,885 paintings, 1,228 sculptures, 2,880 ceramics, 18,095 engravings, 9,293 lithographs/linocuts, 11,748 drawings, 11 tapestries, and 8 rugs. It is truly amazing he had time for bullfights, drinking orgies, three wives, and hundreds of mistresses. Picasso was a destructive force who lived up the description of innovation as "creative destruction." He epitomized this by being largely responsible for the suicides of a mistress, ex-wife, and grandson; the nervous breakdowns of one mistress and ex-wife; and the alcoholism of his son Paulo (Landrum 1996, 179).

Margaret Mead

Margaret Mead, the world's most famous anthropologist, achieved her fame because she believed she could. *Newsweek* wrote in the late 1930s, "The most impressive thing about Mead is not that she has become the world's most famous anthropologist, but rather that it never occurred to her that this would never happen." She wrote in her autobiography, *Blackberry Winter* (1972), "In school I always felt special." An example of her awesome self-confidence is related in an anecdote about a trip Mead was taking. At the time of the incident, Mead had written three books. When she arrived at the airport, the plane was full. Mead thought nothing of telling the ticket agent, "But I'm Margaret Mead," fully expecting someone to get off and give her the seat. (As with most of these subjects, her confidence bordered on arrogance.)

That enormous self-image allowed Margaret to become the first Ph.D. in anthropology in America and to go alone into the jungles of Samoa and New Guinea to research her field. She took her findings and married psychology, sociology, and anthropology in her most successful books, *Coming of Age in Samoa* (1928), *Growing Up in New Guinea* (1930), and *Sex and Temperament* (1935). A high self-esteem and manic work ethic enabled Mead to produce 39 books, 1,139 publications, 10 films, and 40 awards, and to receive 28 honorary degrees.

Mead radiated self-confidence that made people believe her even when she was at the edge of her expertise. Mead was so sure of herself she kept her own name through three different marriages, one of which was to world famous anthropologist Gregory Bateson. When her father asked her why, she responded, "Because I plan to make the name Mead famous." Psychologist Jean Houston tested her cognitive and intuitive powers and said, "She could move in and out of her unconscious with ease." She had boundless energy and her husbands were incapable of keeping up. When Gregory Bateson said, "I can't keep up," She responded, "But I can't stop pushing." Her style was "too much of everything," but it is what made her great because she believed it to be her destiny. One biographer said, "She was goal oriented even when there wasn't a goal."

Frank Lloyd Wright

Frank Lloyd Wright made himself the world's preeminent architect through a resilient personal belief system. The real reason he was so good at marrying form with function integrated with the environment was because he believed he knew what was right for mankind. Wright never doubted that he knew what was best and refused to allow clients to tell him what they wanted in their building. The classic case of this was in his world famous Fallingwater home built *over* a creek even though the millionaire owner had asked to have his home looking *at* the creek.

Wright was so confident he was arrogant. One time he found himself testifying as a key witness and had the audacity to refer to himself on the witness stand as a genius. As he exited the courtroom a reporter stopped him and asked how he could be so bold as to call himself a genius. Without hesitating the ever-confident Wright responded in his inimitable fashion, "I was under oath, wasn't I?" and walked off. Wright's favorite aphorism was this: "Early in life I had to choose between hypocritical humility and honest arrogance. I chose arrogance." A Dutch admirer met him and said, "the man is a bigger egotist than me and I thought I was the limit." Such is the mental image of the truly great.

How did he become so self-confident? Wright's mother decided early in life to mold him into a world-renowned architect. She surrounded his cradle with pictures of the Acropolis, Sistine Chapel, and Notre Dame Cathedral. She thought of him as a little messiah and actually told him he was the reincarnation of the Welsh mythical god Taliesin—something she truly believed. She was certain he was a god and destined for greatness, and she repeatedly told him so. Wright began to believe he was special and acted like it.

Wright's named his two most famous edifices in Wisconsin and Arizona Taliesin, and he often referred to himself and his estates as the same. It is no surprise that this famous architect became an overconfident adult who thought he could defy all traditional architectural design. His biographer Meryle Secrest wrote, "Taliesin and he were synonymous concepts." She called him "a model of brazen self-confidence." He was imperious and designed his great masterpieces with imperial splendor. One only has to look at the Guggenheim Museum or the Marin County Civic Center, both designed when he was ninety, and see the majesty that was an external manifestation of his internal image.

Ayn Rand

Rand wasn't her name—it was Rosenbaum. The woman who defected from Stalinist Russia when she was twenty-one took an American-sounding name off of her Remington-Rand typewriter rather than use the name of her husband, Hollywood leading man Frank O'Connor. She adamantly refused to take his name and when asked why replied, "Because I plan to be famous someday and I want my name to be in lights." This self-confident woman wrote the greatest philosophic epic novel in history—*Atlas Shrugged*—and it then spawned a whole new philosophical system known as objectivism and a new political party called the Libertarian party. Her two famous protagonists, Howard Roark of *Fountainhead* and John Galt of *Atlas Shrugged*, both epitomize the ultimate self-confident overachieving ideal man.

Self-confidence, optimism, and Ayn Rand were all synonymous. These terms were at the root of her ethical philosophy, which was based on egoism and was poignantly described in her book *The Virtue of Selfishness: A New Concept of Egoism* (1964). She spoke of her true belief in the art of selfishness by saying, "I am. I think. I will," to disavow Descartes's famous saying, "I think, therefore I am." Rand believed self-adoration and self-image were godly. She wrote, "a man who accepts the role of a sacrificial animal will not achieve the self-confidence necessary to uphold the validity of his mind, and the man who doubts the validity of his mind will not achieve the self-esteem necessary to uphold the value of his person" (Sciabara 1995, 305).

Ayn Rand personifies a super-achiever whose success was a byproduct of her intransigent sense of self, a trait often found wanting in the average housewife. She was a self-confident visionary whose dedication to high self-esteem and the defense of egoism is best delineated in an early work, *Anthem* (1938), and in *The Virtue of Selfishness*. Her love affair with the ego is best stated in this passage from *Anthem*:

> And now I see the face of god and I raise
> This god over the earth, this god for who men have
> Sought since men came into being, this god who
> Will grace them with joy and peace and pride.
> This god, this one word: I.

Martin Luther King Jr.

The man who had more to do with an integrated American society than any other, Martin Luther King Jr., was optimism incarnate. He believed in himself to such a degree that he was often seen as an insufferable optimist by his adversaries. What other kind of man could make speeches like "I Have a Dream" or "I've Been to the Mountain Top"? This was a man who was speaking to his people as someone who *knows* the way and expects to be followed. King implored his race to follow him in a Gandhian tradition of nonviolent resistance. One example of his belief in developing a strong sense of self comes from his wife Coretta's autobiographical book on their life together:

The individual should strive for completion within himself. The first dimension of a complete life is the development of a person's inner powers. . . . Love yourself if that means healthy self-interest. (King 1993, 6–7)

It is interesting to note that Martin Luther King Jr. was named Mike until he was five. At that time his father took a trip to Germany and was so inspired by the "Here I Stand!" speech of religious reformer Martin Luther that he came home and changed both his name and his oldest son's to Martin Luther King. Junior would live out the true destiny of that name and challenge historical traditions for what was right and fair. He adopted the motto "growth through struggle," and won the Nobel Peace Prize in 1963 for his enormous contributions to reforming race relations in American society.

King's lifetime hero and fantasy mentor was Mahatma Gandhi who King believed was correct in his nonviolent resistance to British authority in India. Martin Luther King Jr. dedicated his life to that same proposition and paid the ultimate price for daring to change society—his life. Without consummate self-confidence Martin Luther King Jr. would never have achieved so much in such a short time. His "I have a dream" belief system armed him well for his struggle, which he finally won, but he had to die to achieve it.

The Dark Side of Self-Esteem—Violence

The American Psychological Association published an article in 1996 in the *Psychological Review* suggesting that raising a person's self-esteem could actually be dangerous. They reported, "People [with high self-esteem] turn aggressive when they receive feedback that contradicts their favorable views of themselves." The association's conclusion was that people who refuse to lower their opinions of themselves tend to be those who commit violent crimes in society.

I have found this to be true with a number of the subjects in this book. The high self-esteem found in Napoleon, Balzac, Dostoevsky, Hitler, and Picasso had a flip side—arrogance—and each of these men turned out to be quite destructive in both their private and professional lives. Their egomania appears to have been a critical factor in their need to destroy. All four men had been doted on as children by adoring women who worshiped them like gods. Excessive indulgence imprinted them with high self-esteem but also appears to have contributed to their dark side. All of these men grew up with a love/hate view of women and classified them as either Madonnas or whores and nothing in between. It is strange that all of these men adored their mothers but seemed to hate other women, and both Picasso and Hitler have been cited as responsible for the suicides of numerous women. Hitler was sadomasochistic and couldn't be happy unless he beat his women and they did the same to him, but in many ways Picasso was even more deviant. He once said, "I'd rather see a woman die any day than see her happy with someone else." He told a reporter, "There are only two kinds of women— goddesses and doormats," and told all his male friends, "You cannot be my friend unless I sleep with your wife." His most famous works were demeaning to women and sacrilegious. His internal rage knew no bounds. He was nihilistic, satanic, perverse, sadistic, and irreverent. The most graphic examples of his destructiveness in art were *Les Demoiselles*, which portrays five prostitutes, soon followed by *Weeping Woman*, *Three Dancers*, *The Minotaur Carries Off a Woman*, *Guernica*, and *The Peeing Woman*.

Picasso has been eulogized as documenting the psyche of the twentieth century in a surrealistic manner bordering on nihilism. He had a psychological conflict between the need to create and the compulsion to destroy. His art has been characterized as a nihilistic decent into hell and an orgy of destructiveness. Ex-wife Francis Gilot once described him as "evil." His mistress Maria-Theresa and last wife Jacqueline both committed suicide because of him. Long-time mistress Dora Maar was institutionalized, and his grandson committed suicide during Picasso's funeral. His son Paul was an alcoholic. His greatest work, *Guernica*, was a study in destructiveness and the demeaning of women. If anything, Picasso was more destructive than creative and that was a difficult undertaking since he was arguably the most influential and productive artist in history. Jung categorized Picasso's art as schizophrenic.

The word "sadism" comes from the name of the Marquis de Sade (1740–1814), a French author who enjoyed whipping and hurting women for his own sexual gratification. de Sade was a brilliant and talented writer who blamed his sadomasochistic tendencies on his early childhood. He said, "I was told I was a superior being and a god, which allowed me to think I did not have to abide by society's rules." He wrote, "I believed from the time I could reason, that nature and fortune had joined together to heap their gifts upon me. I believed it because people were foolish enough to tell me so. . . . It seemed that everything must give in to me, that the whole world must flatter my whims" (Lever 1993). His arrogance was supreme and obviously came out of his early upbringing, which led to a life of debauchery.

All of these men, including Frank Lloyd Wright and Howard Hughes, were doted on as children, thereby promoting abnormally strong self-esteems that bordered on egomania. Because of their strong egos there was little they didn't believe they could master and consequently they accomplished many extraordinary things. They were convinced they were superior beings and outside the bounds of societal rules that restrict ordinary men. Such self-image can lead to great success, but it also contributes to destructiveness.

As mentioned, the *Psychological Review* ran a story ("The Dark Side of Self-Esteem," March 1996) validating the close relationship between high self-esteem and violence. This article made quite a stir among America's psychologists, social workers, and teachers, who had previously believed low self-esteem was the primary cause of violence. Baumeister, Smart, and Boden wrote, "It is threatened egotism, rather than low self-esteem that leads to violence" (1996, 29). The authors went on to say, "Individuals who carry out political violence are either indoctrinated with the view of their own superiority [Napoleon, Hitler, and Hughes are examples of this] or marked by narcissistic traits [e.g., de Sade and Picasso]." The authors concluded that "Aggressors seem to believe that they are superior, capable beings. . . . Violent and criminal individuals have been repeatedly characterized as arrogant, confident, narcissistic, egotistical, assertive, proud, and the like."

The Positive Aspects of High Self-Esteem

High self-esteem does more good than bad in most cases. For example, Maria Montessori used her strong sense of self to create the Montessori method of education. In much the same way, Frank Lloyd Wright used his indomitable self-confidence to defy the traditions of architecture and marry buildings with the environment. Margaret Thatcher's strong belief in economic transformation—privatizing the steel, coal, airline, and auto industries—allowed her to defy the establishment and implement what came to be known as Thatcherism in England. She was personally responsible for turning the British economy around in the late 1970s and early 1980s. Martin Luther King Jr.'s positive force and optimism changed America for the better in a similar manner. All of these are positive examples of people with strong self-images using their confidence to help mankind.

Gender Differences in Self-Esteem

According to a survey done by New Woman in 1992, "More men (42%) than women (34%) have high self-esteem." It was apparent in the research on the females in this book that for them, confidence was harder to come by than for the males. These women were more naturally articulate but had lower self-images than the men. The women were also more concerned with forming solid, emotionally gratifying relationships than the men. It almost appeared the women's feelings on their personal appearance—hair, grooming, and other beauty factors—were far more a factor in their self-confidence than the men studied. Ted Turner would appear on television looking like a bum while Margaret Thatcher always worried about her hair. These are just two examples of hundreds found in these subjects.

Diedra Landrum is a career counselor in Naples, Florida, who administers personality tests and writes clients' résumés as part of a career counseling practice. She has produced approximately one thousand resumes for a wide range of clients, including attorneys, engineers, technologists, marketing executives, and secretaries. Over half of her clients have been college graduates and many have master's degrees. She has even worked with a medical doctor interested in changing professions.

An interesting gender difference in confidence and self-esteem was found among Landrum's subjects: The women frequently understated their ability and talent while the men overstated theirs. Landrum would attempt to get both genders to outline those things they did best, but found a vast chasm between the two genders. The females, even those with master's degrees, understated their achievements, including their level of responsibility and authority. They demeaned their talents, work experience, and accomplishments on the job. Landrum found herself attempting to raise the self-image of the women to fit their true ability. She was forced to literally pull their successes out of them. The men, however, almost universally overstated their qualifications, talent, and experiences. She had to find a diplomatic way of bringing the men's perspective back into reality. In other words, she was forced to raise the female's sense of achievement and lower the men's. Thus, the conclusion can be drawn that the internal self-image of women is fragile and the females reading this should probably work at becoming more assertive and raising their sense of self to parity with their male competition.

I found a similar trend among the subjects covered in this book. The majority of the women studied were less assertive, less egoistic, and had a lower sense of self than the males studied. However, the women were far more confident than what is seen in the general population of females. Isadora Duncan was one such example. The mother of modern dance was totally confident in her abilities. At age sixteen she decided to make her fortune in Chicago, and she brazenly walked up to the great theatrical impresario Augustin Daly and told him he had better hire her because she was going to be famous. Here was a young girl who had never had a dance lesson, had only made it to the fifth grade, and was telling the head of a theatrical agency that he was in trouble if he didn't hire her on the spot. She told him, "I have discovered the dance, the art which has been lost for two thousand years. . . . I bring you the idea that is going to revolutionize our entire epoch. . . . I will create a new dance that will express America." Taken aback by her impassioned outburst, Daly hired Duncan in self-defense. Such is the power of confidence.

Cultural Nuances of Self-Confidence

Americans measure higher in self-esteem than most other nations, which has resulted in the "Ugly American" reputation. In contrast, Asians subjugate their egos to the best interest of the company or the group. Mao Tse-tung, who believed he was omniscient, was an exception to this. Soichiro Honda, the founder of Honda motor company, who will be discussed in chapter 8, fit the Asian mold but always moved ahead on innovative ideas without consensus and did so despite having only an eighth-grade education in a field dependent on engineering expertise. He was certainly an anomaly. The nations which test as having the strongest sense of self are Italy, Israel, United States, Australia, Canada, and Sweden.

Summary

Self-confidence is the external expression of our inner view of our self. We can do most anything if we believe we can and are incapable of performing the simplest tasks if we are insecure or fearful. The primary difference between a president and a bum is self-esteem, although other factors are always at work. Likewise, the internal belief system is the only true difference between a prime minister and a prostitute. There is a fine line between consummate success and abysmal failure, and the difference resides in our self-esteem.

I am convinced success is a self-fulfilling prophecy. Success does beget success, making it incumbent on all of us to practice successful activities until they become so ingrained that we believe success is synonymous with ourselves. Sometimes there is a fine line connecting (or separating) the three sides of the issue—timidity, self-confidence, and arrogance. Those without a strong sense of self are usually timid and feel unsure of competing. Those with strong self-esteems are capable of Herculean achievements, and those who get so caught up in their own self-importance become arrogant and egotistical. The ability to operate in the middle of this trichotomy is the secret to living a successful and fruitful life.

CHAPTER 4

Drive

GREAT PEOPLE LIVE LIFE IN THE FAST LANE

"I worked 20 hours a day, every day, including Sundays."
Helena Rubinstein

Most of the subjects in this book were driven far beyond what the normal person considers sane. In relation to the norms of life, these people were off-the-wall Type A workaholics afflicted with a kind of rushing sickness. They were in a hurry. The individuals personifying this quality came from four of the six disciplines. There were two writers, one inventor, one politician, and one entrepreneur, although Madonna is used later to give credence to the entertainment aspect of drive. All operated as if they were double-parked on the highway of life, they had no time to dally about looking for parking spaces, and refused to devote but a fleeting moment to anyone. This lifestyle was self-destructive but was a positive force in getting them to the very top of their field. Honoré de Balzac, Fyodor Dostoevsky, Thomas Edison, Bill Gates, and Margaret Thatcher personify this character-istic, but a few others like Bill Lear and Madonna will be discussed since they are personalities who suffered from what I call a manic-success syndrome. Their mania contributed greatly to their success until the frenetic lifestyle became a self-perpetuating addiction.

We think we are driven when we work for seven straight days without a weekend break. But think about these subjects who worked seven days a week for many years without a break. Many led such a manic existence for the better part of their professional life. The irony is that they didn't see their hyperactivity as unusual since they were pursuing a labor of love. Picasso did not see what he was doing as work, he was pursuing an internal dream. Balzac,

Edison, and Lear were doing the same when they locked themselves in a room and refused to come out until they had completed their project.

Most people are drained if they put in a two-shift work week (sixteen hours a day) and refuse to sacrifice their golf game, tennis match, bridge game or other diversions like the movies. Catherine the Great, Marie Curie, Maria Montessori, Nikola Tesla, Mao Tse-tung, Amelia Earhart, Walt Disney, Howard Hughes, and James Michener, on the other hand, worked eighteen hours a day practically every day of their adult life. Balzac and Tesla claimed to have worked closer to twenty hours a day every week of their life and from the amount of their research it appears they did. Edison once locked himself in his lab for sixty straight hours without food or water to insure he was not rewarded until he had completed his task. Walt Disney remained at his studio for weeks when producing *Snow White* according to biographer Marc Eliot (1993). He slept on his desk, drank coffee, and had to be on top of his animators at all times. When Disneyland opened he didn't leave the park for almost three months. Mao often went forty-eight hours without sleep and was famous for his 6,000-mile Long March across the barrens of 1930s China—the equivalent of walking across the United States twice.

Characteristics of Manic Personalities

Insomnia

We think we are driven when we miss a few hours' sleep, drive recklessly in order to work, or forego time with our family to earn a promotion. These actions pale, however, when one considers that Tesla allowed 2 million volts of electricity to flow through his body on stage at the 1893 Chicago World's Fair in order to disprove Edison's claim that his power generators were dangerous. If that wasn't enough for the obsessively driven Tesla, he claimed to have slept but two hours a night, not for a few weeks, but for over forty years, so as not to miss out on any creative insights. Others who had the same predilection for little sleep include Margaret Thatcher, who said she only slept four hours a night, Michael Jordan, who says he sleeps little, and Balzac, who drank coffee by the gallon to stay awake. Napoleon, Dostoevsky, Edison, Isadora Duncan, Marie Curie, Howard Hughes, Maria Callas, Earnest Hemingway, and Michael Jackson also say they seldom sleep more than four hours a night. Is that a sacrifice you would be willing to take for greatness? It certainly appears to be critical to the process based on these subjects.

Compulsive Workaholism

Great people are compulsively driven. When Alexander Pontitoff, the founder of Ampex and father of the magnetic recording industry, told Bill Lear in the fall of 1964 that Lear would not be able to create a stereo cassette for an automobile, Lear was unable to refuse the challenge to his ego. Pontiff told Lear, "You can't do it. You just can't squeeze that much information on [a cassette]." That was all the incentive Lear needed. He locked himself in a lab with an audio engineer (Lear had only an eighth-grade education) and refused to leave until he had solved the problem and "many nights we worked all night" (Rashke 1985, 254). He emerged two weeks later with the Lear Stereo Eight.

Thomas Edison had a similar penchant for locking himself in his lab with others. These men seemed to understand the psychology of challenging their associates to keep up with their frenetic need to win. Edison often remained in his lab for weeks while his wife brought him food. He didn't bother to change clothing but his associates told of his catnaps between long vigils that had become known as the "Faust laboratory." It shouldn't have surprised me to read that he spent his wedding night with his second wife in the lab, forgetting to come home to consummate the marriage. Such compulsion is the driving force behind the rich and famous.

Picasso had a similar need to work without stop. At least three biographers describe his personality and style as having an "inexhaustible vitality." Even Catherine the Great was hyper and she had no reason to be, since the empress had dictatorial powers and could have lived a leisurely lifestyle had she wished. But her personality seems to go with the territory. Catherine was a workaholic, "firing off drafts [of letters, edicts, etc.] at a speed that surprised and vexed her copyists." During the years at Motown Records, Berry Gordy Jr. said, "I was so obsessed, I couldn't wait to get to work in the morning and didn't want to leave at night." His protégé, Smokey Robinson, saw the inner side of the man and once told him, "You are a madman." Even the passive and shy Agatha Christie was an addicted workaholic, producing at least one and sometimes two books a year for fifty-seven years.

Mania and Health

Successful people often abuse their bodies more than others but for some reason their bodies rarely falter. Michael Jordan had to lean on his Chicago Bulls teammates and draped over the basket apparatus because he was so sick he wasn't able to stand on his own, but even so, this driven superstar dominated the Utah Jazz in the final game of the 1997 NBA finals winning a fourth world championship for his team. When the coach asked him if he wanted to come out of the game, Jordan said no. He stayed in and hit a three-point shot with twenty-five seconds left on the clock, scoring thirty-eight points and winning the game. Jordan had been in bed for two days before the game with a viral flu, but he was voted the most valuable player in the playoffs. How can you be most valuable when you can't even stand up? It appears that some inner drive relegated illness to other mere mortals when Jordan needed his body to respond to the challenges of the game.

An even more remarkable story is that of Babe Didrickson Zaharias. Zaharias had beaten all competitors until at age forty-two she contracted cancer. In April 1953 she underwent a colostomy, but she had only about a year to live, since the cancer had spread throughout her body. Unaware she was slowly dying (the doctor didn't tell her how much the cancer had spread), she went out and won the Beaumont Open six weeks after her operation, and then won another five pro tour events in 1954 when she was "supposed" to be dead. Talk about sickness being more in the head than in the body.

Napoleon Bonaparte astounded most people with his hyperactivity but none more than his personal valet, Constant. The Little General lived life in such a hurry it is truly amazing he lived to be fifty. Once in a manic, non-stop ride across Europe, this frenetic man killed five horses in five days. Constant said of the experience, "I never comprehended how his body could endure such fatigue, and yet he enjoyed almost continuously the most per-fect health," adding "and he never even stopped to change clothes." An English colonel with Napoleon at Elba wrote, "I have never seen a man in any situation of life with so much personal activity. . . . He appears to take much pleasure in perpetual movement and in seeing those who accompany him sink under fatigue" (cited in Landrum 1996, 129). Napoleon would dic-tate memoranda to six secretaries simultaneously on different subjects. He drove himself and his men to superhuman efforts on the field of battle and because of that he won many battles he was not supposed to win. His mania dominated his life and work and it led him to the brass ring.

Most of these subjects had similar hyperactive lifestyles that not only didn't affect them physically but even seemed to empower them. Because of their manic natures, what I call "rushing sickness," such personalities tend to be trim and ready for action. Perhaps they do not have time to overeat, or perhaps their manic natures burn off all the calories they consume. Balzac was gluttonous: his mania caused him to do everything in excess including work, sex, drinking, smoking, eating, and writing. Ted Turner was so hyper he refused to check baggage when he traveled since it was a terrible waste of time. You would think such Type A behavior would cause these people to catch infection and to break down often, but they do not get sick as often as the average population and do not frequent doctors. It almost seems they were too busy to get sick or even to die. Maria Montessori, Nikola Tesla, Mother Teresa, Edison, Picasso, Frank Lloyd Wright, Helena Rubinstein,

Mary Kay Ash, Joseph Campbell, Estée Lauder, James Michener, and Nelson Mandela all worked well into their eighties and nineties despite lives spent abusing their bodies.

Psychosexual or Libidinal Energy

Psychic energy is the life energy that emanates from within. Many of the subjects included here were manic, on a mission, as driven to satiate their sexual appetites as their creative ones. Berry Gordy Jr. had eight children by five women, only two of whom he married, but even that doesn't adequately describe his sexual activity. One of his recording stars said, "Gordy was the freakiest man I'd ever known. He could make love to five different women a night." F. Scott Fitzgerald noted, "I have a theory that Ernest [Hemingway] needs a new woman for each big book." Hemingway was a profligate who married four times and had mistresses during each marriage. He apparently was incapable of curbing his need for seduction.

Catherine the Great, Napoleon, Balzac, Hughes, Lear, Picasso, Hemingway, Honda, Robeson, Golda Meir, Nelson Mandela, Ted Turner, and Madonna all had strong libidinal drives that dominated their lives. Biographer Huffington described Picasso as having "an inexhaustible passion and energy for work and sex." Paul Robeson, according to one critic, had an emotional power that was terrifying. He said, "In the jealous scenes [he played] he literally foamed at the mouth." Madonna described her success in terms of sexuality. The Material Girl told *Vanity Fair* (October 1992) that the secret of her success was "Pussy Power." What was she saying? That she was able to use her sexual attraction to gain power, to open doors, and to get things done once she was inside. Madonna felt a strong need to rebel against societal restraints on homosexuality (some of her best friends were homosexual), bisexuality (she was into it), incest (she admitted to an unresolved Electra complex), and her book *Sex* was aimed at revealing some semblance of truth in these areas. The book earned $50 million in the first week of its release in 1992.

Freud defined psychic energy as the life force or sex instinct which he also labeled "psychic energy" or the pleasure principle. He believed that all ingenuity flowed from recharged sexual energy and that creative energy was sublimated libidinal drive. What does that mean for an aspiring creative genius? It means those with a strong sex drive may be more capable of making it to the top. Sex and power are truly inextricably intertwined and the Kennedy and Clinton sexual escapades in the White House were not an accident of fate but instead were highly predictable. There are no strong leaders without a high sex drive.

Freud claimed that "what is repressed in sexual life will reappear—in sublimated form—in daily life." At another time he said, "Unsatisfied libido is responsible for producing all art and literature." A number of these subjects demonstrate both these points. Balzac didn't marry until age fifty, Disney was asexual, Freud himself supposedly didn't have sex after age forty, although he continued to be preoccupied with it and strangely, according to Jung, had an intimate relationship with his wife's sister. Tesla claimed in his autobiography to have never had a date let alone sex, and Mother Teresa took a vow of chastity as a teenager. Their lack of sexual activity was offset by the hypersexuality of Catherine the Great, Mao Tse-tung, Isadora Duncan, Howard Hughes, and Ernest Hemingway.

The most sexually provocative females in this book are Catherine the Great and Isadora Duncan. Catherine spent $1.5 billion (in 1990 dollars) on a long line of paramours. She was a notorious man-izer with insatiable sexual appetites. To Catherine, men were merely "instruments of pleasure." Isadora Duncan was also quite the seductress. She had three children by three different men, none of whom she married. She did this at the turn of the century, when sexual mores were far more restrictive than they are today. Mary Desti, Duncan's friend, wrote, "Isadora could no more live without human love than she could without food or music." Madonna is notorious for her use of sex in her performances. She told a reporter that her life was the summation of her sexuality, that it was her life force.

Mao Tse-tung, Howard Hughes, and Ernest Hemingway were all infamous for their need to assuage their sexual energy through continual conquests of the opposite sex, in- or outside of marriage. Mao and Hughes didn't care if their partners were females or males, as long as their desires were sated. All spent an inordinate amount of their energies and time making sure they were sexually satisfied. Mao loved to have multiple girls in bed at the same time and actually set up a bed in a room next to the ballroom for the sole purpose of finding nubile girls to sleep with. There was no limit to his decadence. He was married four times, but was never faithful to any of the wives. A political foe accused him of having a harem of 3,000 concubines.

Howard Hughes left trails of women in his path. It has been said that Hughes would sleep with Ginger Rogers at breakfast, Bette Davis at noon, Katharine Hepburn in the afternoon, and Lana Turner in the evening. Later that night he might find time for a bisexual relationship with Cary Grant or Tyrone Power, or if they were unavailable he could end up with Susan Hayward or Rita Hayworth. Hemingway, like Mao, had four wives and was never faithful to any of them. F. Scott Fitzgerald said that he could tell when Hemingway was about to start on a new book because Hemingway would simultaneously start to seduce a new woman.

What is Mania or Hypomania?

The American Psychological Association defines "hypomania" as a mood disorder falling somewhere between euphoria and mania, a disorder that is "characterized by unrealistic optimism and a decreased need for sleep." The definition goes on to say that some people "show increased creativity" during such states. Writers Balzac, Dostoevsky, and Hemingway, all manic-depressives, admitted they were more productive and creative in such states. Another symptom of hypomania is super energy. Gustl Kubizek, Hitler's only friend in his early years, said, "He never tired and never slept." Dr. Hermann Rausching, president of the Danzig Parliament under Hitler's regime, wrote, "he [Hitler] neither tires nor hungers; he lives with morbid energy that enables him to do almost miraculous things."

Mania is known as the playground for the overachievers. Why? Because in this state a person is persistently elevated, expansive, and can experience symptoms like grandiosity, inflated self-esteem, flights of ideas or insights, and the need for less sleep than most people. Creative and manic people tend to be exceptionally articulate, speak rapidly, and have great flexibility regarding their ideas. They have an intensified sense of self and emotions with heightened sexuality. These people experience high energy that often results in higher productivity and greater risk-taking propensity. Hypomanics have wills of iron. They are so "on" they cannot find any peace, causing Goethe to say, "In my 75 years I have not known four weeks of genuine ease of mind."

Psychiatrists Hershmann and Lieb say, "Hypomania is of special value to poets, humorists, entrepreneurs, inventors, scientists, and others whose work requires creativity" (1994, 22). Kay Jamison studied poets and writers who had bipolar disease and in her book *Touched with Fire* and confirms that such abnormality was found to be most prevalent in poets, musicians, painters, sculptors, and architects. Jamison says hypomania has a strong relationship "with increased achievement and accomplishments." (1994, 87). This confirms the findings on many of these subjects. Mao stopped taking baths because he felt it was a waste of time. Balzac did the same but his logic was that he feared the warm water would prove to be too relaxing.

Isadora Duncan was manic to the point of obsession. Mary Desti wrote of one night spent with her:

> She acted like a person demented; that nothing could stop. Isadora would not sleep a wink and was in a state of the wildest excitement. She decided not to go to bed but to go from restaurant to restaurant, night club to night club, anywhere, and everywhere for excitement. . . . She had an awful inner torment from which she never ceased to suffer. (1929, 133)

Speed—A Type of Rushing Sickness

Speed is synonymous with the manic personality. Manic personalities have some internal need to work, talk, walk, eat, and think fast. They get an inordinate number of speeding and parking tickets since they are in a constant hurry. Most are incapable of waiting in lines and cannot tolerate traffic jams. Research shows they are involved in three times the number of traffic accidents as the normal population. Author Anne Rice confirms this with, "I work best when I work fast, extremely rapidly." Mark Twain said, "I was born excited." Babe Didrickson Zaharias's biographer, Susan Cayleff (1996) wrote, "She had boundless energy." Both Agatha Christie and Stephen King said they were obsessive about their writing and once started could not stop or slow down.

Manic-Depression (Bipolar Disorder)

An unusual number of the subjects studied here were bipolar personalities.* When manic they could do anything, but when down (depressed) they were totally incapacitated. According to psychiatrists Hershmann and Lieb, "Manic depression is almost indispensable to genius because of the advantages it can supply, and that if there have been geniuses free from manic-depression, they have been a minority" (1988, 11). That statement confirms much of my research. Not all of the subjects included here were bipolar, but those who were not were for the most part manic or in some way abnormally driven or uniquely different from the norm.

Balzac, Napoleon, Disney, Dostoevsky, Twain, Edison, Duncan, Hemingway, Hitler, Mao, and Turner were found to be suffering from manic-depression, and Agatha Christie, Anne Rice, Berry Gordy Jr., Honda, and Bill Gates were borderline cases. The eleven card-carrying bipolar subjects represent 28 percent of all the subjects. Eighty-eight percent were hypomanic, and 85 percent were Type A personalities. The only men who were not hyper were Darwin, Einstein, and Joseph Campbell (see a detailed analysis in Chapter 10), and even these three had their moments.

Kay Jamison writes, "Who would not want an illness that has among its symptoms elevated and expansive mood, inflated self-esteem, abundance of energy, less need for sleep, intensified sexuality, and sharpened and unusually creative thinking and increased productivity?" Dostoevsky confirms this, saying, "I can always do more and better in this condition." One writer said of

---

*People suffering from bipolar disorder (formerly known as manic-depression) are volatile. They experience widely fluctuating mood swings ranging from euphoria, excessive drive, competitiveness, and urgency to states of severe depression.

Hemingway, "He needed to be the biggest, most powerful man in the world. He was hyper-aggressive and hyper active with potential for sexual indiscretions." Of course, these "positive" by-products of bipolar disorder are only present in the manic phase—suicide is possible for the severely depressed.

These Type As were obsessed with time and getting things done so as not to feel personally defeated. They typically confused success with self-worth—if they were not successful, they did not feel they were worthy of existence. Time dominated their whole being. Most confused self-worth with winning, which is the primary trait of the Type-A personality. They were all self-starters and workaholics who were driven from within and seldom needed any external motivation, a quality critical to entrepreneurs and political aspirants.

Workaholics—More a Hobby Than Work

The average subject in this work spent a minimum of eighty hours each week working. Most did not take time off on weekends and seldom differentiated a Sunday from a Wednesday or Christmas from any other day. Work was their god, their only god. Hemingway would revise his manuscripts five times and revised his book *The Old Man and the Sea* (1953) more than two hundred times. While in Paris he once wrote eight of the greatest stories he would ever write in a three-month period and then collapsed from nervous fatigue. A prime example of such a driven personality is Berry Gordy Jr., who was so engrossed with building his empire that he "was unaware of the realities of time and space." In his autobiography he wrote, "Work was the thing that brought me the most pleasure. Music was never work. It was like my hobby."

James Michener became independently wealthy from his many books and movies, yet he continued to write seven days a week and refused to take a vacation. Rupert Murdoch also was a very successful media mogul who could go anywhere yet didn't do anything but work. He is still doing so as he nears seventy. Anne Rice is the same. She told a reporter "work is my life and passion." When Michael Jackson collapsed on stage preparing for an HBO concert in 1995 his nephew Taj told the press, "I'm not surprised. He's a workaholic. . . . He works day and night, night and day, sometimes missing meals . . . sometimes without sleep for three or four days." Helena Rubinstein told reporters that her success was based on "working twenty hours a day, every day, including Sundays. . . . Sleep was never important to me. Work is your best beauty treatment. . . . I believe my own success is due primarily to a combination of luck, hard work, and perseverance." Her assistant Patrick O'Higgins called her "a human whirlwind," and she was in her eighties at the time.

Polyphasia—Balancing Many Balls

As has been mentioned, these subjects were expert at multi-tasking, to use a computer term, for their propensity to balance many balls in the air at the same time. For example, Frank Lloyd Wright could not work on one job at a time during his whole life. He had to keep many going simultaneously to keep his interest at a high level. The "greats" discussed here perpetually scheduled more work or appointments than they could possibly keep. They were impatient with ineptitude, intolerant of mediocrity, and impulsive to a fault.

During one period of grandiosity, Balzac started many books that he never finished. Thomas Edison had one grandiose scheme after another and the most prolific inventor in history (he held 1,093 patents) normally had thirty to fifty projects under way simultaneously. Most of these subjects had that unique, but distracting, ability to watch TV, read a magazine, and hold a conversation without missing a beat.

Examples of the Driven Personality

Balzac was arguably the most manic of these subjects, although it is a tough call. Balzac was the most prolific writer of the nineteenth century. Dostoevsky, his near contemporary, was another manically driven writer who could achieve virtually anything when in that elevated state. He wrote "The fiend (mania) is party to every work." Later he would comment on his need to hurry every book, chapter, paragraph, and sentence. "It is possible that something good might have developed out of my writing if I had time to write without hurrying." Margaret Thatcher, the "Iron Lady," described herself in her memoirs as "a driven person." Bill Gates is the richest man in the world but still rocks with frenetic emotion whenever he gives a speech or has a business meeting. Madonna has said she is not married because no one could tolerate living with such a driven personality.

The bottom line is that the subjects chronicled in this chapter are not the types you would have over for a quiet dinner and a fireside chat. They would not be able to tolerate the inactivity and when these people did accept such invitations, they were frenetic and disruptive and ultimately off somewhere else in their heads. They wear you out just by being around them. Type As may not be socially attractive, but they are the people you would want to employ to complete a job with time constraints.

Honoré de Balzac

It is only appropriate that the examples of driven personalities begin with Honoré de Balzac, a man who personifies insatiable energy. When Balzac walked into a room the walls shook from his booming voice and raucous laughter. He was the center of attention as he was energy incarnate. Because he had to be center stage, many people found him intimidating, thus causing him to spend a lot of time alone similar to the other subjects.

Biographer Graham Robb (1994) said Balzac "filled up the room." He was like some kinetic energy machine gone amuck. He did everything in excess, whether it be creating, working, investing, laughing, walking, smoking, talking, eating, or womanizing. He ate and drank ravenously and devoured coffee like a man possessed, a habit which only served to expand his universe and spur on his fits of mania. His hyperactivity wore out his mistresses and friends; they were unable to keep up or bear his frenetic activity. He was loved or hated, but no one ever found him in the ascetic middle ground.

Balzac said "All excesses are brothers," and he appeared to attempt to exert an influence on many disciplines all at the same time. He was a prolific writer, publisher, printer, and newspaper editor simultaneously. He was vitality personified, consuming everything in his path.

Afraid too much romance would interfere with his work, Balzac remained single until age fifty. He was aware of his driven nature and told his friend Alexander Dumas, "A night of love costs half a volume [book]. No woman alive is worth that." Despite this fear, he was wild and crazy and a passionate pursuer of wine, women, and song writing, saying "My orgies take the form of books." Despite Balzac's claim, Robb says Balzac knew of orgies first hand. A friend, Horace Raisson, describes Balzac's encounter with six women during one wild soirée in Paris during the 1830s. Balzac was true to his statement that "dissipation is a way of life." He wrote, "If I'm not a genius, I'm done for" and proceeded to prove it by killing himself with work.

Balzac is considered the founder of the realistic novel. His most famous work was the prodigious masterpiece epic that included over one hundred volumes, *The Human Comedy*, completed in 1850. He would become entranced with an idea and lock himself in the room for days saying, "demons drive me." One night while seriously ill he wrote 15,000 words. After years of manic activity he knew he was burning out and wrote, "I'm wearing myself out in a horrible fashion."

Balzac was impatient to a fault and admitted it. "I'm incapable of waiting. It is an incorrigible fault in my nature." His work became a huge influence on later writers such as Dostoevsky, Marx, William James, and Engels. Engels wrote, "I've learned more from Balzac than all the professional historians, economists, and statisticians put together." History has recorded his contribution by referring to him as the chronicler of nineteenth-century French Society, a feat Balzac accomplished with ninety-two novels, six plays, and dozens of short stories, plus many newspaper editorials.

Balzac's day typically began at 1:00 A.M. when he would begin to work feverishly until 8:00 A.M. At that point Balzac began consuming voluminous cups of coffee that only fueled his hyperactivity. He worked nonstop until 4:00 P.M. before stopping for dinner with friends and would go to bed between 8:00 and 9:00 o'clock, only to repeat this maniacal schedule seven days a week. Robb wrote, "He had an excruciating devotion to a single task to the point of physical breakdown. His was a kind of self-induced madness." It is no wonder he died at fifty.

Rodin's bust of Balzac was a true Promethean representation of this man of many excesses. Robb describes his hyperactivity as making him great but contributing to his downfall. "His creative mind—the prison cell, where he first saw at once the wonderful vision and the enormous cost of that vision— his was a slow suicide" (1994, 294).

Fyodor Dostoevsky

Fyodor Dostoevsky, the great existentialist writer, was a nihilist who saw the weaknesses in man and described humanity's foibles with such passion that Somerset Maugham called him "one of the supreme novelists of the world." Dostoevsky was an epileptic who was prone to wild swings of mood that ranged from wild euphoria to complete depression, and his novels represent his journey through misery.

Dostoevsky refused to fail, and used his periods of mania to produce some of the great novels in history. Freud said, "*The Brothers Karamazov* is the most magnificent novel ever written." Andre Gide gave virtually the identical assessment. Dostoevsky's *Crime and Punishment* (1886) has often been cited as the greatest psychological novel ever written, as it demonstrates how one can commit a ghastly impassioned crime and get away with it but then be unable to live with the ensuing guilt.

A driven nature was at the root of both Dostoevsky's successes and failings. He called his manic-depression "the mystic terror," and was unable to control his drives any more than he could control his epilepsy. Most writers have described Dostoevsky's work as a function of his epilepsy, but Freud and others believed instead that he was a prime example of the guilt-ravaged hypomanic who was unable to come to grips with his raging unconscious. Freud described Dostoevsky's pain as a function of his father's gruesome castration and murder when the author was a teenager. No matter, without Dostoevsky's obsessive behaviors he would never have produced some of the world's great novels. Just like Balzac at least half of his works were created in order to keep him out of debtor's prison and he once fled to Italy to keep from going to jail.

Thomas Edison

Edison was the most prolific inventor who ever lived and much of his success resulted from his Herculean work ethic. He wanted to solve all the mysteries of life and approached his goal with a furor, as he demonstrated by his childhood enthusiasm for the library. When he was ten, Edison started at "A" and worked his way through the whole library, attempting to learn everything about nature and man. It was his indomitable will that drove him and he was never able to quite understand why other men were unable to keep up with his frenetic pace.

Biographer Josephson (1992) characterized Edison as "The Father of modern electronics," saying "his own mental and physical endurance . . . seemed to be without limit." The Wizard of Menlo Park worked nonstop, sometimes for days, taking catnaps to keep his senses keen. He only needed three or four hours of sleep a night and refused to give up on a new project until he had exhausted all possibilities. When a reporter asked why Edison experienced so many failures, the inventor responded, "They are not failures. With each one I am that much closer to the solution." He told reporters, "The trouble with other inventors is that they try a few things and quit. I *never quit* until I get what I want."

Edison was self-motivated in a manner similar to Balzac. Both men would describe their successes long before they even had any idea if they could master them. Balzac would describe a new book as soon as he had the spark of an idea about it. Edison would call a press conference immediately after conceiving of an idea, announcing that he was close to a new technological breakthrough. He did this with the microphone, phonograph, and incandescent light bulb. Even though he had no idea how to solve these great mysteries when he announced their "discovery," he used the press conferences to attract capital and motivate himself and his staff. It worked, and Edison was in constant demand in the media. Once announced he was forced to work like a maniac to solve the problem or lose face. Much of the inventor's work ethic was based on this unusual self-motivation technique.

At age sixty-five Edison tracked his work hours in his lab with a time clock—during that year he averaged 112 hours per week. On one project he didn't leave the lab for weeks at a time and only went home to change clothes once each week. At age seventy-five he was still working two full shifts each day. The electric light bulb can be seen as testimony to his drive. When the experts didn't see a market for it, he created one. He said, "If there are no factories to make my inventions, I will build the factories myself. Since capital is timid, I will raise and supply the products. . . . The issue is factories or death." In fact, the great man supplied 90 percent of the required capital to build his dynamos, electric lamp factories, and circuit plants. That is a driven man who made himself successful through sheer force of will.

Bill Lear

Bill Lear was a man on a mission and was unstoppable. He was driven to achieve, especially when so-called experts told him it couldn't be done. Lear was a man with only a grade school education who defied the aeronautical engineers—they said his Lear jet would never fly. He was dedicated to revolutionizing executive aircraft with his own innovative design, which violated all the rules of aviation at the time. It is not surprising that he was unable to find financial backing in the investment community (bankers said his product concept wasn't financially sound), but he was dumbfounded when the technologists demeaned his dream. Not to be defeated so easily he decided to go it alone and finance his own projects. He proved the engineers and the bankers both wrong and told them, "You watch, I'll fly it" and fly it he did at age sixty. And within twelve months of his maiden flight the innovative plane had revolutionized the executive aircraft industry.

The detailed story of the development of the Lear jet is pure Hollywood. The board of directors of Lear, Inc., turned their founder down when he proposed developing the plane within the confines of his corporation. Irritated, Lear sold the $100 million dollar operation to a competitor, Siegler, Inc., and it became Lear-Siegler. His received $14.3 million and promptly invested it all into his pet project. He then sold his homes in Switzerland, Greece, and Wichita, Kansas, to help finance the plane. He built the plane, flew it, and then ran out of money once again when he attempted to build numerous versions of the popular plane. At age sixty-five he sold out for $21 million. Only a man with his drive and determination could have created the Lear jet—a plane that flew higher and faster and had more amenities than any other private plane of its time (see Landrum 1993).

Margaret Thatcher

Margaret Thatcher, the first female prime minister of Great Britain, was intransigent. She was driven like a man in many respects, prompting her friend and political ally Ronald Reagan to say, "She's the best man in England." The "Iron Lady" knew exactly where she was going. She was a workaholic who liked to say, "I'm a born hard worker . . . I've never had more than four or five hours' sleep. . . . Some people live to work. I live to work." School friend Margaret Wickstead said, "I have never met anyone with Margaret's infinite capacity for work."

As Great Britain's prime minister, Thatcher was an indomitable spirit and an argumentative and combative opponent. The Iron Lady loved a fight and never backed away from any confrontation. Her biographer Young (1989) characterized her as "hardworking, single-minded, and a fierce antagonist in argument." She approached every issue as if it were being played out on the field of battle.

Henry James, Thatcher's press secretary, said, "It's impossible to get Mrs. Thatcher to relax," which she confirmed with her statement "I like to pack each minute with sixty seconds' worth of distance run." She was inflexible but honest, strange traits for a politician. During the height of her political career she told Parliament, "We shall not be diverted from our course. To those waiting with bated breath for that favorite media catch-phrase, the U-turn, I have only one thing to say: you turn if you want; the Lady's not for turning." Her inability to be swayed demonstrates an integrity rare among politicians.

Bill Gates

Bill Gates, the founder of computer giant Microsoft Corp., used his manic nature and obsessive drive to become the richest man in the world—his wealth was estimated at $40 billion in early 1998. Executives at Microsoft know when Gates is excited since he rocks with emotion while talking. Despite having more money than he or his heirs could ever spend, he still goes into his office every day and asks himself, "Am I on top? Am I losing market share? Can I compete?" (This is a man with the most dominant market share in any industry since Rockefeller.) It is difficult to understand such passion, but that is the one factor that has kept him on top of a highly competitive and dynamic industry.

The Microsoft mystique was born of Gates's bravado in challenging IBM's dominance of the computer industry by using their operating system, which he produced on contract, and offering it to the world of computer clones. This made MS-DOS (and Intel) the only common element in the ubiquitous personal computer.

In early 1998 the media asked Steve Jobs of Apple Computer what he though about Microsoft and Gates. In the inimitable style of a fellow entrepreneur, Jobs responded, "I like Bill, but I think he would have benefited greatly when younger if he had dropped a bit of acid." In other words, Gates's peers think the man is too wired, too manic, too driven for the industry's or for his own good.

Gates is the classic Type A entrepreneur who is so driven he walks, talks, eats, and thinks fast. *USA Today* characterized Gates as "being competitive even at parties." He admits to having worked day and night to get Microsoft started and hasn't slowed down much since. The *Los Angeles Times* referred to him as a "megalomaniac." *Inc.* magazine wrote that he is "a fidgety bundle of kinetic energy. Behind the boyish demeanor lies a ruthless competitive entrepreneur." A friend, Vern Rayburn, characterized him as "competitive-plus. Race drivers have a phrase for it: red mist. They get so pumped up, they get blood in their eyes. Bill gets red mist" (*USA Today*, January 16, 1991).

Madonna

The Material Girl, born Madonna Louise Ciccone, broke all the Beatles' records for successive number one singles even though many consider her a mediocre singer. She was a hit in many rock concerts where she profiled her dancing skills. The Lady of Perpetual Motion has homes in Los Angeles, Miami, and New York and sports a net worth over $100 million. Most show business experts agree that she has very mediocre talent, but her albums have sold millions of copies and her movies generated millions of dollars. How did she become so rich and famous? Madonna is the consummate example that success has nothing to do with talent. She has the other necessary characteristics and these are led by her drive. Seymour Stein of Warner records signed Madonna to her first recording contract. He described her as a woman who can "walk into a room and fill it with her exuberance and determination. I could tell she had the drive to match her talent." Her agent, Liz Rosenberg, describes her as a person "who isn't interested in wasting a lot of time." She has admitted to using and then discarding anyone and everyone who could help her rise to the top. The Material Girl told the media, "I have the same goal I've had since I was a little girl; I want to rule the world." That tells the whole story.

Madonna is a chameleon who changes her image every two years. She was brilliant at understanding the faddishness of the entertainment industry and purposely changed to stay fresh. The creator of the Boy Toy (her corporate name) image is incapable of relaxing. She must be on the move and seems to have a bottomless well of psychosexual energy. Kinetic energy is her forte. She must be in constant motion or die and she epitomizes the person living life in the fast lane. And nobody had better get in her way. Madonna told Vanity Fair in 1992, "I've been striving for power all my life." When asked about her role as a single mother she responded caustically, "I am a workaholic and I'm extremely ambitious. I have insomnia. And I'm a control freak. That's why I'm not married. Who could stand me?"

The Down Side of Manic Behavior

Our strengths are also our weaknesses and we always pay a price for our indiscretions. In the case of mania speed wins and speed destroys. In Napoleon's case the very mania that made him great doomed him. He used his superior energy and speed to destroy the armies of Prussia and marched right into Moscow after trampling the out-manned Russian armies. The delusions of grandeur resulting from his manic-depression enhanced his ability to win over great odds. He was in the manic state when he marched triumphantly into Moscow in October. But when he found a burned city with no animals or provisions he went into a terrible depression that debilitated him for six weeks. Napoleon expected a grand entrance as a conquering hero and when he was confronted with the dismal Russian winter he was incapable of making a decision. By that time it was too late in December and Napoleon lost 200,000 men to the harsh conditions of the Russian winter.

Emotional breakdown, suicide, and severe anxiety are the down side of the bipolar personality. Balzac, Dostoevsky, Twain, Hitler, Hemingway, Disney, Hughes, and Maria Callas all paid a heavy price in terms of emotional collapse. These visionaries climbed to euphoric heights only to collapse into morbid lows. When high they were able to conquer worlds and accomplish impossible tasks. When low they were incapable of the simplest tasks and were impotent. Balzac spent his life recovering from ridiculous investments he made. When he was down in one field he would make wild and frivolous decisions that a naive teenager wouldn't consider. The deeper in debt he became the more foolish was his decision-making. His grandiosity led him from one debacle to another, forcing him to write feverishly to stay out of debtor's prison. He spent the last fifteen years of his life fleeing from his debtors and the anxiety killed him. Like Dostoevsky he was made and destroyed by feverish ambition.

Thomas Edison became wealthy at a young age, but his manic need to conquer more and more led him to lose $2 million on an iron ore project, forcing him into bankruptcy at age fifty-three. Bill Lear became insolvent in his sixties due to his lavish spending after the success of his Lear jet. He was forced to sell out and then he blew those monies on other bizarre projects and died a poor man. Nikola Tesla did the same.

Dostoevsky sold the lifetime rights to his works to get out of debt and then went out and bet it all on the spin of a roulette wheel. He wrote his friend Turgenev, "I have lost everything. I am completely broke. I even gambled away my watch." As with most compulsive and driven people he sat down and wrote about his experiences in *The Gambler* (1867), which he completed in only sixteen days in a valiant attempt to get out of debt. Dostoevsky had a tragic life that would have been a wonderful model for one of his existential novels. He paid a horrible price for his indiscretions but he wouldn't have been successful without them. Biographer Joseph Frank (1990) said, "He had a volcanic eruptedness that drove him to excesses in most things that proved self-destructive." The introspective Dostoevsky saw this trait in himself and wrote, "The will-to-power leads inevitably to ruin," and in reference to his obsessions, "The fiend is party to every work of art."

Summary

Successful people often live their lives in the fast lane. That is why they succeed and it is often the reason for their demise. They are driven, emotionally, intellectually, libidinally, and physically. They are energy incarnate and often those energies are an outgrowth of a bipolar personality. Their defining characteristic is speed. Ninety percent eat, drink, think, talk, work, and drive fast, so fast they outrun their competition and sometimes crash. The majority (84 percent) are Type A personalities who are incapable of finishing second for fear of losing self-respect. Ninety percent are hyperactive or hypomanic and a product of a manic-success syndrome. Mania made them great and often simultaneously debilitated them.

According to Kay Jamison, "Mild mania and depression are the best states for creativity because they increase both the quantity of completed work and its quality." That sums up these driven subjects. Most of them fit the *Diagnostic and Statistical Manual*'s definition of hypomania: They had highly elevated self-esteems, grandiosity, high-energy, enthusiasm, extreme impatience, impulsiveness, reckless driving, and intense and impulsive romantic or sexual liaisons, in addition to creative thinking and prodigious productivity. Foolish business investments and frivolous spending sprees are found in the hypomanic and these subjects were no exception.

These subjects were aroused beyond the norm and obsessively driven, which caused them to be seen as workaholics and to take imprudent risks. Drive was responsible for their great success, but it also burned them out prematurely. It had short-term benefits and long-term liabilities. The drive was not good for them physically in the long term, but they were uncommonly healthy, demonstrating that physical well being is as much mental as physical. The mental and emotional demands of these hyper-driven personalities often caused breakdowns, but these were merely temporary. These greats would recover and return to their frenetic overacheiving. In some, like Napoleon, Balzac, Dostoevsky, Hughes, and Disney, the manic drive was responsible for much of their fame and the breakdowns were mere diversions. The one thing that is certain, drive and hard work are the elixir for great success, as these subjects prove. These traits also correlate to fame and fortune although many had to die to become great.

CHARISMA

Napoleon Bonaparte

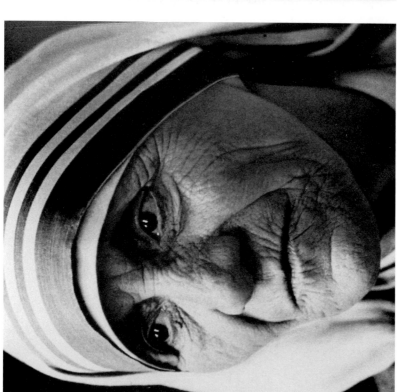

Mother Teresa (All photos courtesy AP/Wide World)

COMPETITIVENESS

Ernest Hemingway

Mildred "Babe" Didrickson Zaharias

CONFIDENCE

Frank Lloyd Wright

Maria Montessori

DRIVE

Thomas Edison

Margaret Thatcher

INTUITION

Albert Einstein

Margaret Mead

REBELLION

Karl Marx

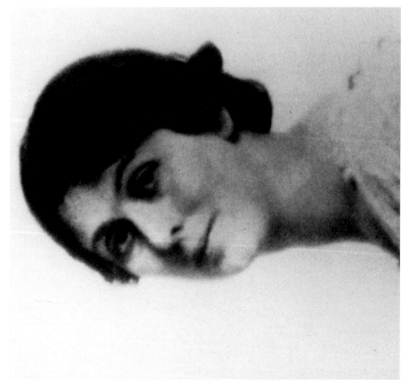

Isadora Duncan

Berry Gordy

RISK-TAKING

Marie Curie

TENACITY

James Michener

Catherine the Great

CHAPTER 5

intuition

SEEING THE FOREST THROUGH THE TREES

"The sense of certainty and revelation comes before any definite belief."
Bertrand Russell

Holistic Vision: The Elixir of Greatness

Great visionaries see the big picture and use that image to implement their dreams. Myopic people tend to get mired in the details and seldom emerge from that morass to see the whole of anything. Visionaries are able to tap into their inner vision. Isadora Duncan is a prime example of a superstar tapping into her unconscious where she believed "truth of greatness" was hidden. It was this internalized "spiritual vision" or "will" that she believed needed "awakening" in order to find "beauty." Her autobiography was the most erudite and introspective that I have read on any of these subjects. She wrote, "Life is a dream where the inner force of the will becomes the driving force of life. . . . I followed my fantasy and improvised in creating modern dance." Her friend and biographer Mary Desti quoted her:

> I feel the presence of a mighty power within me which listens to the music and then reaches out through all my body, trying to find an outlet. . . . Sometimes this power grew furious, sometimes it raged and shook me until my heart nearly burst from its passion. (Desti 1929, 224)

Lillian Vernon, America's entrepreneurial catalogue queen, says, "I never rely on price/performance statistics in my acquisition decisions. I depend on

129

my Golden Gut." Michael Jackson has the same predilection for selecting his music and dance material. He wrote in his autobiography, *Moonwalk* (1988), "A certain force tells me what works. Other people don't see what I see. I rely on instinct." Stephen King agrees, saying, "What I write comes from the gut instead of my head, from intuition rather than intellect. My books are visual movies in my head" (Baehm 1992, 82). Seeing the big picture was the methodology of Darwin, Einstein, Freud, Mao, Tesla, Frank Lloyd Wright, and Joseph Campbell, who are the shining examples of how intuition can lead one to the very top. Visionary females, namely Golda Meir, Maria Callas, and Oprah Winfrey, will be analyzed to provide some insight into how they operated.

Napoleon became one of the most extraordinary military geniuses who ever lived by violating traditional military tactics and relying on his "feel" for the battle relative to his holistic view of the battlefield. As a young general he won battle after battle he was "supposed" to lose by following his instinct instead of the more rational strategy taught in military academies of the time. Napoleon became Emperor of France because he was seen as a mystical leader who could not lose, as belief derived from his lopsided wins against insurmountable odds. How did he do it? By looking at the battlefield as a chess board and then proceeding to do the outlandish, the bizarre, the unexpected. Napoleon was aware that he would lose if he fought battles by the rules of others when they had the advantage. When fighting a sumo wrestler one must not fight on the opponent's terms or the loss is preordained. Innovation is the name of the game and that is what made Napoleon rich and famous. Napoleon always took the divergent path using his holistic vision to guide him. He saw the "whole" field of battle and deployed his troops where he perceived weaknesses in the lines. When he was successful at exploiting those weaknesses he won many battles others would have lost.

Big Picture Types

Those using the gestalt—the whole—to win are unique. They classically analyze the details in the context of the whole in order to see unique opportunities. These right-brain dominants are the people usually making great breakthroughs and creating new paradigms. Why? Because visionaries are able to remove themselves from the clutter of the detail and envision the totality of existing systems. Only when you are able to stand back are you capable of seeing with total clarity. Problems, dysfunctions, and errors are never seen when one is immersed in them. They are only apparent when one is removed from the details—that is why great innovation and insight comes from the fringe and the "flaky" right-brain types like Einstein, Darwin, and Marx. It would be more logical that these geniuses would have been left-brain dominant number-crunchers, but they were not. They were all immersed in the details only to the extent it made sense in the whole. The revolutionary contributions of these people—the theories of relativity, evolution, dialectical materialism, alternating current, psychoanalysis, the Cultural Revolution, and ecological architecture—were all born of holistic insight, not analytical dogmatism.

The important thing to understand is that all of these concepts were intuited, not deduced. These visionaries used induction, not deduction, to arrive at their great breakthroughs. They began with the answer and only then worked out the methodology. Darwin had enormous data but intuited its meaning. Freud kept hearing about childhood dysfunctions from his patients, causing him to make the leap to an *unconscious* source of the problems. If intuition worked for these earth-shaking concepts, think of the possibilities for less erudite concepts. Other eminent scholars have validated this same thing. Nobel Prize winners Linus Pauling and Jonas Salk both said, "We know the answer before we work it out." What are they saying? That they start with the answer and work back to the question in the exact way we program computers. You can't get to your destination until you determine it. Once that is confirmed then you can meticulously work out the details. Unfortunately, most people believe that arduously accumulated details will lead you to a solution.

James Michener wrote in his biography, "I discovered at an early age that I saw spatial relationships better than other children." Dr. Charles Garfield, a Berkeley research psychologist who wrote *Peak Performance* (1986), helped train the first astronauts. In that endeavor he discovered, "Great accomplishments are always the result of imagination. Almost all world class athletes, astronauts, and other peak performers are visualizers. They see it, feel it, and experience it, before they do it." No subject better illustrates this than world-renowned physicist Albert Einstein. He often likened himself more the artist than scientist. He wrote, "Intuition is the gift of the gods, logic is its faithful servant. It is the really valuable thing. The gift of fantasy has meant the most to me." Only "clerk mentalities"—those mired in their own tunnel vision—don't get it; albeit most have great difficulty envisioning nonconcrete concepts. Even highly trained scientists refuted flight until they saw a plane fly.

Myopic Experts—The Bane of the Visionary

Some people never see the big picture even when it is shoved under their nose. Have you ever had a problem with a new product, called for assistance, and had the clerk at the other end of the phone say, "That's not my department"? I call these types a *clerk mentality*. These individuals have such a myopic view of their job, and the firm's mission, they will always be clerks if they remain with the company for twenty years. They are incapable of seeing the forest for the trees. These clerk mentalities will bury any new concept if allowed. They are so mired in their own little world they are incapable of seeing the whole and without such a vision it is impossible to be effective in any organization. Winners always see problems and attempt to resolve them even if they are beyond the purview of their responsibility. Why? Because visionaries are holistic not myopic. They are macro not micro, qualitative not quantitative, analog not digital, and operate inductively not deductively.

How are Visionaries Different?

Visionaries are different because they don't sweat the details of any undertaking and are able to tap into the right hemispheres of their brain, where all creative discoveries are born. Most of the world is pre-programmed to worry about the details; most people worship at the altar of numbers. They have been told repeatedly in school or business to do it by the numbers! Minutiae has proven to be the rallying call of the late twentieth century. Most organizations train their employees to honor the budget. Consequently, everything else is secondary, and while the executives are wandering in the land of the trees their competitors are viewing the forest. Research has shown that 80 percent to 85 percent of people in the Western world are left-hemisphere dominant, which means the majority of Western leaders are overly analytical and do not come up with creative solutions easily. Einstein is an example of one whom you would think would be numbers dominant due to his profession as scientist. In fact, he was not, which is why most scientists didn't like him. His favorite admonition to his Princeton students was "Not everything that counts can be counted, and not everything that can be counted counts."

Psychiatrist Daniel Cappon, the author of an article titled "The Anatomy of Intuition" (1993), says, "Those who are intuitive move their eyes differently. Their eyes zigzag quickly over a picture and make an accurate perception." He calls intuition "the essence of common sense," and used Einstein as an example of someone who was intuitive because he was able to immerse himself into his dream. Cappon correctly believes that intuition is denigrated by a Western culture obsessed by facts and science and consequently it is lost on many people. He goes on to say, however, that "intuition can be trained." The essence of all success and creativity is the freedom to think and refusing to be locked into a single-dimensional force-field prescribed by our teachers, parents, and bosses.

The inability to see the world holistically is the major difference between average people and extraordinary visionaries like Darwin—who was very ordinary by virtually every account. Darwin saw a pattern in nature and extrapolated that pattern into a whole system, thus deriving the theory of the evolution of humanity through natural selection. In attempting to defend his ideas he said, "I did not expect to convince experienced naturalists, whose minds are stocked with a multitude of facts, of the theory of evolution." It is truly ironic that Darwin, a man trained for the ministry, had used his intuitive powers to develop a theory that denied any literal interpretation of the Bible. He wrote in the *Origin of Species*, "I owe the general law to my imagination." Darwin's biographer Frank Sulloway confirms Darwin's intuitive powers in *Born to Rebel* (1996). He wrote, "The best way of understanding creative genius is through the remarkable insights that Darwin's own theories provide."

Frank Lloyd Wright was known as the Anarchist of Architecture due to his iconoclastic nature. He is the epitome of the visionary who never bothers with the details. These types need someone to follow behind them to pick up the pieces they drop in their quest for the gestalt. That is why the Johnson Wax Building, Guggenheim Museum, Marin County Civic Center, and Fallingwater all had leaky roofs and inoperative plumbing. Wright was so immersed in designing the building to blend with the environment, form over function, that he didn't bother dealing with the small stuff. As with most creative geniuses, Wright's greatest strength was his greatest weakness.

Einstein was another who didn't care about the details. When he arrived in America a reporter asked him, "And how far is it to the moon, Mr. Einstein?" The great physicist looked at the young man and said, "I have no idea." The reporter was taken aback that a man considered the brainiest in the world did not know what every high school student is taught and asked, "Why, every student knows that answer, Mr. Einstein." The great man said, "I don't have time to bother with such trivia. If I need that information I know where to find it."

Entrepreneurs like Hughes, Turner, and Gates, scientists like Einstein and Tesla, innovators like Darwin and Wright, and political visionaries like Napoleon and Mao were able to see the big picture. All were prone to planning their ventures in a very logical or quantitative way. For example, Napoleon played at war like he was playing at chess. He spent hours on detailed planning and with that well in hand rode to battle and deployed troops (the details) in context of the whole. Ted Turner meticulously computed the opportunities for CNN (quantitative analysis) but used his gut instinct (qualitative analysis) to launch the all-news station. Ironically, they operated in just the reverse, in a very qualitative manner. Such behavior is diametrically opposed to what is taught in school, probably because the teachers must operate in a very tradition-bound system that prefers structure to chaos, the known to the unknown, and the rational to the esoteric. In school numbers become sacrosanct and modeling exercises on existing systems and regimens is the standard. Unfortunately, this is not the way of a dynamic world. Regurgitating facts is comfortable and validates performance, despite being counterproductive to experimental learning.

Right-Brain versus Left-Brain Thinking

Why do most of our great inspirations come at night, in the car, on the beach, or in the shower? Simple! Because that is when you have put your left brain in neutral and have allowed free reign to your right brain, where creativity resides. It is very important that one escape from his or her immediate environment in order to see it holistically. When in the middle of solving a problem, or in the field of battle, it is virtually impossible to see all the aspects of a problem, but without examining all sides of a situation, it is impossible to be creative. That is why press boxes are located on the top of the stadium and not on the field of play.

The right brain controls the left side of the body and the left brain dominates the right side of the body. The left side governs logic, rational thinking, sequence, analysis, and quantitative thought. The right side is more sensual, governing intuition, spontaneity, gestalt, and qualitative thought. One is digital the other analog, one micro the other macro, one the trees the other the forest. When the quantitative left side is hard at work dealing with the day's problems, the right side is dormant. It only becomes activated when the left is allowed to rest, which is why the "Eureka" ideas occur on the beach or in the shower.

How to Become More Creative

Leave your Desk and Go Straight to the Beach

Visionaries walk on the beach while myopics slave at their desks. Myopics spend their time exploring details while visionaries dedicate their life to the possibilities and opportunities that surround us daily. Visionaries worship at the altar of opportunity, myopics at the altar of numbers. Minutiae is the mortal enemy of anything innovative, unfortunately most of us were trained to worship budgets and to live our lives "by the numbers." Sound familiar? Details and structure dominate our lives at the expense of the new and innovative. Unfortunately, living your life among the trees doesn't allow any view of the forest. Einstein discovered this truth quite early in life and refused to conform despite training to be a scientist. His refusal to adapt got him expelled from high school and he was refused entrance into engineering school.

Stop Being a Slave to Numbers

Demand freedom from all internal and external structures and allow your brain free reign away from all immediate problems. It is important to put your controlling left brain in neutral for your creative right brain to function. While your left brain is in control of your actions there is no way for you to be creative since imagination, fantasy, and innovation are found in the right hemisphere of the brain. Creativity can only occur when the left brain is dormant, but relaxing can sometimes prove to be difficult; often the harder we try to relax the more tense we become. The only solution may be to act "irresponsible" and go to the beach, leaving your problems on your desk. You will be shocked to discover how many solutions can be found when you are not actively looking for them. The late Victor Frankl came upon his theory of "paradoxical intention" while working with the impotent. The harder his male patients attempted to get an erection the less chance they had for success. Only when they stopped trying were they able to perform. Success can only come from relaxing and allowing nature to take its course in sex and other creative processes as well.

Flakes

Are visionaries flakes—irresponsible, flighty individuals? No. But many people erroneously think they are because they can often be observed living by their intuition, something mistakenly seen as emotion. Intuition is the manner in which we perceive the world, not how we deal with what we see. We can be deductive or intuitive, left-brain or right-brain dominant, and no matter our predilection we can make our decisions either rationally or emotionally. The two are mutually exclusive. Therefore, intuition is seeing the big picture and not an emotional or gut decision, as we sometimes refer to it. Intuition is our view of the world and can be either emotional or rational. It has nothing to do with making emotional decisions. One dimension has to do with how we see life, the other with how we deal with what we see. Those who confuse intuition with emotion are confusing two independent states.

We make decisions based on how we *feel* or *think*, but we base those decisions on how we perceive the situation—*intuitively* or *sensorially*. One view is quantitative, the other qualitative. Neither is wrong but one is usually more appropriate. Emotional decisions come from the heart, rational ones from the head. Deductive decisions emanate from the left side of the brain and intuitive ones from the right side. Do you see this important distinction? We equate "gut" type decisions as emotional ones when they are really a right-brain view of a decision that can be either emotional or rational. How we envision the world, or any idea, can be dealt with either emotionally or rationally. In other words, our methodology is based on how we see things and then how we act on them. Intuitive decisions are more spatial but certainly not emotional. For example, Freud's conclusion on psychoanalysis—talking cure—was not an emotional one but was based on vast amounts of experimental data from his past work and his own dysfunctions. By shutting down the cynical left hemisphere and permitting the frivolous right side to function you are opening yourself up to creativity. If you have a problem you had better put on your creative hat and allow your right brain some chance to enter the equation. On the other hand, when you want to balance your checkbook, the last thing you need to do is be creative and it is imperative to turn off your creative side and allow your digital side to take over.

Psychologist Marcia Emery defines intuition as "knowing without knowing how you know." Emery means we can tap into our internal database and from that information make either emotional or rational decisions. What is important to remember is that we make them based on how we see the problem either empirically or intuitively. As I have said before, neither approach is right or wrong but unfortunately the world has become so quantitatively driven the qualitative has been lost to many people. The pathway to creativity comes by turning off your need to quantify everything and start living life more qualitatively. Dynamic environments demand dynamic solutions. That is what change is all about—sacrificing the present for a better future. Great visionaries are famous for following their dreams at the expense of everything present.

Carl Jung's Archetypes

In his system of personality types, Carl Jung defines the "feeling" types as those inclined to making emotional decisions. This is the opposite of the person who prefers to make "thinking" or rational decisions. Another dimension of our personality is how we see the world. In this he describes the "sensor" type who see life as a bunch of details—what I have described as the left-brain dominant people who are more comfortable operating in highly structured environments and should be responsible for maintaining order and control since they resist all change and disruption. These types make the best CPAs, police officers, and bankers. Their opposite is the "innovator" type, who are the right-brain dominant personalities who see the forest in all things and refuse to be tied down to structure. They are the artists, entrepreneurs, and scientists.

The above two archetypes represent two distinctly different bipolar means of interacting with the world. When you make an emotional decision your are allowing your *feelings* to be the defining factor and when you make a rational decision you are allowing your *thinking* to take precedence. It is important to recognize your preference and not place yourself in a position or job where you must make feeling-type decisions, such as nursing or a kindergarten teacher, if you are a very strong rational thinker. Conversely, do not take a position where you are expected to act rationally when you prefer to allow your feelings to decide. You are setting yourself up to fail if you are a visionary and take a job shuffling papers or you need structure and place yourself in a job without any.

Remember, emotional decisions come from the heart, thinking ones from the brain. Rational decisions emanate from the left side of the brain and intuitive ones from the right side. Do you see this important distinction? Intuitive decisions are holistic, not emotional. You must shut down the censoring left-brain that bombards your mind with empirical information if you ever expect to have a creative idea. Psychologist Stuart Vyse says, "Intuition is a reflection of what we have experienced in the past. There is no special power associated with it. There are better ways to make decisions." What he is saying is that we can make emotional or rational decisions and we can also make them based on our senses—(empirically), or based on our gut—(intuitively).

In a dynamic world it is imperative that we allow dynamic people to lead us through change. That is not possible with people who are so wrapped up in the numbers, budgets, and analysis-paralysis that they cannot see the larger picture. Such people mortgage our futures for present solace. Visionaries are more apt to mortgage the quantitative present for a more qualitative future. Harvard researcher Burton Klein put this in perspective in a work called *Dynamic Economics*:

> If the entrepreneur wants to give himself the best chance of putting the law of large numbers on his side he will use his intuition to leap to new hypotheses. The entrepreneur's riches are his hints. But if his hints are not to be squandered the entrepreneur must trust his intuition. (1977, 264)

Recent research has shown that intuition can be taught, but first it must be assessed. Ask yourself the following questions in order to test your intuition (these reinforce Leonardo Da Vinci's aphorism, "the limit of vision is simultaneously the limit of comprehension"):

1. Do your hunches come true?
2. Do you have flashes of insight?
3. How are your anticipation skills?
4. Are you able to empathize accurately?
5. Can you sense when something is amiss?
6. Are you good at abstract problem solving?
7. Do you have a feeling as to how a movie or book will end?
8. Can you see the forest while others are lost in the trees?
9. Are you able to see a pattern in abstract pictures and art?
10. Have you thought of a person and found a letter from him or her in the mailbox?
11. Have you ever felt precognitive—sensed an accident about to happen?
12. Have you ever thought about a subject and suddenly had it come up in conversation?
13. Do you sense what another person or audience wants to hear before saying it?

Having some or all of these sensations or what Jung labeled "synchronicities" says you are intuitive. You should develop your "hunches" (rather than dismissing them) by going with the flow and letting your fantasy have free reign. Go with it despite internal (fears and guilt) or external (anal-retentive friends and family saying no!) road blocks and refuse grounding. Do you think Einstein cared that he was laughed at for concocting the theory of relativity based on imagining himself flying through the air on a spaceship? We should all take a cue from Dr. Seuss (Theodore Geisel), whose "logical insanity" was the basis of his creativity. He told the media, "when I dropped out of Oxford, I decided to be a child," and that proved to be his image. Such zaniness and whimsy could never have come from someone too grounded.

Subjects Who Personify Right-Brain Vision

The visionaries discussed here were virtually all right-brain dominant. Those who best personify this important trait are Ayn Rand, Charles Darwin, Albert Einstein, Nikola Tesla, Sigmund Freud, Golda Meir, Maria Callas, and Joseph Campbell. These individuals all saw the big picture that was often lost on their peers or associates.

Ayn Rand

Ayn Rand, a Russian immigrant, spent her life preaching that the idyllic man operated with what she termed "rational self-interest." She created a system of thought that became the basis for a new philosophical system—objectivism (rational self-interest)—which in turn became the ideology behind the Libertarian party, which held rational selfishness to be the essence of an optimum economic system—politically of personally. What is interesting is that Rand's rationality appears on the surface to conflict with the intuitive process but in fact it does not. This obsessive advocate of capitalism concocted her whole objectivist philosophy based on a system of "psychoepistemology" that was purely intuitive. In other words, the philosophy presupposes that a person must see the wholeness in any system to be able to operate on it rationally. The vision is qualitative or speculative; the decision-making is what is quantitative or rational. Rand wrote, "Creators work *intuitively*, allowing their subconscious to integrate evidence that not even their conscious minds grasp immediately." Her philosophy was based on her intuitive sense of what was right for the world and espoused her theory of enlightened self-interest. She describes her basic premise in this way:

The mind is more than immediate explicit awareness. It is a complex architecture of structures and processes. It includes more than the verbal, linear, analytic processes popularly if misleadingly described as "left-brain activity." It includes the totality of mental life, including the subconscious, the intuitive, the symbolic, all that which sometimes is associated with the "right brain." (Sciabarra 1995, 194).

Rand used Frank Lloyd Wright as the model for her protagonist in *The Fountainhead*, her best selling novel about an iconoclastic architect named Howard Roark. Roark was the quintessential visionary who defied the bureaucrats and the establishment, just like a modern Prometheus. *The Fountainhead* became a popular movie in the late 1940s and memorialized Wright as the defiant visionary who would rather destroy his creations than have them bastardized by the establishment. Because of the success of the book and the movie, Wright himself became known as "The Fountainhead"—a symbol of defiant vision.

Charles Darwin

The father of evolution, Charles Darwin, was quite ordinary by most accounts. He was "dogged," in his words, and that doggedness is what allowed him to accumulate such a wealth of geological, biological, and anthropological data that meant little alone but once he was able to combine the information into a totality it made eminent sense. Darwin was a man with an obsessive interest in nature, was inquisitive to a fault, and had a work ethic that knew no rest. But it wasn't until he was able to formulate his theory of "natural selection" that he came up with the answers surrounding the descent of man. His theoretical insights altered the way the world envisioned man's evolution. Darwin did not publish his *Origin of Species* until 1848, twenty years after he had conceived the theory, due to the emotional turmoil he faced in a Victorian society personified by his god-fearing wife and family. The publication of Darwin's theories caused an uproar that tormented him the remainder of his life.

Darwin was from a devout family and had graduated from college with a divinity degree. While awaiting assignment to a ministry he took a five-year voyage on the *Beagle*, a journey that changed his career path and altered humanity's belief in the scriptural view of creation. Darwin was a man of average intelligence but great curiosity. It was his ability to put together the pieces in an intuitive puzzle that ultimately made him rich and famous. At first Darwin struggled for absolute proof of his hypotheses, but eventually he went with his intuition since he had no concrete proof that could be exercised. He had used induction to solve a problem that would have been insoluble deductively. The logic of the patterns Darwin observed in his vast store of information became the intuitive answer he sought.

Darwin described his mind as "a kind of machine for grinding general laws out of large collections of facts." After years spent accumulating random facts, Darwin's "survival of the fittest" hypothesis and his overall theory of evolution arose after he read Thomas Malthus's theory of population. He had a "catalytic" flash of insight in 1838 which led to the formulation of his theories on the descent of man:

> It at once struck me that under these circumstances favourable variations would tend to be preserved, and unfavourable ones to be destroyed. The result of this would be a new species. Here, then, I had at last got a theory by which to work. (Darwin 1958, 120)

Golda Meir

Golda Meir, the Golden Girl, was truly the savior, if not the creator, of the Israeli state. If not for her efforts Israel may have perished in its early years when there was never enough people, weapons, money, or political support. It was Meir's charisma and intuition that made her a unique female leader in the bastion of male power. Her incredible "sense" of what was right and her eloquent definition of problems allowed her to become the first female prime minister of Israel at the age of seventy. Meir was known as "Goldie" as a child, which evolved into the "Golden Girl" after she immigrated to Milwaukee from Kiev, Russia, in the early part of the twentieth century. She was educated in the United States prior to relocating to Palestine where she would dedicate her life to Zionism. When her husband of six months said "I'm not sure I want to go off to a foreign nation to live," Meir responded, "Then you stay. I'm going." Such was the emotional commitment of the woman known as a "zionut" to her friends.

Biographer Ralph Martin described Meir as possessing "an unerring instinct and intuition . . . both logical and intuitive at the same time." The most poignant example of this occurred just prior to the Yom Kippur War in 1973. Meir had just taken over as prime minister and was preparing for Yom Kippur—the Day of Atonement, the most solemn of Jewish holy days. Many of Meir's cabinet members had gone on holiday when reports of Russians moving out of Arab territories sent a message to this visionary leader. She sensed something was amiss but her advisors told her, "Don't worry. There won't be a war." But Meir's gut told her otherwise. On the day before Yom Kippur she decided to follow her instincts and called an emergency cabinet meeting and told them, "I have a terrible feeling that this had all happened before. I think it all means something." Her chief of staff, minister of defense, and chief of intelligence and commerce all told her no problem existed. Meir wrote in her memoirs, "I should have listened to my heart and ordered a callup. I knew that I should have done so, and I shall live with that terrible knowledge the rest of my life." The Yom Kippur War began the next day and 2,500 Israeli soldiers died within a week, many of whom would have been spared had the men heeded Meir's warnings, or had she acted despite their bad advice.

Sigmund Freud

Sigmund Freud, the father of psychoanalysis, as a practicing neurologist in Vienna, had a feel for what was happening in his anxiety-torn patients. As a medical doctor Freud was trained to believe in the senses and what was scientifically provable. But his intuitive feel for what was actually happening to his patients, in conjunction with his premonition from dreams and other coincidences, led him to concoct his controversial theories of the unconscious as a driving force for man's nature.

Freud's creativity emerged out of his insight into the emotional causes of the physical symptoms and traumas he witnessed in his patients. No matter what opinion one has of psychoanalysis, it is a fact that Freud has had an enormous impact on the language and methodology of psychology. In fact, it is nearly impossible to open a magazine or newspaper without some reference to Freud's view of the human condition. Freud had an enormous influence and it was mostly intuitive hypothesis since little of his theory is based on empirical findings. Our daily conversations include words like "unconscious," "ego," "subliminal drive," "libido," "neuroses," "psychic energy," "sibling rivalry," and "subconscious." All of these we owe to Sigmund Freud.

Freud published *The Interpretation of Dreams* in 1899. Ironically, the famous book sold only a few hundred copies in the first three years. It was in this book that Freud undertook the task of defining what makes us tick within instead of without. He wrote, "Dreams are the royal road to the knowledge of the unconscious. . . . Insight such as this falls to one's lot but once in a lifetime." He said the unconscious drove all of our actions and that sexual motives were behind all we did. Such a thesis is truly ironic since Freud himself led an ascetic life and did not have sex. Wish fulfillment really motivated us, according to this visionary, who believed that "What is suppressed in sexual life will reappear in distorted form in daily life." Freud used Leonardo Da Vinci as an example to validate this principle, which has affected millions of people, including Nikola Tesla. Tesla never married, and says he never had a date, because he believed, as Freud did, that sexual activity and romance would detract from his creative potential.

According to Howard Gardner in *Creating Minds* (1993), "Freud attained the heights of creativity through the use of an intrapersonal examination of his own thoughts and feelings." Gardner used Freud as the example of using a personal linguistic intelligence to create and innovate. Freud validated his approach to the creative process by saying, "I have very restricted capacities or talents. None at all for the natural sciences; nothing for mathematics; nothing for anything quantitative" (quoted in Gardner 1993, 74). In many respects Freud put more stock in dreams than in experimentation and was sure that dreams were just "wish fulfillment" emanating from the *unconscious*. Freud's whole creative output was based on intuitive concepts based on his work with emotionally disturbed people, mainly women. He clearly understood his use of the intuitive process to create, as illustrated by this statement:

> Every child at play behaves like a creative writer in that he creates a world of his own, or, rather, rearranges the things in his world in a new way which pleases him. . . . The creative writer does the same as the child at play. He creates a world of phantasy which he takes very seriously—that is, which he invests with large amounts of emotion—while separating it sharply from reality. (Gardner 1993, 24)

Albert Einstein

It is telling that Einstein was booted out of high school and failed to qualify for an electrical engineering college. How could that be? Because he was a visionary being evaluated by bureaucrats caught up in the analysis paralysis that is viewed as godly in that environment. Einstein taught himself Euclidean geometry and went on to create his own vision of the electronic world of the atom. Most of the quantitatively oriented scientists were unable to comprehend his view of space, time, and energy. Einstein graduated from Switzerland Polytechnique but was such a renegade intellectual that he was unable to find a teaching job anywhere after graduation. Einstein found work at the patent office as a clerk and that is where he wrote his special theory of relativity in 1905. He presented his theory to the Switzerland Polytechnique and was granted his doctorate, but they still refused to hire him.

The father of relativity always contended that he had developed his complex theory of relativity using childlike imagery such as riding on a rocket through space. He said, "I used childlike questions, then proceeded to answer them." That was the simple intuitive methodology he used to develop the theory of relativity ($E = MC^2$), which was beyond the comprehension of the scientists of his era. Einstein relied on fantasy to create and on his imagination to base his innovative concept on intuitive vision rather than facts. Einstein truly believed that "The most beautiful thing we can experience is the mysterious. . . . The gift of fantasy has meant more to me than any talent for absorbing positive knowledge." He expanded on this point by saying, "I think physicists are the Peter Pans of the human race. They never grow up and they keep their curiosity. Once you are sophisticated, you know too much—far too much." He once said he had not had an original insight after he was thirteen. He credited intuition for his theories of relativity and his Nobel Prize in physics. Einstein believed that all creativity came from a childlike imagination and always credited intuition for his insights into space and time, writing, "The really valuable factor is intuition. . . . A theory can be proven by experiment, but no path leads from experiment to a theory."

Nikola Tesla

Nikola Tesla created the electrical and engineering designs by which the world moves. His power stations drive the factories and machines of the world. Like his contemporaries Freud and Einstein, he came up with his ideas through intuitive insights that were not based on scientific experimentation. Tesla's patents on alternating current power generators and the induction engine were used by men such as George Westinghouse to build America's power distribution stations. The innovations were also the basis for the myriad of everyday household appliances used around the world.

Tesla was a truly remarkable human being, a titan, even compared to the wunderkinds in this book. The media of his era called him a cosmic visionary. This renegade scientist envisioned each one of his great breakthroughs prior to putting them into practice, and then determined how to make them work, the reverse of most other scientific exploration. Tesla wrote of his unusual methodology, "I could visualize with such facility. I needed no models, drawings, or experiments. I could picture them all in my mind" (O'Neill 1968, 257).

New Age writer Anton Wilson gives further credence to Tesla's approach, saying, "A genius is one who, by some internal process, breaks through by painting a new somatic map, builds a new model of experience." While in school, Tesla committed the logarithmic tables to memory and was infamous for walking up to the blackboard and writing the answer to a complex differential equation and then returning to his seat without giving an explanation of his solution. This annoyed his teachers since he would refuse to show the details of his computation. While in school, Amelia Earhart had a similar penchant for solving complex problems intuitively much to the chagrin of her teachers and other students. Tesla never received the acclaim due his enormous contributions, in part because he refused to accept a joint Nobel Prize with his mortal enemy Thomas Edison. His refusal to capitulate has left him a relative unknown even though he is arguably one of the truly great inventive minds in history.

Maria Callas

Maria Callas, a world renowned diva, changed the world of opera by daring to be different. Callas was infamous for refusing to follow traditional approaches to singing an aria. She used instinct to negotiate her away around the stage because she was nearsighted almost to the point of being blind. She refused to admit her problem and wear eyeglasses, and therefore had to rely on her intuitive powers and personality, characteristics that made her great.

Few singers provoked such controversy as "Cyclone" Callas. Many purists were offended by her husky voice, which didn't meet the standards of operatic tonal quality. Her signature was not in the qualitative aspects of her music, however, but in her delivery, her persona, her individualistic style. Her *Barber of Seville* at La Scala was considered a failure when it was performed, but today the 1956 recording is considered a benchmark for such performances. Callas was aware of her flaws and never allowed the traditionalists to defeat her. She said, "Generally, I upset people the first time they hear me, but usually I am able to convince them of what I am doing." Posterity has proven that she and her intuitive approach to a very definitive art form worked.

Joseph Campbell

Joseph Campbell is considered by most to be the father of modern mythology. Of all the eminent individuals researched, Campbell is the most erudite in my opinion. The son of a sales agent become so enlightened by burying himself in books, searching the world for the answers to the mysteries of life, and spending time with the likes of Freud, Carl Jung, Fritz Perls, Abraham Maslow, John Steinbeck, James Joyce, and human consciousness guru J. Krinshnamurti. Campbell once dropped out of school and spent one year alone at Woodstock reading the classics. At age fifty he went to Japan and learned to read and write Japanese in order to better understand their myths. Campbell's explorations into the land of the mystics, psychologists, and mythology were based on his search for the derivation of myths and his study of how they reflect the culture that created them.

Campbell collected vast amounts of data (as did Darwin, Curie, and Edison) before using intuition to arrive at his hypotheses. In many respects he was a Jungian, saying, "Our archetypes are acquired through identity with myths and myths create heroes out of those who heed them." He saw the unconscious as the source of our collective drives and needs, and as the source of our mythical belief systems:

> Myths are models for understanding your life. . . . Like dreams, myths are reproductions of the human imagination. . . . They are revelations of the deepest hopes, desires, fears, potentialities, and conflicts of the human will. (Segal 1987, 51)

Campbell said "myth is metaphor," and he believed "mythology is symbolic of spiritual powers within us." In other words, he saw intuitive vision as the source of creative energy and success. He admonished everyone to "follow their bliss," that inner knowledge we often acknowledge as "insight" or "intuitive vision," no matter where it led. Campbell believed our psyches to be the cave containing all the true jewels in life, and said, "unless we are willing to rely totally on that inner treasure we will get lost on the highway of life." Most people are afraid to follow their bliss, and consequently opt for the safe and secure. "Experts" become the gods of such people even though such people have such a psychological investment in the present they can seldom grasp the potential of the future. Campbell saw the error in this and knew intuitively that "if you have the guts [intuitive vision] to follow the risk, life opens . . . up all along the line."

The Down Side of too Much Vision—Fantasy!

Those with the fortitude to give free reign to their intuition are capable of flights of fantasy that often end in self-actualization or an epiphany. Picasso told reporters, "I have the revelation of the inner voice," often escaping into an orgy of artistic surrealism that erupted from deep inside his raging psyche. The Spanish painter was a nihilist whose paintings documented the dementia of the twentieth century. His work is a study of the sociopathic fantasies of a demented personality. Hitler was equally as guilty of releasing his inner rage on the world. Even Stephen King saw the down side of allowing free reign to the unconscious. He is quoted as saying, "If I weren't writing, I might be a mass murderer. I make up horrors to help me cope with the real ones. It is a cathartic release for me."

The *New York Times* labeled Frank Lloyd Wright the "Anarchist of Architecture" and "Frank Lloyd Wrong." Most of the media could not understand his iconoclastic nature. Wright refused to conform to anything, allowing his fantasies free reign. His most impulsive action may be his decision to run off with the wife of a client, abandoning his thriving Chicago business and a faithful wife and six children. Much of his work represented elegant masterpieces that married function with the environment, but Wright was so concerned with the essence of his creations he didn't pay attention to the "small stuff" like roofs and plumbing. Manhattan's Guggenheim Museum, the Marin County Civic Center, and Fallingwater all won awards for artistic distinction, but their roofs leaked and the plumbing seldom worked. It took someone with Wright's prescient vision to create such edifices but in the end it was his strength—melding a building with its environment holistically—that became his weakness—refusing to acknowledge, or even care about the details like safety or integrity.

Other facets of Wright's life were also affected by his macro vision. For example, he was often on the verge of bankruptcy since he refused to replicate any of his work, which is where all the real money is made in any business. Earning from previous work is the way to earn money, but Wright preferred creating new designs to financial security that would result from re-using old plans, considering commercialization below him. When he was sixty, his dream home, Taliesin, was repossessed. He never began to make any real money until he was in his eighties, when his reputation was such that he commanded enormous fees for his designs.

Wright suffered from the same disease that ails many visionaries: Once he had built a castle in the sky he preferred to begin work on another rather than move in and enjoy the fruits of his creation. Such men prefer to be off in Neverland, creating new edifices as testimony to their genius. Wright paid a terrible price for his beliefs and was bankrupt at sixty, losing his namesake estate, Taliesin, three different times. Such individuals don't seem to understand that profits never come from the first of anything. The money comes with the ability to exploit past works and to replicate what you have already created. The overhead costs for the first of anything are quite high whether one is creating a burger stand or a work of art. Most astute business people know this basic axiom but it appears to be lost on the visionaries. All economic wins come from reproductions and copying is the cornerstone of capitalism since all products move inexorably from specialty to commodity.

Nikola Tesla paid an even larger price than Wright for his fantasizing. The man the *New York Times* named the "cosmic visionary" died a pauper because he preferred to invent rather than commercialize. He had fluorescent lights working in is lab in the 1890s, but refused to commercialize the product, which was not introduced to the market until 1943. He did the same with radio transmission, remote control boats, electronic transmission systems, wireless transmission, vertical take off and landing, electron microscopes, cosmic rays, guided missiles, radar, solar energy, and many others. He predicted the advent of satellite TV in 1915. But Tesla's most grievous error was tearing up his Westinghouse contract when the company owed him $12 million in back royalties. This contract would have made him a billionaire by the time he was sixty, but more importantly, it would have allowed this inventive genius to create great new products for the world. When his friend George Westinghouse told him J. P. Morgan refused to finance him due to Tesla's royalty agreement, the impulsive Tesla reached in his desk, took the contract that was worth billions, and tore it up without any thought of re-negotiation. He justified his bold move by saying, "My visualization has kept me poor in a monetary sense but rich in the raptures of the mind." This dedication to creativity is one of the most inane in history and one of the sad commentaries of American technology. Money is seldom important to the world's visionaries and Tesla proved this axiom more than most.

Tesla was also prone to allowing his visionary imagination to make the most bizarre statements. He told the *New York Times*, "I can bring down the

Empire State building in a matter of minutes." That was just after he had broken windows and frightened much of Manhattan with his oscillators (high-tech vibrators) that were causing power outages and shaking buildings. He told the media in the 1920s and '30s "I am capable of splitting the earth, and can transmit energy in large amounts from one planet to another." Once he attached a tiny electro-mechanical oscillator to an iron pillar in his Manhattan lab and the police became alarmed when buildings started shaking and people began panicking in the streets. The police rushed to the lab of the man known as the "mad scientist," and the embarrassed Tesla smashed his oscillator.

Intuition—An inner View of the World

Carl Jung saw intuition as a function of a *collective unconscious* that manifested itself as an archetype—that personality type that sets us apart or what some behavioral psychologists have labeled "lifetypes"—in each of us. Freud called this genetically predetermined manifestation *instinct*, but agreed it was but a form of insight based on inductive reasoning. Freud believed that many truths that had been repressed from early traumas were revealed in our dreams. He wrote extensively about the value of visualization, believing that thinking in pictures was more akin to the unconscious processes than thinking in words. Jung called this process *active imagination*, in which the person meditates to enhance the flow of mental images.

Joseph Campbell synthesized the above concepts into a "mystical hero" hypothesis. His theory was based on what he described as epiphany or "an intuitive grasp of reality." Campbell refined the psychologists' system into what he believed to be fundamental to living an adjusted life, claiming, "Myths are models for understanding our own life." He spent most of his life exploring the unconscious symbols of intuitive exploration. He wrote, "Life potentialities are innately unconscious. The imagination develops symbolic experiences recording them as mythical scripts on the unconscious." This unconscious adoption of heroes as driving forces from within will be discussed at some length in later chapters but suffice it to say here, intuitive ability comes from within. Campbell believed myths were the secret of a blissful life. "Each individual must find the myth which is fundamental to his internalized needs. Only a myth can help one live a systematic life with meaning." He believed the identification with a hero was the way to find peace and contentment. His thesis is fundamental to my belief that fantasy mentors from books or music can show one how to find a greater understanding of life.

Gender Implications: "Women's Intuition"

Numerous studies have shown female leaders to be twice as likely to be visionary than males. The term "women's intuition" is not just a fabrication. Women appear to have a special antenna allowing them insight into truth or fiction. Women have evolved from societal traditions permitting them to show emotion, be intuitive, and nurture without retribution, arming them with a talent for premonition based on body language, eye contact, voice, and other subtle, nonverbal clues. They sense altered behavior in their mates who are often shocked at their prescient vision.

Recent studies have shown that the brains of females are different from those of males. Research from both UCLA and Berkeley demonstrate the superior holistic thinking of females. UCLA neuroscientist Melissa Hines tested the verbal abilities of twenty-eight women, measured the abilities relative to the hemisphere of the brain used for language, and found that women are more likely than men to use both hemispheres for verbal tasks. She called women's brains "paragons of holism" and men's brains "paragons of specificity," providing females with better access to both sides of the brain, thus making it easier for a woman to express emotions than a man. A woman's strength, however, often becomes a weakness when she is unable to separate emotion from reason. An article in *Newsweek* (March 1995) claimed that this inability may have physical causes: "A woman may be less able to separate emotion from reason . . . since the back part of their brains are 23 percent bigger than men's."

Cultural Nuances of Intuition

Asian cultures are more inclined to be intuitive than those in the West, according to Fritjof Capra. Enlightenment in the world of Zen becomes a holistic system or experience that differs dramatically from the West. Buddha taught that intuition was the ultimate source of wisdom and truth and that is why Eastern religions are far more mystical than those prevalent in the West. The Chinese place a strong emphasis on searching for the truth in nature and life. Taoism is a philosophic system aimed at discovering "The Way"—the method or norm to be followed, especially in conduct. Adherents of Hindism search for enlightenment and intuition via yoga and meditation. The Japanese use Zen to reach a state of awakening—a life aimed at naturalness and spontaneity. All these religions are more focused on the integration of the mind, body, and spirit as the path to enlightenment. Adherents of these religions believe their gods exist everywhere, consequently they view business far more holistically and long-range than their

Western counterparts. This has contributed enormously to the Asians' success in mass consumer product. Asian companies, such as Honda Motor Company, have come to dominate since they are not concerned with instant gratification or quarterly reports, as American companies are. Asians produce over 85 percent of all consumer electronic products in the world because they worry about doing what is necessary to own those markets rather than making this quarter's numbers. They are willing to delay profits and build manufacturing plants and distribution networks for the future instead of for the present. The future opportunities are far more important than the existing security.

Summary

Visionaries operate in the gestalt—the whole—never in the details. That is why Darwin, Einstein, Tesla, Freud, Wright, and Campbell became rich and famous. They were all holistic rather than mechanistic. None ever bowed to the "do it by the numbers" axioms that pervade academia. Consequently, each of these great men was considered a flake by the establishment because they refused to fit in or be constrained to the structure that bureaucrats so cherish. Their behaviors were considered deviant and contentious because they saw the world through a different lens. Ironically, they were all quite good at numbers but only used them to operate on the whole. In Jungian terms they were intuitive-thinkers—right-brain visionaries with an ability to function analytically.

New Age writer Anton Wilson wrote, "The future exists first in the *imagination*, then in the *will*, and only then in *reality*" (emphasis added). What wisdom! Further confirmation comes from America's Renaissance man, Buckminster Fuller, who said, "Again and again, step by step, intuition opens the doors that lead man's designing of more advantageous rearrangements" (Hatch 1974). Psychiatrist Daniel Cappon has researched the impact of intuition on creativity and writes, "I am convinced that intuition is the older, wiser and perhaps greater part of human intelligence."

Were Darwin, Einstein, Tesla, Freud, Wright, Rand, and Campbell born intuitive? Hardly! They learned that relaxation is conducive to the intuitive process. Tesla wrote that he discovered the secret to the induction engine when he was in the throes of a nervous breakdown. His personal trauma appears to have released his mind to float free without which he would not have found the answer to a problem he had been researching for months.

Even Freud experienced such diversions. Freud was abandoned in 1895 by his closest allies—Josef Breuer and Wilhelm Fliess. These departures left him alone on the fringe with no one to share his counsel. During this time he allegedly had an emotional breakdown, that, like Tesla, coincided with his epoch-making discoveries regarding the human psyche.

There is little argument that success necessitates tapping into the imagination. Fritjof Capra speaks of "spontaneous insights" in his book the *The Tao of Physics*: "The rational part of research would, in fact, be useless if it were not complemented by the intuition that gives scientists new insights and makes them creative" (1977, 286). The great people in this book are further validation of Capra's hypothesis. Everyone would be better served if he or she learned from these great people and learned to shut down their left brains so that their right brains can function.

CHAPTER 6

Rebellion

ABNORMAL SUCCESS DEMANDS
ABNORMAL BEHAVIOR

"Innovators and creators are, at best, mildly sociopathic, and at worst, completely insane."

Erik Winslow, Educator

Eccentricity—The Elixir of Greatness

The history of technological advance, scientific breakthrough, creative genius, and entrepreneurial vision is a study in rebellion. Virtually all innovation comes from the fringe of society. It is shocking how few of our product innovations emanate from the Fortune 500 or those with the greatest resources and talent. Likewise, seldom does the person with the best voice become the greatest singer, the politician with the finest credentials get elected president, or the scientist with the highest IQ win the Nobel Prize. Superstars rarely come from the mainstream but are iconoclasts with will power, drive, and temerity.

If you want the best chance of success, find the pack and then go elsewhere. There are no big wins where everybody else is located, but it takes someone comfortable with ambiguity, nonconformity, and a renegade lifestyle to operate in such a hostile environment. The subjects of this book fit the mold. Most suffered at the hands of the establishment for daring to be different and defying tradition. They were Prometheans chained to a bureaucratic rock with myopic naysayers preying on their psyches. It is interesting to note, however, that most relished the role of the renegade and thrived on the dynamics of change that permeated their life. Tradition-bound people

151

are devastated by change but these visionaries were empowered by it. Einstein is one example of the renegade scientist who relished his nonconformist role in society. Psychiatrist/author Anthony Storr said, "Einstein provides the supreme example of how schizoid detachment can be put to creative use" (Storr 1983).

Karl Marx is another example of a rebellious college student who became a radical Young Hegelian—a follower of philosopher G. W. F. Hegel—and then spent the rest of his life paying for his daring philosophical stand against authority. Young Hegelians were *persona non grata* in nineteenth century Germany but Marx refused to allow the establishment to win and set out to destroy them with his prosaic pen. German society never accepted him and he was never able to find work. After earning his doctorate in philosophy, Marx sought a teaching assignment but was denied a post due to his radicalism. What does a man do to earn a living if he has a doctorate in philosophy? He becomes a radical revolutionist who creates his own ideology to justify his philosophy. He then goes out and attempts to overturn the existing system and, in this instance, calls for the "workers of the world to unite" against traditional authority. Marx would spend his whole life creating a dogma that would overturn capitalism, and his obsessive energies earned him the epithet the "father of Communism."

Other examples include Mark Twain, who was so radical in his early years in Virginia City, Nevada, that he feared for his life. He would not use his own name (Samuel Clemens) on the articles he wrote for the local papers even though his brother was governor of the state. Paul Robeson became America's greatest Shakespearian actor for his *Othello* performances around the world, but he was such a radical he moved to Russia. Isadora Duncan also moved to Russia. She told reporters, "I'm not a Bolshevist, I'm a revolutionist." Anne Rice is an occult writer who is as unusual as her vampire creations. She told a reporter, "I don't know, most of the time, what gender I am . . . but Lestat is the man I would love to be."

There is a fine line between eccentricity and insanity. That Alexander Graham Bell covered the windows of his house to keep out the "pernicious rays of the moon" did not detract from his positive and creative contributions to society. In fact, he probably was only successful because of his strange views of the world. Howard Hughes's eccentricities make Bell's look conventional. Hughes painted the windows of the Las Vegas Desert Inn's penthouse to insure no one ever saw him walking around nude swathed in tissue paper to ward off the germs. He wore no clothes for years and hired a full time employee whose only job description was to catch flies. Hughes spent thousands of dollars on catching flies and dissecting them in a pathological need to understand their makeup. His aversion to germs led him to wear gloves in his penthouse to open doors, and if the gloves were unavailable, he would kick the doors open. All of Hughes's food had to be delivered in paper bags by Mormon employees wearing surgical gloves who were not allowed to speak to the boss. The only allowable communication was through written notes. He regularly held business meetings while he sat on the toilet.

In some respects the ingenious Nikola Tesla was even more eccentric than Hughes. Tesla would not stay in a hotel room unless its number was divisible by three, and he had a compulsion to compute the cubic contents of each bite of food before eating it. He ate nightly in a ritualistic ceremony in the main dining room of the Waldorf Astoria Hotel in New York City with eighteen napkins laid out so he could meticulously clean each piece of silver and crystal. He wore white gloves to each meal and threw them out after one wearing. His phobias included earrings and pearls on women.

Tesla was arguably the most inventive genius who has ever lived and the most bizarre. He was known in media circles as the "electrical sorcerer" for his life-threatening stunts. The media called him "an arch conspirator against the established order of things." One example of his odd behavior was his need to refute Edison's claims that alternating current was too dangerous for use in the average household. Tesla stood on a stage at the 1893 Chicago World's Fair and allowed two million volts of electrical current to enter his body, causing it to glow while lighting a light bulb held in his hand.

This genius had highly perceptive senses. According to his biographer, Margaret Cheney, Tesla was able to hear thunderclaps at a distance of 550 miles, a watch tick from three rooms away, a train whistle twenty miles away, and could sense the presence of a fly twelve feet away in the dark. He was precognitive and obsessive-compulsive, but a man with "ethereal genius." Tesla never lived in a normal residence; hotel rooms were his home throughout his long life. If he walked out the door of the Waldorf Astoria, his Manhattan home for many years, and accidentally turned the wrong way, he was incapable of turning around. He had to walk all the way around the block. In any era, by any definition, Nikola Tesla was not normal.

Even Walt Disney was abnormal. According to biographers, Uncle Walt was an FBI informant, obsessive-compulsive, manic-depressive, and suffered eight nervous breakdowns during his long and illustrious career. His compulsive need to create and obsessive need for perfection made him one of America's great creative geniuses but it also contributed to his problems.

Eccentrics

The results of a 1995 British study was published in *Eccentrics: A Study of Sanity and Strangeness* by David Weeks and Jamie James, who found, "An eccentric is creative, curious, idealistic, and obsessive about some special interest." The study found, as I have, that the eccentrics discussed here knew they were different around the age of eight, lived lonely early lives, and had "feelings of superiority." The study found that eccentrics tend to be more intelligent than the average population—"one standard deviation higher, in the 115–120 range" (Weeks and James 1995, 38), and suffer less stress because they "do not have to worry about conforming." Eccentrics also "go to the doctor only once every eight or nine years," and appear to have no time for illness.

Break the Rules

Sam Walton, the founder of Wal-Mart stores, wrote in his memoirs, "Break the rules. Swim upstream. Go the other way. Ignore the conventional wisdom. If everybody is doing it one way, there's a good chance you can find your niche by going in exactly the opposite direction. I always pride myself on breaking everybody else's rules" (1992). Michael Jordan echoed this when he told a sports reporter, "I never listened to the coach in the huddle my whole life. . . . My mind is totally somewhere else." Nietzsche was most eloquent in the defense of rule breaking: "Whoever wants to be a creator in good and evil must first be an annihilator and break values. Thus the greatest evil belongs to the greatest goodness; but his is—being creative" (Kaufman 1967, 327).

Maria Callas persistently broke important theatrical engagements, and she was also unreliable with personal appointments as well. Her faithful husband, a devout Roman Catholic, once arranged an audience with the pope that the Diabolical Diva promptly broke. Her reasoning? "I don't want to see the Pope this morning. It's raining, a gray day, and wearing black would irritate me." Her irate husband told her, "No one stands up the Pope." Maria did.

Both Mark Twain and Frank Lloyd Wright broke all the rules in their professions as well as in their personal lives. Neither cared for the establishment and showed their disdain by their bizarre choice of clothes. Both were dapper dandies and models of sartorial splendor. Twain wore a white suit, white hat, white gloves, and white shoes all year round and defended his attire by saying, "I have certain mental and material peculiarities and customs." His wit came through in describing why mavericks such as he succeeded in the world: "It is strange the way the ignorant and inexperienced so often and so undeservedly succeed when the informed and the experienced fail." Wright was even more unconventional in his dress. He walked into meetings adorned in a broad-brimmed hat, cane, and swirling cape. Wright is the personification of The Fountainhead. Ayn Rand's protagonist of the book of the same name was fashioned after Wright because he epitomized "rational-self-interest," a man who would rather destroy a new creation rather than allow it to be defiled by the establishment.

Singer Madonna learned early in life that breaking the rules could lead to success. At age nine she walked on stage with nothing on but a skin-colored bikini. Her conservative father and the nuns were mortified, and the student body was titillated by her daring. She said, "I was practically naked, but the talent show was my one night of the year to show them who I really was and what I could really be." Winning that contest imprinted this woman with the knowledge that she could use shock to succeed, as she has continued to do so in her lyrics, performances, and her personal life.

The Eminent are Loners

Carl Rogers, the famous research psychologist, wrote in 1980, "Creative man is a loner—and so is the innovative man, for once he departs from consensus he is on his own." All of the individuals discussed here were loners, even the extroverts. Those who find themselves out in front of the pack are alone and must find support via their own counsel. They must be capable of relying on their own evaluation of what is right and not have to call in so-called experts. Self-sufficiency is the hallmark of all creative success. You must be prepared to destroy what presently exists in order to create the new. A new romance is always born out of the ashes of an old one just as all new products must arise from those presently in vogue. If you resist the destruction others will do it for you.

Hypomaniacs

Renegade visionaries are not only different, but are often considered abnormal emotionally with "neurotic" and "sociopath" the most often-used terms. Ninety percent of the subjects in this book were diagnosed with mood or emotional disorders that ranged from hypomania to manic-depression. Ninety percent of these visionaries qualified as hypomanics and were in a constant state of hyperactivity. They did everything in a hurry, including eating, talking, walking, driving, and working. Their clinical symptoms were euphoria, mania, and unrealistic optimism. They were many things but normal was definitely not one of them.

Eighty-four percent of the subjects were Type A personalities who, according to the *Diagnostic and Statistical Manual* of the American Psychiatric Association, are individuals characterized as having excessive drive, competitiveness, and time urgency. Over one-third of the subjects were manic-depressives, including Mark Twain, Michael Jackson, Walt Disney, and Ted Turner. All of these individuals went through wide ups and downs in their life. While in the up state they were capable of extraordinary achievement. In the down mode they were incapable of anything and many ended up with nervous exhaustion or an emotional collapse. All of the individuals were subject to wild mood swings which contributed to their success but also left them emotionally scarred. (See chapter 4 on Drive for a more detailed analysis of the bipolar and hyper personality.)

Avoid All Experts

The great people of the world avoided all the experts and had good reason to refuse to listen to those who thought they knew the way. Even though they would one day be considered experts they were ridiculed early on. Consider the head of the U. S. patent office, one myopic Charles Duel, who recommended in 1897 that the office be closed since everything that could be invented had been. "Experts" have such a psychological investment in what *is* they are never able to see what *might be*. Henry Ford described an expert as "someone who knows all the reasons an idea will not work." Walt Disney refused to listen to the Hollywood experts who thought *Snow White* was a stupid idea. Even the Board of Directors at Disney Studios and Walt's own brother, Roy, demeaned most of Walt's creative ideas.

When Walt came up with the idea to produce the full-length animated film *Snow White* in the mid-1930s, Roy told him "you're trying to ruin us." Then the movie moguls, Louis B. Mayer, Jack Warner, and Harry Cohn, told the media his idea was "Disney's Folly." Walt never listened to the so-called experts who also told him *Pinnochio*, *Dumbo*, and *Fantasia* were stupid ideas. When he decided to build an amusement park that would be a fantasy destination for the whole family, his board of directors refused to finance the project and Roy told him, "Walt, you have finally gone over the edge."

Disney was forced to sell his Palm Springs home and cash in his life insurance policy to buy the land in Anaheim, California, that would become Disneyland. The experts told him, "It's a fantasy and won't work," and proceeded to contract other experts to validate their claims. The Stanford Research Institute even produced a study that told the board not to invest one penny in the idea since they would lose it all, citing as justification the very reasons the park has been such a sensational success. Disney finally became alarmed if management or experts said his new ideas were good. It was when they hated the the ideas that he proceeded with great haste.

Writer/intellectual Marilyn Ferguson wrote in the *The Aquarian Conspiracy*, "New paradigms are nearly always received with coolness, even mockery and hostility. . . . Discoveries are attacked for their heresy" (1976, 68). Such was the plight of Ted Turner when he launched CNN. His accountant quit, believing Turner was destined to lose everything over such a stupid venture. The *Washington Post* agreed with the networks, who all predicted CNN's early demise. The paper wrote, "The industry doubts Ted Turner knows his ass from a hole in the ground. . . . His going ahead will help those of us who can do it better." The industry experts were the very ones who should have been establishing a twenty-four-hour-a-day news network but they were mired in their own myopia. ABC, CBS, and NBC all told the print media, "It can't be done!" Ted ignored these experts and pulled off a feat that made him a billionaire, but more importantly his gamble made the "global village" a reality and transformed the former billboard salesman into the Godfather of Cable.

Most creative geniuses are ridiculed by self-proclaimed experts who prefer to protect their own knowledge and expertise than to accept the new and different. Aeronautical engineers told Bill Lear his jet idea was stupid and would not fly. The sixty-year-old eighth grade dropout built it and flew it and responded, "They said I would not build my plane, well I did. They said my plane would never fly, well it did. They say we won't succeed, well we will." When Thomas Edison perfected his incandescent light bulb, most of the scientific world told the media it made no sense. The respected Dr. Henry Morton of the Stevens Institute told the press, "the development of an electric lamp is an absurd claim attributed to sheer ignorance and charlatanism."

Such "experts" believe they are purveyors of truth but in reality they are purveyors of doom. The Catholic Church ostracized Galileo for daring to suggest the earth circled the sun. They were wrong, but it took them almost four hundred years to admit their error. J. P. Morgan, the most powerful financial banker in the world at the turn of the century, told Alexander Graham Bell, "Your telephone invention has no commercial value." The respected magazine *Scientific American* proclaimed the Wright brothers' flight a hoax. IBM engineers in the late 1970s told reporters the personal computer makes no sense. Now in 1998 we find that according to a New Zealand study, what most people consider the three worst written books were all written by professors of English. How ironic! Thousands of such myopic examples exist, therefore it is very important to ignore anyone who thinks he knows the potential for any radically new concept because chances are, he is protecting his own sacrosanct knowledge base.

Sometimes Stupidity Pays

Ignorance is bliss because when we don't know what can't be done we are able to accomplish more than would otherwise be possible. Our predetermined limitations, not our ability, are our natural enemy. Many of the great wins in life result from entering the wrong door. People who aren't so smart that they know exactly where not to go often stumble into the most awesome opportunities in life. It doesn't pay to know too much about anything, and it is equally important to admit when we don't know something. The only people who get in serious trouble in life are those who don't realize how little they know. If you don't know something, but are aware of that limitation, you will survive in dire circumstances. But if you act like you know when you don't, you will have your head handed to you on a plate. It never pays to be too smart and pre-judge life's opportunities.

Jacques Barzun wrote in "Paradox of Creativity" (1989), "Being too good a student can limit creativity." He was confirming that it is not good to be too smart, to be too arrogant, and to become too indoctrinated regarding what we can accomplish and what we cannot. The biggest failure of education is the way it stifles creativity. It is designed to place our children in boxes of mediocrity, teach them what is possible, and, unfortunately, what is impossible. But it is accomplishing the impossible that is what made the visionaries included here great. Einstein got kicked out of school for pursuing concepts considered impossible. Fred Smith was told at Yale that his overnight package delivery idea made no sense. One of the reasons for Margaret Mead's enormous creative success in life was the fact she was not permitted to attend normal primary schools until she was a teenager—and her parents were both Ph.D.s. Mead was taught to write poetry, weave, sculpt, and solve all types of abstract problems. This early training developed one of the most holistic-thinking women in history.

Subjects Who Succeeded by Being Different

Socrates wrote, "The poet has no invention in him until he has been inspired and is out of his senses." Hershmann and Lieb write, "manic-depression is almost indispensable to genius. If there have been geniuses free from manic-depression they have been in the minority" (1988, 20). Psychiatrist Arnold Ludwig researched the link between creativity and deviant behavior and found that "mental disturbances may provide individuals with an underlying sense of unease that seems necessary for sustained creative activity." His study was conducted on 1,004 eminent individuals, including Darwin, Marx, Picasso, Einstein, Hemingway, Hitler, and Freud, to name some subjects included here. Ludwig found "such people harbor an ingrained contrariness and opposition to established beliefs, which frequently antagonizes other people."

All of these subjects were unusual in some way, and many were unusual in many ways. Rupert Murdoch had a bust of Lenin in his room at Oxford. Amelia Earhart refused to conform to any stereotype, wearing long pants and short hair when feminine styles called for dresses and long hair. Earhart did what other women feared and went where even men would not dare go. She defiantly wrote, "I will not live a conventional life." Hitler was a sado-masochist and Ayn Rand had a fifteen-year sexual liaison with a man twenty-five years her junior. Tesla, Hughes, and Disney were all obsessive-compulsives. Bill Gates, the world's wealthiest man, was analyzed by a psychic for a 1991 USA Today article. Psychic Catherine Duncan concluded, "Gates has felt like a misfit since early childhood, always taking the unbeaten path."

One of the more telling examples of being different comes from Nelson Mandela. His given name in South Africa was Rohihlahla, which translates to "troublemaker"—a name he lived up to in his volatile life as a rebel fighting Apartheid. Madonna admits her radical behavior is aimed at changing the mores of society. Karl Marx, Mark Twain, Paul Robeson, Michael Jackson, Isadora Duncan and Anne Rice all rebelled against the standards of their field.

Karl Marx

Karl Marx was a radical from his teen years in college. He spent his whole life attempting to get even with the establishment, who refused to allow him to express himself. His response was a life spent writing an ideology—dialectical materialism—aimed at destroying the bastions of capitalistic power that he envisioned as his mortal enemies. At his funeral Friedrich Engels described Marx's effect on the world by saying, "He was the best hated and most calumniated man of his time."

Marx renounced his homeland, Prussia; his religions, Judaism and Protestantism; his economic system, capitalism; and his family, none of whom he saw again after he graduated from college. Now that is rebellion. His opening line in the *Communist Manifesto* (1848) reads, "Workers of the world unite, you have nothing to lose but your chains." In a valiant attempt to destroy the vile bourgeoisie whom he blamed for the despicable state of the world, he concocted a dictatorship by the proletariat. His singleness of purpose was obsessive, causing him to sacrifice money, family, and his health for his dream of a managed society. Marx fought with a prolific pen but never once lost his "obsessive enthusiasm" and "profound conviction" that he was right. Engels said, "He was intoxicated with enthusiasm and had an unfailing optimism."

Marx's father described him as a "demonic genius." The facts that Marx never had a real job, lived his life in perpetual poverty, was imprisoned, defiled by the establishment, lost three children to illness, and was exported by three different nations stand as testimony to the truth of this statement. In every respect Marx was a rebel who attempted to use revolution to correct the world's problems. His political ideology blended economics, politics, and sociology into the theory of dialectical materialism, which was modeled after Hegel's dialectic philosophy of being (thesis), non-being (antithesis), and becoming (synthesis). Marx built a whole system based on conflict between opposing economic forces. His most naïve and radical idea was that the working classes could understand his intellectual ideology which called for the working classes to take control and change the world for the better. Revolution was at the heart of his whole scheme and violence was to be invoked when and if necessary. Karl Marx's political adversary, Michael Bakunin, sums up this radical intellectual's personality:

He is immensely malicious, vain, quarrelsome, as intolerant and autocratic as Jehovah and like him, insanely vindictive. There is no lie, no calumny, which he is not capable of using against anyone who has incurred his jealousy or his hatred; he will not stop at the basest intrigue if, in his opinion it will serve to increase his position, his influence, and his power. He also has many virtues. He is very clever, and widely learned. . . . Very few men have read so much and so intelligently. (Berlin 1978, 80)

Mark Twain

Mark Twain (Samuel Clemens) was an irreverent humorist who documented the social conscience of the Gilded Age of America. He was a mythical sage of the nineteenth century and his colloquial humor was part philosophy, part storytelling, and a strange mix of tragedy and comedy. His first book, *The Celebrated Jumping Frog of Calaveras County, and Other Sketches* (1867) was written when he was thirty-two, by which time he had already lived in New York; St. Louis; Philadelphia; Cincinnati; New Orleans; San Francisco; Sacramento; Honolulu; and Virginia City, Nevada, and had worked as a printer's apprentice, journalist, riverboat captain, silver miner, sugar farmer, reporter, and lecturer. The one thing Twain wasn't was traditional or predictable."

In northern California and Nevada Twain adopted his pseudonym as a means of staying healthy (he wrote and reported on con men and feared for his life, so a new name helped him hide). He produced *The Gilded Age* in 1873 with Charles Dudley, and two years later his first classic, *Tom Sawyer* (1876) was published, chronicling the adventures and misadventures of a boy on the Mississippi. *The Adventures of Huckleberry Finn* (1884), a book describing life on the Mississippi in the vernacular of the time, is considered his greatest work. His attempt at describing realism with a satirical and flamboyant cynicism was met with complete antipathy by the educated elite on the East Coast of the United States. No less a personage than Louisa May Alcott took it upon herself to have both of his masterpieces banned in Boston. She wrote, "The books have a blood-curdling humor, gutter realism, coarseness, and total unsuitability for young people. . . . They are demeaning, immoral, and no better than dime novels." The banning was a boon to his work and his unconventionality turned out to make him rich and famous.

Twain was a risk-taking renegade who lived on the edge in everything he did. He lost hundreds of thousands of dollars in all kinds of wild schemes in publishing, mining, patents, and a myriad of new inventions. An intrepid entrepreneur at heart, he started a publishing company and contracted with President Ulysses Grant to publish his memoirs, but was forced into bankruptcy in 1893 at age fifty-eight. Always the rebel, Twain defied the writing traditions of his era, using satire to portray the cynicism of man's dilemma. Courage, honesty, and common sense were his forte. He refused to conform to anything, including his clothes, wearing white suits all year round. In

1867, newspapers called him "the son of the devil," "miserable scribbler," and a "man lost to every sense of decency and shame."

Twain had all the symptoms of manic depression, alternating between euphoric highs and dismal lows for much of his adult life. He admitted his personal turmoil, writing, "I was born excited." One biographer characterized him as "obsessed." For all of his travail Twain was quite successful in communicating the psyche of the common folk in a very readable form. Tribute of his ability comes from Ernest Hemingway, who wrote, "All American literature comes from one book, *Huckleberry Finn*. There was nothing before. There has been nothing since" (Kaplan 1966).

Isadora Duncan

By age five the mother of modern dance was telling her teacher, "There is no Santa Claus," and then she proceeded to say "there is no god and marriage is a joke." Isadora Duncan wrote in her autobiography, "I was always in revolt against puritanical tyranny. . . . I'm a Puritanical Pagan." This iconoclast believed she was a modern Aphrodite destined for greatness. Very early in her life she decided "I'm a revolutionist. All geniuses worthy of the name are. Every artist has to be one to make a mark in the world today." Further confirmation of her renegade nature comes from historian Daniel Boorstin. In his book on creative heroes, *The Creators*, he wrote "Isadora shocked society audiences in London and Paris by her bare feet and legs, her clinging and revealing costume, and her free movements, and then gave an irreparable jolt to the classic ballet of Imperial Russia" (1992, 495).

Duncan was the consummate renegade who liked to refer to herself as a "Promethean visionary." She lived her philosophy by living a life of rebellion against marriage, religion, and the establishment. Ballet was also her mortal enemy. She also was a confirmed atheist and joined the Communist party, for which she took a great deal of flack. When her career was threatened, she told the media, "I'm not a Bolshevik, only a revolutionist."

Duncan lived on the edge to such a degree her life reads like a Greek tragedy. Two of her children drowned when the car they were in spun out of control into the Seine in 1913. Shortly thereafter, Duncan gave birth to another son in Italy, but he died soon after birth. The grande dame of dance died as she had lived, in an obsessive love affair with freedom. She was on the French Riviera, dressed in her typical attire, a long, free-flowing dress and a six-foot scarf, and jumped into the backseat of a Bughatti convertible. Duncan waved to her friends, calling out, "*Adieu, mes amis. Je vais a gloire*" (Farewell my friends. I go to glory). During the drive, Duncan's scarf became entangled in the rear axle, and in one bone-crunching snap broke her neck, killing her instantly.

Paul Robeson

Paul Robeson, perhaps America's greatest Shakespearean actor, was in fact a Renaissance man of enormous talent. He dominated every discipline he attempted, earning a Phi Beta Kappa key at Rutgers University, where he was also voted the first black All-American football player in the school's history. He went on to earn a law degree from Columbia before receiving accolades for his Broadway and movie rendition as Joe in *Show Boat*, where he sang Jerome Kern's "Ol' Man River" to wide acclaim. He then moved on to play Shakespeare's tragic Moor, Othello. During his career Robeson performed *Othello* in the movies as well as in twenty-seven different nations—in the native languages of each, which he taught himself.

Robeson was one of the truly gifted men of the twentieth century, but his renegade nature destroyed both his reputation and his life. When called before Joe McCarthy's Congress on charges of being a Communist, he said "I am a radical and I am going to stay one until my people get free to walk the earth" (Foner 1978, 221). He also proclaimed his "contempt for the Democratic press." After such pronouncements he found himself in a battle that he couldn't win with the Washington politicians. Robeson had spoken out against blacks serving in the military in World War II and Vietnam War and the politicians blackballed him, took away his passport, destroyed his career, and ruined him financially, physically, and emotionally. It was then that this indomitable spirit changed the lyrics of his signature song, "Ol' Man River," from "I'm tired of livin' and feared of dyin'" to the more rebellious "I must keep fightin' until I'm a dyin'." How did he become such a radical?

Robeson desperately wanted to be an attorney in New York City. After graduating from Columbia University Law School magna cum laude, he attempted to get a job as a lawyer, but no firm would hire him due to his color. One firm finally gave him an opportunity, but the white secretaries refused to take dictation from him. Frustrated and incensed, Robeson accepted a job on Broadway, another remarkable feat since he had never had a singing or acting lesson.

His first successes came on Broadway and in London, where he made an enormous impact for his role in Eugene O'Neill's plays *Emperor Jones* and *All God's Chillun Got Wings*. Robeson spent some time in Hollywood, but he knew there he was a token black and would never get a role other than a stereotyped one. He began to hate the system and started reading about Marx's dialectical materialism on a visit to St. Petersburg, Russia, where he performed *Othello*. After a visit to war-torn Spain in 1939 he became a political activist, an action that led to his being branded an anti-American "Communist sympathizer."

After a controversial speech at the 1949 World Peace Conference in Paris in which the American Othello told the press, "In Soviet Russia, I breathe freely for the first time," Robeson was labeled a communist and became a casualty of that despicable McCarthy madness. The U.S. State Department then saw fit to take away his passport, robbing him of his earning power and self-respect. Robeson's renegade nature contributed to his greatness, but it destroyed him, making him a victim of the McCarthy era witch-hunting and the myopic bureaucrats who broke him because he dared speak his mind.

Anne Rice

The queen of the occult, Anne Rice, was christened Howard Allen O'Brien at birth because her parents so desperately wanted a son. She has spent the rest of her life in a desperate search for her gender identity. Rice was so embarrassed by her boy's name when she started to school she picked the name Anne and kept it, although she has remained androgynous. In high school the other girls referred to her as "that weirdo." She went on to college in Texas and San Francisco where she learned what "weird" was really about. The queen of the occult and husband Stan Rice lived in Haight-Ashbury, a well-known home of "flower children" during the volatile 1960s and early 1970s. Rice fit right in with the flower-children of the era as she has always been obsessed with sex, gays, androgyny, and the supernatural. As testimony to her renegade nature she wrote, "My characters all represent longings and aspirations within myself. I am obsessed with the marriage of horror with the erotic."

She made her mark in the world of writing with *Interview with a Vampire* (1976), which *Publishers Weekly* said was an "extraordinary first novel." The book was written after her daughter, Michelle, died tragically at age five of leukemia. Rice began writing to exorcise those ghosts and her obsession with the supernatural and existential mysticism is due to an inner need to find immortality. Lestat is Rice's heroic vampire who personifies the qualities of a Nietzschean Overman. She was attempting to delve into the soul of the unknown and unknowable and says, "I wanted a hero and it was Lestat. Louis [the protagonist] was certainly me when I wrote *Interview* and then later Lestat was more me." Rice is the consummate example of Jung's syzygy, where tapping into the opposite gender can optimize behavioral interactions.

Rice has said "I've always loved the images of androgyny. . . . I think I have a gender screw-up to the point I don't know most of the time what gender I am" (Riley 1996, 222). She told one biographer, "I'd be a man in a minute. I would cheerfully be a six foot, blonde-haired man wearing a size thirty-eight." Her protagonist vampire hero Lestat "is the man I would love to be." She wrote, "You are the man in me: rule-breaker, anti-god, male energy symbol."

Michael Jackson

Michael Jackson, the Peter Pan of Pop, is the consummate rebel. Skin bleaching, hyperbaric chambers (a health-enhancing "apparatus") in an attempt at perpetuating life, and an obsession with remaining a perpetual teenager in the fantasy likeness of his hero Peter Pan have all led to an eccentric image. Jackson has perpetuated that image by his on-stage persona of white gloves, crotch grabbing, white socks, and sunglasses—all symbols of overt defiance. His personal life is far more bizarre. The King of Pop has had his chin, nose, eyes, and mouth done in a valiant attempt to look like his mentor Diana Ross. He described in his autobiography, *Moonwalk* (1987), "My attitude is if fashion says its forbidden; I'm going to do it."

Jackson's great success has grown out of his independent nature. The album *Thriller* (1984) was a radical departure from more conventional pop music, as was his signature dance, the Moonwalk. A lyric from his 1996 album *HIStory* tells the story of his life on the fringe. Jackson sings, "Life isn't so bad after all, if you live it off the wall." He went too far with the lyrics of his *Scream* album and was forced to change the words due to public furor over anti-Semitism. In reality Jackson has few prejudices, and most of his eccentricities have been a positive contribution to his enormously successful career. His proclivity for an alternative lifestyle makes Jackson a media icon but also has led to much anxiety in his life. Nothing he does conforms to the mores of any society, including his 1996 marriage to former nurse Debbie Rowe, who bore him a son he named Prince Michael Jackson.

"Wacko Jacko" is one of the media's favorite nicknames for Jackson due to his unusual lifestyle. He believes in magic and is very spiritual, saying, "I don't do many things until a certain force tells me to do them." Jackson is probably bipolar and is obsessed with remaining a perpetual teen. He suffers from panic attacks, experiences violent mood swings, and is a Type A personality to the nth degree. All of these attributes or maladies have contributed to his enormous success on stage but have caused him to live the life of a recluse. When she interviewed Jackson and his first wife, Lisa Marie Presley, Diane Sawyer referred to him as an "industry within an industry. He is a fascinating combination of art and commerce, of self-invention, of something mysterious and something recognizable." Jackson's album *Thriller* was the best selling album of all time and his Moonwalk dance moves audiences to hysterical adulation.

The Down Side of Iconoclastic Behavior

People who are different frighten the establishment. Napoleon was purportedly poisoned by his British captors, Martin Luther King Jr. was assassinated for daring to challenge the system, Darwin was tormented, Duncan ridiculed, Robeson destroyed, Marx exiled, Wright derided, Mandela imprisoned, Callas and Madonna banned from performing, and Ted Turner scorned.

When Frank Lloyd Wright ran off to Europe with another man's wife, leaving his own wife and six children and his thriving architectural business in Chicago, Wright's family and the world of architecture were not understanding. Many nations banned Madonna's book, *Sex*, even though the Material Girl was only flaunting her right to publish it. Picasso said the painter must destroy what *is* in order to create the *new*, to give it another life. All of these people paid an enormous price for daring to be different and violating society's rules, but their uniqueness led them to the very top of their discipline.

It's Okay to be Different

Ralph Waldo Emerson wrote in *Self-Reliance*, "Who would be a man must be a nonconformist." That has certainly proven to be a valid statement. Most of the renegades included in this study were labeled kooks, deviants, misanthropes, or worse during their trek to the top. Those reviewed in this chapter were certainly unreasonable. All were renegades who defied the establishment and used their differences to further their careers. No one better epitomizes this than Margaret Thatcher, who refused to capitulate to the established order. She learned to be independent quite early in life from her father, who told her, "You are a leader and leaders are independent. It is okay to be different, Margaret." Thatcher took him at his word and grew up to be different and that quality catapulted her to the top of the British political system.

Gender and Renegade Behavior

The majority of these subjects were rebellious, and had to be, in order to rise to the very top of their discipline. The most defiant was probably Karl Marx, who spent his life attempting to destroy the establishment both politically and economically, but Paul Robeson was a close second. The Shakespearian actor lived in exile in Russia for many years rather than conform to American expectations. Isadora Duncan was known as the "Pagan Revolutionist" while Rand earned the epithet as the Radical Russian. Babe Didrickson Zaharias violated every social norm and dared any male to challenge her at golf or arm wrestling. Zaharias, Amelia Earhart, and Anne Rice were all defiantly androgynous, refusing to comply with traditional modes of dress and hairstyle, while Twain, Wright, and Tesla were fastidious to a fault in their top hats and canes.

A study on eccentrics found that "about two-thirds of America's current eccentrics were women" (Weeks and James 1995). Why? The authors contend women have stronger spirits and are far more independent, more rugged and assertive than male eccentrics. They say women have "the courage to swim upstream." This study found the majority to be renegades regardless of gender and didn't find a big difference in their need to flaunt tradition or established values. Being different is critical to success when one is attempting to alter paradigms and gender is not a factor. Most people are able to tap into their opposite gender—what Jung labeled the syzygy. Virtually all of the women and many of the men in this book had this ability. Examples are Margaret Mead living alone in the jungles of New Guinea as a single female in order to acquire her research data and Catherine the Great donning a Colonel's uniform and mounting her steed like a man to defeat her husband. Amelia Earhart refused to fly with other women just as Babe Didrickson Zaharias refused to play sports with other women—both were convinced they could only improve by competing with males. Conversely, Freud, Tesla, Campbell, and Martin Luther King Jr. were highly sensitive males who were adored by their female disciples for their nurturing natures. Even the often vile Mao Tse-tung was described as having many female qualities (Zhisui 1994). Other data substantiates the gender shifts with *Fortune* (August 8, 1994) saying, "Women entrepreneurs are more like men entrepreneurs than they are like other women," and *Psychology Today* (July 1996) writing "Creative and talented girls are more dominant and tough than other girls."

Summary

Success doesn't come from the pack. It blasts its way out of the fringe and can only be found where the pack isn't. Therefore if you are an eccentric, maverick, or renegade, you have a much better chance at the brass ring than those conformists who would never think of rocking the boat. One reason for the success of nonconformists is their refusal to abide by "expert opinions." Fear and security are antithetic to the creative process. Fear of change is the driving force behind all bureaucratic decision-making and is not a factor for the rebel. Bureaucrats protect the present with a passion and fervently mortgage the future. These are the type people who poisoned Socrates for daring to preach change and truth. They are the mortal enemy of innovation and creativity. Rebels are the innovative geniuses who change the world. Change is their god and it makes them successful.

According to Weeks and James (1995), the "eccentric is largely immune to the physiological toll of stress, because they do not feel the need to conform." Success comes from not conforming, the diametric opposite of what is taught in school and church. In the opening lines of Darwin's *Origin of the Species*, the father of evolutionary theory says, "a high degree of variability is obviously favourable." Even more prophetic are the words of the eminent philosopher John Stuart Mill, who said, "That so few dare to be eccentric marks the chief danger of our time."

There is no abnormal behavior—there is only abnormal times and places for the behavior. Screaming and standing on your chair in a five-star restaurant will get you summarily ejected. The same behavior at a football game will gain you new friends. The vitriolic rhetoric of Karl Marx in China or Cuba would gain respect and adulation. The same behavior in Singapore, Tokyo, or Cincinnati would get you arrested. Mark Twain's white suits in Southern California or Florida in the year 2000 will probably not even bring a second glance, but in nineteenth-century London or Tokyo they were seen as quite odd. Paul Robeson's objection to the Vietnam War was twenty years too soon, but the bad timing destroyed a great man. Duncan's bearing of children out of wedlock would hardly bring a comment today but she was despised for it at the turn of the century. Abnormal behavior is in the eyes of the beholder, but never allow anyone to make you conform since they are only inhibiting your creative potential.

CHAPTER 7

Risk-Taking

THERE ARE NO GREAT WINS
IN LIFE WITHOUT GREAT RISKS

"Life is either a daily adventure or nothing."
Helen Keller

Living on the Edge: The Way to Greatness

Great people appear to have a death wish due to their willingness to bet everything on their dreams. The subjects in this book were all high rollers, willing to bet the farm or risk their lives to succeed. They didn't take occasional risks, they took huge risks almost daily. Comedian Bill Cosby admitted to a biographer that he often lost more money gambling in Lake Tahoe than he made performing. Amelia Earhart and Howard Hughes would take off in planes destined to crash in an attempt to break some airspeed record or to prove they had the power to cheat fortune. Marie Curie worked with radioactive materials knowing their dangerous nature, ultimately dying of leukemia due to exposure to radiation.

Rupert Murdoch told a reporter, "Business is a life of constant calculated risks," and he set out to prove it by risking his media empire every week of his life. Berry Gordy Jr. was a high stakes gambler who wrote in his autobiography, "I made a game out of everything." His games included playing ping-pong in Motown's offices for $10,000 a game or $100,000-evenings at the blackjack tables in Vegas. The great writer Fyodor Dostoevsky received 1,000 rubles from the sale of a novel and gambled it all away and the next day had to borrow money for food. Ted Turner bet $100 million, including the Atlanta Hawks, Atlanta Braves, and TBS on his CNN venture. Had his gamble come up snake eyes he would have been a pauper. It came up a seven and he is now a billionaire and known as the Prince of Cable.

Risk-Takers, Care-Takers, Under-Takers

I have found only three kinds of leaders in the executive suite and other venues. The first type are *risk-takers*—visionaries who use innovation to foment change. These types include the people profiled in this book, those individuals who are always willing to bet the farm on their beliefs. Such individuals are critical to progress in any dynamic society.

The second type are the *care-takers*—followers who are very dependable and insure the status quo in any organization but are unimaginative. This group also encompasses the myopic bureaucrats who protect assets and tradition at the expense of innovation. Such individuals stifle progress by resisting change.

The third type are the *under-takers*—misplaced individuals or losers who use up valuable space in business and other organizations. They seldom contribute to progress and are ill-suited for their positions for many reasons including addictions, ineptitude, and dishonesty. Such people are dangerous to any organization if they are allowed to remain. Many have Peter-Principled* and should be removed immediately prior to destroying future opportunities.

The above three types represent a bell curve distribution with the risk-takers making up about 8 percent to 15 percent of any large organization, care-takers compromising about 74 percent to 90 percent, and the under-takers the remaining 8 percent to 15 percent. Risk-takers can be found in any discipline. Einstein, Tesla, and Marie Curie were adventurous scientists; Napoleon, Mao, and Hitler were bold politicians; Martin Luther King Jr. and Margaret Mead were live-on-the-edge humanitarians; Rubinstein and Disney were fearless in business; and Robeson and Isadora Duncan were intrepid entertainers.

No one would think of an artist like Picasso as a risk-taker but he lived right on the edge of the art world professionally and personally engaged in dangerous activities, such as running with the bulls in Pamplona. He said, "My whole life has been a struggle against reaction and the death of art." His works *Les Demoiselles d'Avignon* and *Guernica* are testimony to risk taking of the highest order, since they pushed all limits of artistic expression, defying dignity and morality (death and prostitutes are grotesquely depicted). Using the metaphor of jumping rope he said, "If you jump you might fall on the wrong side of the rope. But if you're not willing to take the risk of breaking

---

*The "Peter Principle" refers to those individuals who keep getting promoted until they reach a point where they are incompetent for the position they hold.

your neck, what good is it? You don't jump at all." To him that was far worse than a broken neck. Because of insights like this, art historian William Rubin called him "perhaps the greatest psychologist of the twentieth century," something that would not have been possible if he had not lived on the edge.

Soichiro Honda, the founder of Honda Motors, almost died as a race car driver. He told a university audience that winning was but a function of risking and failing. He told the student body, "To me success can only be achieved through repeated failure. In fact, success represents 1 percent of your work—which results from the 99 percent that is failure." William James, America's father of psychology, was even more elegant. "It is only by risking our persons from one hour to another that we live at all. And often enough our faith beforehand in an uncertified result is the only thing that makes the result come true." George Gilder, an economist and writer, confirms James's comment with this elegant definition of success:

> The investor who never acts until statistics affirm his choice, the athlete or politician who fails to make his move until too late, the businessman who waits until the market is proven—all are doomed to mediocrity by their trust in a spurious rationality and their feelings of faith. (Gilder 1984, 147)

Comfort with Ambiguity

Risk-takers are people who feel comfortable in unknown environments. They have what psychologists label "comfort with ambiguity." Such people thrive in creative and innovative environments and become frustrated and anxious in risk-averse organizations. Risk empowers them rather than disarming them, unlike the care-taker types. These live-on-the-edge personalities are inspired by the unknown and take capricious risks. They are easily bored when not challenged or if danger is not present. Their escapades involved flying their own planes (Hughes, Earhart, Honda, and Smith), racing sports cars (Wright, Honda, Berry, Gates, and Jordan), competing in the America's Cup races (Ted Turner), and trekking through jungles (Mead, Mao, and Hemingway). If dallying with someone else's spouse is considered dangerous, which it can be, then nearly all the subjects discussed placed themselves at risk. Many also relaxed by living on the edge through alpine skiing, big game hunting, drag racing, and skydiving.

Eminent people seem to know they cannot conquer other worlds until they master their own. These subjects all seemed to understand the risk-reward trade-offs in life. (Reward without risk is a delusion.) Consequently the truly great have opted for the home run instead of the base hit, and were prepared to pay the price for reaching for the fences. Babe Ruth struck out more than any other player of his era, but he also hit the most home runs.

That trade-off is an immutable law not just in baseball but in all facets of life. Base hitters don't strike out often but they are also relegated to the also-rans when paychecks are printed. The Cy Young Award is given each year to the top pitcher in baseball. It is named for Young because he won more games than any other pitcher in baseball history, in fact, he won over one hundred more games than his nearest challenger, Warren Spahn. That statistic is a well-known fact to baseball fans. What is little known is that Young also lost the most games. The moral here is that you cannot get to the top without risking being on the bottom.

Risk-Reward Curve

Figure 1 illustrates the concept of risk and reward in graph form. Rewards and risks are inversely related: As you move down the curve from high risk-taking to low risk-taking the rewards decline in direct relationship to your propensity to risk. That is the immutable law of success both personally and professionally. Locking your child in a room makes it less likely he or she will ever get a bloody nose or skinned knees, but it also insures he or she will never have the chance to experience the important lessons of life and learn how to cope in a competitive world. Our greatest education in life comes from our losses, not our wins, therefore we must risk in order to win and it is imperative we risk big to win big.

As I have mentioned, one of the problems of our educational system is that we not only learn what we can do but we are also advised as to our limitations. Accountants are taught how to reduce risk in any business. Unfortunately, that is wrong. Removing risk is not the answer; managing it is. As the accountant removes risk he or she is simultaneously removing opportunity. Two of our most respected professions in business are accountants and attorneys, and both are trained to mitigate risk for their clients. Removing risk only removes the potential for a big win as is illustrated in the risk-reward curve. In the vernacular of Las Vegas, it is much safer to play a nickel slot machine than a dollar slot, but you had better be satisfied with the lesser wins associated with the lesser bets.

Physical, Financial, and Psychic Risks

There are three kinds of wins and losses: physical, financial, and psychic. We normally associate risk-taking with financial and physical opportunities only and forget the psychic wins and losses, but psychic wins and losses follow the same curve. If you are only willing to ski on a bunny slope you will reduce your chance of breaking a leg but you will also forego the euphoric experi-

Figure 1
Risk-Reward Curve
An Immutable Law: There are no
Great Rewards without Great Risks

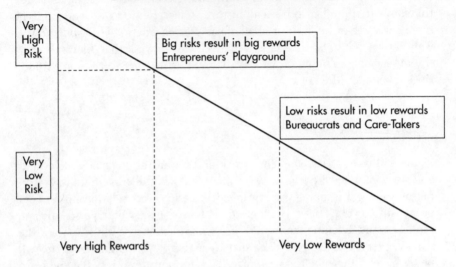

Very High Risk

Big risks result in big rewards
Entrepreneurs' Playground

Low risks result in low rewards
Bureaucrats and Care-Takers

Very Low Risk

Very High Rewards   Very Low Rewards

- Risk and reward are a zeo-sum game. Risks decline in direct proportion to the risks taken both professionally and personally

- Removing risk from any venture only results in reducing the potential

- Psychic, financial, and physical risking are all subject to this law

- There are no big wins in life without big risks

- Risk-taking declines with aging and accumulation of assets for the average population. This does not apply to either entrepreneurs or bureaucrats. The former continue to risk regardless of age and assets, the latter never risk.

- Great success—physically, financially, and psychically—demands identifying high risk opportunities and managing those risks.

ence of defying the elements or enjoying the panoramic view from atop a mountain. Why do people mountain climb, sky dive, or bungee jump? Because of the risk involved, and the need to prove to themselves they can beat the odds and overcome the elements. Without the inherent risk no one would partake in such costly and frivolous recreation. Refusing to try snowboarding or whitewater rafting, turning down a trip to Mongolia or Russia, or refusing an offer to make a commencement speech at the local high school only denies you an opportunity to experience a more dynamic side of life. Not risking our self-esteem only keeps us from self-actualizing and the psychic payoff of such risk-taking. Playing it safe removes all risk and simultaneously removes the euphoria that could be experienced had we been willing to live outside the safety of our environments.

Entrepreneurs and Risk-Taking

Entrepreneurs are the best example of risk-taking and appropriately most college textbooks equate the term "entrepreneurship" with risk-taking. The world's great entrepreneurs, men like Andrew Carnegie and Henry Ford and women like Mary Kay Ash and Estée Lauder validate the definition of entrepreneurship as taking risk. Balzac, Edison, Twain, Tesla, Disney, Hughes, Rubinstein, Earhart, Berry, Turner, Smith, Gates, and Jordan were off-the-wall entrepreneurs who were willing to bet the farm on an untested theory.

These entrepreneurs operated at the very top of the risk-reward curve but so did the athletes and most of the politicians. And the amazing thing is that they violated the norm by continuing to risk long after they had no reason to. It is easy to understand why someone might risk everything when there is little to loose, but once these intrepid souls made it to the top, you would think they would become more conservative in their ventures. Not so! They continued to bet everything long after they didn't have to because risk was just as much a part of their makeup as shoes. They lived for the thrill and challenge of proving they could overcome enormous odds and often paid the price. What is shocking is that they risked it all, not only professionally, but personally. Turner and Murdoch bet their whole empires on new schemes when they were in their fifties and sixties even though they were already billionaires, seemingly willing to lose it all for the glory of the new win. They had that inner drive to live on the edge, take the big gamble, go for the home run. It made them wealthy and it often came close to destroying them.

Investing in bonds or finding a safe haven was not in their game plan. It didn't fit their need for arousal and stimulation. All of these people appeared to seek the thrill of the gamble. Risking titillated and motivated them. But in capitalism we keep score in money, which is why Ted Turner's $100 million-dollar bet on CNN improved his net worth to $3 billion and why Rupert Murdoch's insolvency in 1990 has catapulted him into the $4 billion net worth eight years later. Had either of these men protected their asset base like more prudent men they would be wealthy, but not super-wealthy. Turner would be worth a few hundred million but he certainly would not be worth billions. Hughes and Murdoch both became billionaires due to their willingness to bet everything on their ventures. Berry Gordy Jr. didn't do quite so well as these two, but he still ended up with a personal worth in the hundreds of millions for his Motown wager.

Optimism (internalization) versus Pessimism (Externalization)

Optimists win because of their temerity, pessimists lose because of their fear. The pessimists opt for the risk only in negative situations and never on positive opportunities and they lose in both. Optimists internalize their wins and losses and take responsibility for whichever results. Optimistic gamblers and athletes blame themselves for their failures but then perform better after a defeat than their pessimistic counterparts. Research (such as that discussed in chapter 2 regarding competitiveness) has shown that defeat causes Olympic swimmers to swim faster in the race following their loss. Optimistic football and basketball players have been tested and found to do better after recent defeats than pessimistic players. The reason is the internalization versus externalization of the experiences. Optimists unconsciously absorb the experiences and retain the associated emotions, pessimists blow up and then forget the experience. The mind is the only variable in the performances.

A consistent finding among the eminent is that the more risk-oriented their nature, the more optimistic and open they tend to be. Risk drives people and organizations to a higher degree of openness; less risk to lower degrees of openness. In other words, the more risk in an environment, the more openness is required; the less risk, the less openness. This is a warning to be wary of those uptight people who insist on covering their tracks. Most great visionary leaders are optimistic and open. One example is Thomas Edison, who told reporters, "Nothing here is private. Everyone is at liberty to see all he can and I will tell them all the rest." Great people are not paranoid about their creations because of their inner knowledge that they are in control of their destiny.

Fear and Risk-Taking Behavior

Overprotective mothers and bosses inhibit risk-taking in their children and employees. Until bosses or parents can allow error without guilt, they will not groom others to risk or succeed because fear becomes the basis of decision-making for security-driven individuals. Fear dominates their lives and they lead barren existences because of their need to play it safe. Where security reigns supreme risk is nonexistent. Such risk-adversity is counterproductive to all innovation and therefore progress. Where fear dominates innovation ceases because all decisions are based on the least advantageous alternative. The safe path is always chosen to the detriment of psychic, financial, or physical wins. In other words, fear is the enemy because it interferes with one's ability to make objective decisions.

One example of fear influencing rational decision-making is a psychological study on risk-taking behavior. This study offered people three choices on a gamble and ironically, the majority always chose the least attractive alternative due to their fear. A quote from this study gives some indication of what takes place when security dominates: "When choosing between gains, people are risk-averse; when choosing between losses, they are risk-seeking—and both decisions are poor" (Hunt 1993, 547).

Subjects of the study were offered an opportunity to win $80 or the alternatives of an 85 percent chance of winning $100 or a 15 percent chance of winning nothing. The majority chose the $80 alternative even though the best statistical choice would have been the $100 (statistically, the average yield of this choice is $85). What had they done? They chose the least dangerous and actually paid the price for their conservatism. This study was also done in reverse, and a second set of subjects were offered the choice of losing $80 or an 85 percent chance of losing $100 versus a 15 percent chance of losing nothing. In this case, most subjects were willing to take the gamble (loosing $100), perhaps because they saw it as the least dangerous. In this case, they should have been conservative but were not. Once again the majority chose the wrong alternative because fear and security drove their decisions.

What is the moral of this story? The majority of people risk when they shouldn't and don't risk when they should. My research has shown that the great people of the world are optimists who do just the opposite of the average population: They take responsibility for their actions while the security-driven pessimists prefer to blame outside forces for their ineptitude. The risk-takers are willing to bet on their ability to win and the risk-averse are always hedging their bets.

Can You Change Your Risk-Taking Propensity?

According to recent research those people with high testosterone take more risks than those with low testosterone. This will be discussed shortly. Another way to become comfortable with risk-taking is to make it not seem to be a risk. Ted Turner did this constantly. He was famous at CNN for saying, "The greatest risk for me is not taking the risk."

How do you change your attitude toward taking risks? By facing that risk head on. Identify some terribly risky thing in your life and conquer it. In other words, get rid of the inner fear that makes a risk appear to be dangerous. You must transfer the negative into a positive, see the action or decision as fun and exciting instead of an imprudent move. If you are afraid of flying, the only way to eliminate the fear is to stare the risk right in the face and take flying lessons. Until the fear is transformed into pleasure, it will dominate your decision-making process, and you will not be prone to risk-taking since the risk is too threatening. Until you see the risk as nonthreatening, you will not take it. Fear is the enemy, not the risk.

The successful wunderkinds in this book experienced numerous life- or career-ending traumas in their early lives. All overcame those threats and were empowered by their ability to overcome adversity. They grew up viewing risks and adversity as obstacles that are fun challenges to overcome. What most people saw as a problem these over-achievers saw as an opportunity. Early life successes caused them to look at risk with disdain and conditioned them to see difficulties as a challenge, not a deterrent. The best example of this is Amelia Earhart. At age six she learned that risk is but a perception and courage was the thing that arms one to overcome all risks. One day on her family's farm in Kansas, Earhart jumped on a snow sled face down like a boy and raced down the hill at breakneck speed. (In those days girls sat up in a lady-like fashion.) At the bottom of the hill she encountered a horse and buggy directly in her path, but the intrepid girl adroitly guided the sled underneath the carriage. She got off her sled smiling with the knowledge she had narrowly escaped disaster. This daredevil who learned to fly before she could drive was instantly imprinted with a strong need to risk as way of life. This early flirtation with disaster had given her a euphoric sense of adventure. She intuitively knew she could have been decapitated had she been sitting upright like other girls. In her autobiography, Earhart gave credit for this event as a transformation in her life.

Another example of learning from taking risks comes from Ted Turner. His father committed suicide one night after he and Ted had a big fight over the sale of the business. Turner's father left a cruel note to his son saying that he had willed the company to him but went on to say that he had sold it to a conglomerate. Turner spent many months attempting to overturn the sale based on his father's obvious emotional problems and alcoholism. Desperate to keep the company, he went to extreme lengths, transferring all of the assets and employees into a new company he alone controlled. He went to the edge in a wild attempt to win this battle of wits with a huge firm. Turner picked up the phone and advised the firm to take his offer or he would burn the lease contracts and destroy the operation.

The executives and lawyers at the conglomerate were in shock at the boldness of this brash young kid. Assuming he was after a bigger stake they offered him $200,000 and told him to take it or leave it. They gave him thirty seconds to decide. The fearless and impetuous Turner told the lawyers, "I don't need thirty seconds. I will pay you $200,000 to cancel the deal. Now get out of my office." The shocked executives walked out as Turner's accountant looked at him and said, "Ted, you have absolutely nothing. Where are you going to get $200,000?" Turner didn't care. He had made the deal against impossible odds. It proved to be his finest hour and instilled in him the knowledge that he could compete with the big boys and win if he was willing to risk big. Turner never paid all of the $200,000, but the experience gave him the self-confidence that allowed him to make deal after deal with bigger and stronger opponents.

High Testosterone

Being endowed with high testosterone appears to be one of the key ingredients for operating high on the risk-reward curve. Frank Farley, former president of the American Psychological Association, spent much of his research life studying the "arousal value of many mental and physical stimuli" (Farley 1986). Farley labeled high testosterone and thrill-seeking people as "Big T's." He said these individuals "tend to be more creative and more extroverted, take more risks, have more experimental artistic preferences and prefer more variety in their sex lives" (47). He goes on to say that their tendency to seek the novel, unknown, and uncertain, in addition to their high risk-taking propensity, further enhances their likelihood of being creative. Farley believes genetics and nutrition are the primary contributors of high or low testosterone in humans and it is well known that testosterone levels vary not only between individuals, but also in any given individual. Hockey players have higher testosterone after winning a big game than before and men have twice the level of testosterone in the morning as in the afternoon.

"Big T" Thrill-Seekers

According to Farley the Big T personality abhors predictability, low risk, and clarity. Big T personalities are also twice as likely to have driving accidents, eight times as likely to fight, and have more sex partners. Farley defines Big T's as complex, flexible, intense, and capricious risk-takers. He describes the "little t's" as low arousal types who prefer certainty, predictability, low risk, and simplicity.

America is a nation of Big T's. A case could be made that our intrepid ancestors who left Europe and landed at Plymouth Rock were all Big T's. The low risk types stayed in Europe, the Big T's split for America. The little t's formed the communities, but the Big T's moved west to found Ohio, Kentucky, and Illinois. This movement continued westward with the low arousal types forming the backbone of new communities and the high arousal types moving further west. After many generations of this there was no further to go and they had to stop in the land of fruits and nuts. California had been settled by high arousal, thrill-seeking renegades. It should come as no surprise that California is now home to iconoclasts and high-risk personalities that defy the establishment. Further proof is the state's rampant creativity in the arts, technology, and business. Silicon Valley is recognized as the technological epicenter of the world, but the real validation of the state's innate creativity is that over 50 percent of America's Nobel Prize winners have come from there.

Subjects with the Highest Risk-Taking Behavior

The fearless tend to leap before they look. Marie Curie never allowed the fear of radiation from the pitchblende she was working on to deter her from her research on radium. She leaped into her work without looking at the health considerations of her decision. Despite physical evidence that the radium had serious health implications, such as burns on her skin, Curie relegated personal safety to a distant second after satiating her need for discovery. Had profitability been high on his list of priorities, Rupert Murdoch would never have negotiated a contract to televise NFL games that was guaranteed to lose him $150 million in 1994. He told his detractors, "You're not a network without the NFL." No corporate executive would dare make such a deal so it was impossible to compete with him since he was willing to take much greater risks.

Howard Hughes never looked before he leaped. He repeatedly jumped into planes he had no idea how to fly and in many cases crashed them without ever worrying about his safety. Such impulsiveness is found in most daredevil entrepreneurs. Ted Turner told a reporter, "I never even had a business plan for CNN and I bet my whole company [on its success]." Hughes, Murdoch, and Turner all operated at the very top of the risk-reward curve both in business and pleasure. Each was willing to bet everything on virtually every business transaction, which is what separated them from the pack. It is difficult to compete with opponents who have no fear of losing.

Marie Curie

Manya (Marie) Sklodowska Curie was born in Poland, immigrated to France, and became the only woman to win two Nobel Prizes—one in physics and one in chemistry. She also discovered two new elements—radium and polonium—while she was working on her doctoral thesis at the Sorbonne. This woman never worried about her safety while working in a field where radiation had terribly debilitating effects on the body. In 1903, about the time she won her first Nobel Prize, Curie got pregnant and worked through the whole term while exposing herself to radiation poisoning. Eight months into the pregnancy she went into premature labor while bicycling and the baby—a girl—died. This is the way the world's greatest female scientist lived her whole life.

Curie was a driven workaholic who had experienced a nervous breakdown at age fifteen due to the trauma of her sister's death when Curie was nine and her mother's death the following year. Then her father lost his business and she had a difficult time coping. She met and married Pierre Curie and they became a team for about ten years until he was accidentally killed by a runaway horse in 1906. After his death, Curie became the first female professor at the Sorbonne and went on to make her mark in the world through an obsessive work ethic that was "male-like" according to one biographer. Curie was a driven woman who was fearless, which is what made her one of the greatest female scientists to have ever lived. In the early years she worked in abominable conditions that would have killed a lesser person. A friend, George Sagnac, wrote, "I should long ago have gone under if I had maltreated my body in the way you have." She wrote in her autobiography, "I would be broken with fatigue at the day's end." Despite this exhaustion, her need to know and understand the world around her pushed Curie to continue her work.

Amelia Earhart

Amelia Earhart flew airplanes before she could drive and frightened her flight instructor with her daring. Meta Kinner, her teacher, said, "She used to scare me to death. She wanted to fly between high tension wires to prove she could." A short time after Earhart learned to fly an open cockpit plane she quickly became known around the airfield as "That slightly crazy girl," not an easy task in a land known as the home of the fruits and nuts. Later in her life, Earhart rationalized her risk-taking behavior by saying, "I just want to go where no one else has been." A biographer wrote, "If to dare was to die, then she would die."

Earhart loved fast cars and fast planes. In 1928 she became the first woman to fly the Atlantic. In 1933 she became the first to fly the Atlantic twice. She was the first person to fly Honolulu to California in either direction (in 1935) and the first woman to fly an autogiro (a forerunner to the helicopter). The First Lady of the Air was the first female to fly solo across the continent and she set numerous speed records in her short but exciting life. This thrill-seeker had seven major air crashes due to her daredevil antics, which were spurred by an obsessive need to push the window of opportunity.

Earhart was a vagabond who had attended three different high schools. When she was in her mid-thirties and a reporter questioned about settling down as a housewife, she responded, "I've had twenty-eight different jobs in my life and I hope I have 228 more." But it was risk-taking that defined her. When she was considering a flight across the Gulf of Mexico from Mexico City to New Orleans, pilot Wiley Post told her, "Don't do it, it's too dangerous." That was all she needed. She took off with 472 gallons of high-octane fuel from a pot-holed runway and broke the record for that flight.

Earhart was the sweetheart of America in the late 1920s and 1930s, daring to do what few women would, becoming an icon to housewives across the world. She wrote a poem just prior to her first flight across the Atlantic called "Courage," the first lines of which read, "Courage is the price that life exacts for granting peace, / The soul that knows it not, knows no release."

Earhart set her first flying record on October 22, 1922, at an air contest at Rogers Field in California. She was in an open cockpit plane with no oxygen and climbed to 14,000 feet through fog and sleet when her Airster's engine began to falter. The fearless young aviator kicked the plane into a tailspin and came straight down toward land. When she landed, the older pilots asked what she would have done if the fog had reached to ground level. She said that was the chance she had to take to set the record for highest altitude attained in an open cockpit plane.

Earhart's last flight was even more frivolous—to reduce the weight of her plane she refused to carry the most basic communications equipment and she took a known alcoholic as her navigator. She paid the ultimate price for her thrill-seeking behavior; she was lost at sea near the equator. Amelia Earhart is a symbol of temerity winning in her battle against anonymity. Earhart proclaimed, "I will not live a conventional life. . . . I want to dare what all that a man would dare." She did, and became one of the most famous woman of her era as a result.

Howard Hughes

Howard Hughes was even more daring than Earhart. He was a hypochondriac who constantly flirted with death, although he was afraid of the smallest insects. He was not afraid to jump into the cockpit of a new airplane, or to invest millions in wild business ventures, but was deathly afraid of the common housefly. He often took off in airplanes without being familiar with their instrumentation or aerodynamics. He risked his life and fortune virtually every month of his life and came close to dying in a number of violent plane crashes. In all, Hughes survived seven major crashes, the last of which broke him physically, emotionally, and mentally. Prior to that crash Hughes was merely eccentric, but after that crash he became addicted to painkillers, and the drugs came to dominate his whole life.

Flying was an obsession for Hughes and it was also the basis for his first major encounter with economic disaster. In 1928, Hughes embarked on a movie-making venture that made him famous. He had no experience with movies, but was always willing to bet whatever was needed to fulfill his dreams. Hughes decided to produce the greatest flying movie ever made and named it *Hell's Angels*. The movie became the most expensive movie to that time when the impulsive Hughes acquired what was the third largest airforce in the world. This manic risk-taker spent $500,000 acquiring a fleet of eighty-seven vintage World War I fighters to achieve authenticity. The movie took over a year to produce and when finished cost $2 million plus the lives of two pilots who died in one of his realistic air battle scenes. During the production Hughes had fired both the producer and director and took on those functions himself, positions for which he had no experience or training.

Hell's Angels was finished just as the first movie with sound, *The Jazz Singer*, starring Al Jolson, was released. *Hell's Angels* was magnificent, but did not meet perfectionist Hughes's standards. He scrapped the film and started over, breaking all kinds of precedents by hiring an unknown teenage siren named Jean Harlow. He gave his lover the lead role and proceeded to recreate *Hell's Angels* in sound, investing another $2.8 million. Although the film, when finally released, was a smash hit at the box office, Hughes still lost $1.5 million. Hughes viewed the risk as worth the effort, and he chalked his loss up to an investment.

Hughes spent much of his life living on the edge, but never was this so apparent as in the 1960s when he was in his sixties and in ill health. During this period he spent up to $367,579 each day according to biographers Bartlett and Steele (1979). His mad ventures included the acquisition of Las Vegas properties—Desert Inn hotel and golf club for $13.2 million and the Sands Hotel for $14.6 million. He then started spending money at such a rate that the media speculated he was attempting to buy up the state of Nevada as his personal estate. His spending spree has few equals in the annals of business. He purchased numerous radio and television stations, helped finance the 1962 Bay of Pigs invasion, and at one point had a plan to monopolize the Las Vegas gambling casinos and hotels. What made this so bizarre was that he didn't drink or gamble and never once made it to a Vegas show. In just a few years he had acquired the Castaways, Frontier, Stardust, Silver Nuggett, Bonanza, Silver Slipper, and tried unsuccessfully to buy Harrah's.

How did he pay for this spending binge? He had divested his holding of TWA stock for $546 million, then bought KLAS-TV, the Krupp Ranch, Riddle Real Estate, Comstock Mines, various other mining operations, and Air West. During the height of this mania he unsuccessfully tried to buy the ABC network, Paradise Island Resort, National Airlines, Western Airlines, and the Landmark Hotel in Las Vegas. Hughes made some incredibly stupid acquisitions—like gold and silver mines that were hoaxes—and some wonderful ones—like TWA—but the only areas where he truly lost a lot of money is the silver mines and some radio and television stations. Even his debacles, however, were wins, as in the case of the Spruce Goose airplane. That cost him dearly and on paper there was no return. But the enormous media exposure led to Hughes Aircraft becoming the largest government contractor for spacecraft and satellite systems. That was his ultimate goal, although it was lost on his inside executives and the media.

Hughes's risk-taking worked in his business ventures but proved fatal in his personal life. He decided to be the test pilot on a new plane known as the XF-11. Biographer Charles Higham describes his test flight as "recklessness and near-suicidal folly" (1993, 122). Hughes was supposed to fly over an unpopulated area but instead flew over heavily populated Culver City so Katharine Hepburn, one of his paramours, could see him. Higham wrote, "Suicidally, he decided to fly for an hour and a half when the maximum fuel allowed, 600 gallons, would permit only forty-five minutes." Hughes doubled the fuel load to 1200 gallons, a move that proved lethal. He crashed at 200 mph into a home and was pulled from the wreckage with his heart moved to the opposite side of his body, severe burns, and many broken bones. Hughes was not expected to live, but through sheer will power survived. He became addicted to the drugs he needed to assuage the pain, and he was a broken man the rest of his life.

Berry Gordy Jr.

The founder of Motown Records, Berry Gordy Jr., is another of our superheroes who used risk to reach the top. This high-roller was known to bet a thousand dollars on how quickly a raindrop would reach the bottom of a window pane, but perhaps his greatest risk was his 1971 production of *Lady Sings the Blues*, a movie depicting the life of his childhood idol, Billie Holliday. Gordy was set on having his recording star and lover Diana Ross play the lead role as Billie. Ross had never even had an acting lesson, but Gordy insisted she play the leading role in the movie. Paramount Pictures executives had taken on the project with Gordy functioning as "angel"—lead investor on the film—but they rejected his idea of Ross as leading lady since they were unwilling to bet on an unknown singer without experience to carry the movie. (To that time Ross had only had success as a nightclub singer. Her many albums were yet to be recorded.)

The live-on-the-edge Berry stepped up his investment and the studio executives capitulated. Half way through the production however, the costs got out of hand and after much negotiation, Paramount decided to kill the film. To that date, no other film with a primarily or wholly African-American cast, including *Porgy & Bess*, had been made for more than $500,000. *Lady* was going to come in at close to $2 million cost. Such risks are beyond the realm of executives who have zero tolerance for risk. Berry was incensed at the cancellation and said, "That's crazy. We're right in the middle of filming." They executives proposed that Berry pay everything over $2 million to continue the project. Berry asked, what his alternatives were, and the Paramount executive said, "Just bring me $2 million and the film is yours." The next day the high roller took the largest gamble of his life that could have buried Motown Records had he failed. Berry walked into the Paramount studio and threw down a check for $2 million and took over as producer and director in the fashion of Howard Hughes thirty years before. What guts! Here was a man who earned his high school GED while he was in the military and he was now producer and director of a major motion picture. Berry then decided to promote one of his assistants at Motown to direct the film since she had at least been to college. Think about the gamble: Berry was functioning as the producer and knew nothing of the trade, Ross was the star and had never been in a movie or to acting school, and his assistant was the director.

Few people would have the guts to take such a high risk. What turned out to be a $3 million dollar gamble for Berry came up a seven. *Lady Sings the Blues* opened up to rave reviews in October 1972 and was nominated for five Academy Awards. The Magic Man was quite introspective about his wildest wager in his autobiography: "Creative people many times do dumb things. Business people watch for the budget, creative people only for the magic."

Gordy succeeded as an entrepreneur who married pop with soul because he was willing to live on the edge. Gordy wrote in his memoirs, "I had gambled since childhood—dice, poker, horses, commodities, women, and music," and said his success was due to his ability to "lose money if it meant building stars." That helped him build stars like Marvin Gaye, Smokey Robinson, the Supremes, the Jackson Five, Stevie Wonder, Gladys Knight, and Lionel Ritchie among others. Gordy's attorney once called his boss a "reckless gambler. On any given day he could lose between $50,000 and $100,000 frivolously." That mentality is what made Gordy rich and famous.

Rupert Murdoch

Media baron and owner of the Fox network, Rupert Murdoch refuses to allow age or any other obstacle to interfere with his mad dash to becoming the dominant force in worldwide communications. He lost $150 million in the first year of his NFL football TV contract and knew he would when he signed the deal. He proceeded anyhow because, in his inimitable words, "You are not a network without the NFL." It is truly ironic that Murdoch and Turner are such rabid enemies since they are so much alike. Both were at the zenith of their risk-taking mania in the mid-1980s and both nearly perished under the debt of highly leveraged purchases.

In 1982 Murdoch purchased the *Boston Herald* for $16 million and in 1985 acquired Metromedia for $2.6 billion, raising his debt to an awesome $2.3 billion. He did this while in the midst of a life and death struggle in London with the newspaper union at the now famous Wapping plant. In that skirmish he was betting his whole London publishing empire on defying the union at his plant in Wapping and it would have cost him $300 million had he lost. (Murdoch was building an automated plant to replace the union workers who required three times the number of employees—at higher salaries—to do jobs identical to those in other Murdoch plants.) He won and with it came the spoils, as the estimated value of those papers rose to $1 billion. Such are the results of leverage and the willingness to bet everything on your ideas.

In 1988 Murdoch bought Harper & Row publishers for $3.8 billion. He continued buying and by 1990 his indebtedness had reached an amazing $7 billion. Such numbers terrified Murdoch's creditors, and, like a game of dominoes, Murdoch's empire would crumble if the banks began calling in their notes. The most powerful media man in the world was near bankruptcy from 1990 through 1992. Reducing the debt took over two years. Murdoch, who lives by the motto, "Business is war" was not to be destroyed without a fight. He sold off some of his prized possessions, *Seventeen*, *New Woman*, *Mirabella*, and *Racing Form* for $650 million. The most amazing part of this story is this inveterate risk-taker finally crawled out from under this enormous debt and before the ink had dried began taking even greater risks than before. And he did this while in his sixties.

Murdoch is a compulsive gambling spirit in the likeness of Hughes and Turner and like them he has a huge net worth, which *Forbes* magazine in 1997 estimated at $4.5 billion. The thrill of the gamble is what makes these men run and when they succeed they are seen as geniuses. When they fail they also make the headlines but seldom does it deter them from the next great gamble. A *New York Times* reporter asked Murdoch's wife about his success. She responded, "If he was a pilot, I would not board the plane."

Ted Turner

Ted Turner, the man known as Captain Courageous, was even more prone to taking risks, if that is possible, than Hughes, Gordy, or Murdoch. Turner earned the nickname Capsize Kid as a young teen for his many daring sailing exploits but those pale in comparison to his obsessive need to live on the edge in business. It almost appears he has a death-wish when you analyze his early ventures.

Turner's most daring personal risk occurred during a 605-mile long FASTNET sailing race held in Ireland in 1979. This race earned headlines, "THE FASTNET OF DEATH" when 70 percent of the 303 ships were sunk or grounded in 70-mile-per-hour winds. Twenty-five sailors were lost, and everyone except for the irrepressible Turner ran for cover. One hundred and sixty sailors had to be rescued, fifteen died, but Turner refused to capitulate to the elements or his obsession with winning. He insisted the crew keep the *Tenacious*'s sails full and on track to the finish line. He won the race, but jeopardized his own safety and that of his oldest son, crew, and girlfriend. Winning was the bottom line to this media mogul.

The 1980s proved to be the pinnacle of Turner's risk-taking mania.

During a span of five years Turner defied all logic for fiscal safety or even prudence. His risk-taking ventures rivaled any others in modern times. He began by betting his $100-million-dollar business empire on the CNN launch. His bet included TBS, the Superstation; the Atlanta Braves; the Atlanta Hawks; and a number of minor radio and television stations. According to his key executives at the time the venture was "sheer madness, the act of a crazy man." *The Economist* (July 1989) wrote, "He has recovered so often from seemingly suicidal financial escapades that many Atlanta businessmen are now convinced he is indestructible."

Turner came precariously close to losing everything on CNN—during its first eighteen months the network lost $2 million a month. Like his adversary Rupert Murdoch, as soon as Turner was safe and not at risk of bankruptcy he went on an even more maniacal acquisition binge that involved billions. First he acquired the MGM film studios for $1.4 billion and followed that by purchasing an Atlanta white elephant known as the Omni Shopping Mall & Hotel complex for $64 million. Simultaneously he donated $26 million to the Goodwill Games and $500,000 to the Better World Society. His risk-taking included a divorce settlement of $40 million to ex-wife, Janie. He then made what he says was the worst business decision of his life. He offered $5.4 billion to buy CBS. He later admitted later that he would have been bankrupt had they accepted his offer.

Were Turner's bold bets worth the inherent risks? Some were and some were not but by risking he has changed the world more than most. One only has to travel outside the United States to get a feel for the impact of CNN. This network is the communications link to America for Asia, the Caribbean, and the Middle East. CNN is ubiquitous and has become "the" TV network since Bernard Shaw broadcast live from Baghdad in 1990 during the Desert Storm War. Saddam Hussein decided CNN was the medium to talk to the West and ever since the Turner network has become known as the "Diplomatic Pouch." For the past eight years CNN is the network of choice for prime ministers, presidents, and potentates. It has become their surest and swiftest pipeline to deliver the latest propaganda to their adversaries. Turner's estimated net worth of $2.6 billion in 1997 (according to *Forbes*) is testimony that risking can be profitable if one is willing to bet the farm on his dreams. Turner sums up his success by saying, "Every time, I tried to go as far as I could. When I climbed the hills, I saw the mountains. Then I started climbing the mountains."

Leverage—The Ultimate Risk

Hughes, Murdoch, and Turner were all masters of leverage and used it adroitly to build their empires. "Leverage" is a synonym for risk. It is the art of using other people's money to finance your ventures. Once these entrepreneurs had their own assets they used them as collateral to borrow more money in order to expand their empires.

Turner used leverage to acquire both the Atlanta Braves and the Atlanta Hawks. He paid the asking price but forced the sellers to carry the paper and take nothing down.* That is the ultimate leverage and the ultimate risk but it worked for Turner.

Why did he buy those sports teams and why is Murdoch buying the Los Angeles Dodgers? Neither is an avid sports fan, so these were not emotional purchases. Both men are very similar and understand the businesses they are in. Sports teams have the most airtime and both men are in the air-time business. By paying top price they were able to use the assets of the teams as collateral and in some cases their own balance sheets.

Leverage is a double-edged sword in that it maximizes the risk while maximizing the potential for gain. When it works, the rewards can be astronomical, when it fails, the losses can be equally as devastating. Using debt in growing an empire can catapult the empire into huge success or mire it into the quicksand of financial debt. If you cannot pay back the debt, as happened to both Tom Monaghan and Rupert Murdoch, those who loaned you the money will own your business. That is the price one pays for using leverage to finance a new enterprise. Both Monaghan and Murdoch were successful in saving their businesses but it was only due to tenacity, luck, and the complexity of their companies. Had either man had less moxie and more problems, he would have lost his empire.

These men seldom bought companies with cash. Their acquisitions were for paper, using collateral to guarantee their purchases. Howard Hughes used Hughes Tools to finance his movies and his acquisition of TWA. Rupert Murdoch used his two local Australian papers to finance the *Australian*, and then used that operation to finance his entry into television. He then leveraged those assets to acquire the *London Sun*, *News of the World*, the *New York Post*, and the *Boston Globe*. Ted Turner was even more cavalier in the use of leverage. He purchased the Atlanta Braves and the Atlanta Hawks with nothing down. Those early successes bolstered his confidence to such an extent he persisted in using debt to finance all his future investments. The art of leverage catapulted Turner into a strong asset position—$100 million by 1980. Empowered by the process he pledged the Atlanta Braves, Hawks, and the Superstation to finance CNN and the MGM film library. This leveraging frenzy has made him enormously wealthy.

When leverage works you can become rich practically overnight, as Hughes, Monaghan, Murdoch, and Turner did. When it doesn't you can go broke overnight. Leverage was the reason Hughes lost control of TWA in

---

*As in most negotiations, if you agree to pay full price and have other assets to pledge, you can buy without cash. In this case Turner bought two major sports franchises now worth hundreds of millions of dollars without spending one cent of his own cash.

1963, why Turner became insolvent in the mid-1980s when he acquired the MGM film library, and was the reason for Rupert Murdoch's near bankruptcy in 1990–1991. What is amazing is that none of these close scares changed these men or affected their propensity to take risk. Each came out of his debacles with a new passion to bet it all on his next idea and each did so despite advancing age. All were in their fifties and sixties when they made their greatest gambles.

The Down Side of Risk-Taking

Not all risks end up with wins. That is the ultimate truth of gambling. For every Howard Hughes, Rupert Murdoch, Berry Gordy Jr., and Ted Turner there are people who have lost everything. Amelia Earhart said, "I want to go where no one else has been," but paid the ultimate price—her life—for her need to live on the edge. Howard Hughes came precariously close to dying numerous times and his life was effectively over after his near-fatal plane crash in 1946. The death-wish mentality also prematurely claimed the lives of Napoleon, Balzac, Hitler, Curie, Duncan, Hemingway, and Zaharias.

The Positive Aspects of Risk-Taking

Burton Klein wrote a book about risk-taking and competition called *Dynamic Economics* (1977). He found that, "The more certain an environment, the poorer will be the incentives for risk-taking, and the less certain an environment, the higher will be the propensity for risk-taking" (77). In other words, risk-taking will be more common when things are bad and less likely when things are good. As we saw in the risk-reward curve, risk-taking declines as we accumulate assets and as we age and this is true of firms as well as with people.

Since the creative and entrepreneurs are used to living in uncertain environments, to use Klein's analogy, then these types should be the most prone to taking the big risks that are necessary for great success. When you are too fat and happy you tend not to take big risks. Innovation is the province of the uncertain and according to Klein entrepreneurially inclined people should be operating with a high-risk mentality.

One definition of "innovation" is creative destruction. That means that one must be willing to risk the destruction of an existing product to create a better one. One cannot change boyfriends or girlfriends without destroying some existing relationship. That is the price of innovation in business or romance. It is the person comfortable with dealing with the new and unknown that is able to take such risks. Those afraid and unwilling to take high risks should not be entrepreneurs. Those comfortable with risks will

Table 9
Three Types of Individuals
Risk-Takers—Care-Takers—Under-Takers

Risk-Takers
[6%–12% of general population]

Style	$	Work?	Motivation?
Live-on-the-edge entrepreneurs	Money never important—only creativity wins	Gamblers who work best alone since they never allow fear to enter decisions in contrast to security-oriented peers	Prefer to pursue life's opportunities and willing to sacrifice safe present for possibilities of better future

Care-Takers
[68%–86% of general population]

Reliable and stable with a penchant for status quo	Security and money a driving force for all decisions	Best suited to mature firms in traditional industries or highly structured bureaucracies	Prefer to follow lead; typically sacrifice the future for present. Instant gratification with budgets and quarterly earnings sacrosanct

Under-Takers
[8%–15% of general population]

Losers who have Peter-Principled or become caught up in drugs or alcoholism, or are merely misplaced	Money is only reason for existence	Self-serving, with fear and greed dominating all decisions	None in concert with organizational objectives

make good entrepreneurs but it isn't just the risk-taking that will make them successful. There are many other factors in the equation that must be considered. If we can believe Klein's statement, then it is understood that bureaucrats and politicians will never take a risk and consequently never lead us into any promised land. Risk energizes the visionary leader and tends to immobilize bureaucrats.

Gender implications of Risk-Taking

The women in this book were not as inclined as the men to bet it all even though most were far more inclined to take risks than the average female.

Catherine the Great, Marie Curie, Isadora Duncan, Amelia Earhart, Helena Rubinstein, Margaret Thatcher, and Babe Didrickson Zaharias were the most inclined to live on the edge. These women were all willing to risk their fame and fortune to grab the brass ring, and only succeeded because they were willing to do so. In almost any definition, they were not average in risk taking or any other aspect of getting to the top. Amelia Earhart epitomizes the female who lives for the thrill but she certainly didn't gain the reputation as an "androgynous sex symbol" for her femininity.

Summary

It is an axiom that there are no great rewards without taking great risks. It was the catalyst to the top for all these subjects who learned early in life to live by the tenets of the risk-reward curve. These creative visionaries lived by the rule that risk and reward is a zero-sum game with the victors those willing to bet it all on their dreams. They were all awesome optimists who seemed to view the world through rose-colored glasses.

These visionaries were all willing to go for the gold. Many were blessed with high testosterone, others had stared mortality in the mirror and saw no down side since they were already on the bottom, others were competitive freaks, and still others were willing to follow their dreams wherever they led. The entrepreneurs seemed to use leverage as their personal tool and a number became billionaires for daring to risk. The upside of leverage is a double-edged sword. It isn't for everyone, especially the faint of heart. Make sure you have the temperament for sitting at the $100 table of life before you start taking big risks. Maybe the $2 table is more to your taste for adventure. If you don't care to sit at any table then you probably should work on your résumé.

To summarize the findings on creative genius relative to various operating styles of behavior see table 9, which classifies people into one of three categories: risk-takers, care-takers, or under-takers. These subjects were all risk-takers where money was never close to being at the top of their priorities. Creative and innovative success was their driving force—never security or money. They pursued their dreams as a means of seeking opportunity and the possibilities and fear or security never entered into the equation as it does with the average person. Those who seek money only are destined to fail, but those who seek innovative success will be rewarded with financial windfalls since money is the way we keep score in capitalism. Bill Gates is continually badgered about his $50 billion net worth and disdains it, saying he never did it for money and he can still only eat one cheeseburger at a time. Billionaire Richard Branson wrote in his memoirs, "I can honestly say I have never gone into any business purely to make money" (Branson 1998, 43).

CHAPTER 8

Tenacity

IF YOU NEVER QUIT,
YOU CAN NEVER LOSE

"Persistence propels potential to perfection."
Gene Landrum (1993)

One of Winston Churchill's more memorable speeches was a commencement address that contained one sentence. He walked on stage and said, "NEVER, NEVER, NEVER, NEVER, NEVER, NEVER, NEVER, NEVER, NEVER, NEVER give up" and sat down. The great politician knew one of the true secrets of great success in life: tenacity. Hitler's school friend August Kubizek offered some insight into the dictator's success. He told reporters, "Hitler did not know what the word resignation meant. . . . He never tired, he never slept." In a 1931 speech Hitler told an audience "For me the word impossible does not exist. . . . I intend to set up a thousand-year Reich." Mao Tse-tung went into the hills of China in 1923, at age thirty, and spent the next twenty-two years fighting for survival and assembling the team that would bring Communism into power as the People's Republic of China in 1949. What perseverance! During this time he led his army on a retreat that became famous as the Long March, which took Mao and the Red Army 6,000 miles across the hinterlands of his nation.

Ted Turner told a reporter after one of his sailing victories, "I never quit. I've got a bunch of flags on my boat but there ain't no white flags. I don't surrender." Maya Angelou had a similar penchant for surviving the crises in her life. She wrote, "My life is about survival. You may encounter many defeats but you must not be defeated." Darwin's son Francis wrote a biography of his father and said, "Perseverance hardly seems to express father's almost fierce desire to force the truth to reveal itself."

Perseverance Pays Dividends

The history of success is borne of persistence. Amelia Earhart told a reporter, "I'm not the best pilot. What I have is tenacity." What the First Lady of Flight was saying is that other factors were at work and she had more staying power than many of her competitors who often gave up after an initial defeat. What most people don't realize is that even the super great fail at first just like anyone else, but they do not give up. The loss empowers them to try harder, to make themselves better. Picasso's first paintings were not master-pieces and even Michael Jordan got cut from his high school basketball team. And the world-renowned authors like Balzac, Dostoevsky, and Anne Rice didn't quit after being rejected. Balzac was ridiculed for his first attempt at nonfiction. His first book, *Cromwell,* caused him to reevaluate his approach to literature but he kept trying until he got it right, which took him another eight years. Both Dostoevsky and Michener spent twenty years of struggle prior to succeeding as authors.

Think about Thomas Edison working to create the first light bulb and having a renowned professor—Silvanus P. Thompson—tell the media, "He is doomed to failure and shows the most airy ignorance of the fundamental principles both of electricity and dynamics." Now that doesn't seem like much in retrospect, but considering that Edison had but three months of formal education and a highly trained engineering professor denigrated his ideas could have been lethal to his self-esteem. The leading scientists demeaned his idea and one leading expert in the field called his light bulb idea "absurd claims attributed to sheer ignorance." At the time Edison experienced little success after hundreds of failed experiments. It would have been easy to quit but the tenacious Edison kept on with the struggle until he had an incandescent bulb that worked. He told a reporter, "The trouble with other inventors is that they try a few things and quit. I never quit until I get what I want." You can get some idea of the man's doggedness by his statement, "If there are no factories to make my inventions, I will build the factories myself. Since capital is timid, I will raise and supply. . . . The issue is factories or death." That is a man who became great because he refused to lose.

Paul Robeson struggled for years to make it through Columbia University Law School but finally graduated magna cum laude. Then he was unable to get a job because he was black. Many men would have crawled into a bottle or even worse. Instead Robeson walked down to Broadway and made himself into America's greatest Shakespearean actor.

One of the more inspirational stories of tenacity comes from Tom Monaghan of Domino's pizza fame. Tom lost his company to bankers in 1970 because he was unable to repay a bank loan and other debts. He had in excess of one hundred lawsuits and was $1.5 million in debt to 1,500 creditors. The bankers took over his company and became the franchisor (the "parent" organization to which individual franchises pay royalties) and began running Domino's until they could get their money back or sell the firm. Finding himself on the street with no other means of livelihood Monaghan agreed to work for the bankers for $200 a week to help bail out the firm. Tom worked fifteen hours a day seven days a week but by March 1971 the bank decided Domino's was destined for bankruptcy and gave Tom back their stock in the firm in exchange for a store. To Monaghan's lasting credit, and as a tribute to his moral integrity, he spent the next nine years paying off his creditors. He refused to give up and fifteen years later he became the largest home delivery pizza operation in the world and owner of the Detroit Tigers. That is tenacity.

Executives in commercial product sales know that 85 percent of all sales are made after the fifth call. The irony is that most sales people never make the second call. Therefore, the majority of all sales—80 percent in most products— are made by only 20 percent of the sales force—that 20 percent who make five calls. Turner spent his youth as a billboard salesman and learned this truth. After CNN finally made it, he told a reporter, "Never get discouraged and never quit, because if you never quit, you're never beaten."

When Rupert Murdoch found he was insolvent in 1990 with $7.6 billion of debt it would have been easy for him to turn it all over to the courts for resolution. He didn't and regained control over his media empire. He has since created a new television network, Fox, and is once again expanding at breakneck speed. When Murdoch was at the bottom he owed money to 146 different financial institutions in ten different currencies. This nightmare was created as a means of using leverage to grow. Grow he did—he was operating an international media dynasty. Using other people's money had backfired in 1990 and one phone call would have made him a pauper. Citibank was one of his major creditors so they assigned one of their rising young stars—Ann Lane—to help bail Murdoch out. Lane told the media "one phone call could have destroyed his whole life's work, but to his credit he worked harder and more determinedly than anyone I ever met." She told reporters, "He could easily have said, 'I can't do it anymore.' " But like the others in this book Murdoch didn't understand not finishing any race even when there was a serious threat of being beaten badly. At the time Murdoch controlled over 70 percent of the press in Australia, approximately one-third in Great Britain, and TV stations in San Antonio and other cities in America. Had he fallen it would have had enormous financial implications around the world, but the indomitable Murdoch refused to fail.

What Makes Tenacious People Unique?

Tenacious people are not concerned with failing, only with winning. In the sports vernacular, they only think about how to win and never worry about how not to lose. Their optimism defines them since they never see the down side, only the up side of any opportunity. Confidence is on their side in addition to an indomitable will to win. Edison said it best: "It takes a deaf man to hear." He meant that experts often know too much and he wasn't one of those types. Such subtle optimism allowed him to invent the microphone, phonograph, and the first movie picture camera with sound despite the fact that he was nearly deaf. His most famous aphorism gives credence to this. "Genius is 99 percent perspiration and 1 percent inspiration."

Probably the most unique thing about tenacious people is that they refuse to allow adversity to block their way to the top. In fact, it appears that they view problems as opportunities not threats. When reporters asked Golda Meir how 350,000 Israelis could defeat 45 million Arabs in just two weeks, she gave the most succinct response in history: "No choice!" They won because they had to. That was also the driving force behind many of the great novels written by Balzac and Dostoevsky. Both men were constantly writing in a valiant attempt to stay out of debtor's prison. Balzac spent twelve years writing to pay off his enormous debts from all his poor business ventures. Dostoevsky once wrote a novel, *The Gambler* (1866), in just two weeks in order to stay out of prison but was still forced to flee Russia. Another example of such tenacity was Frank Lloyd Wright, whose architectural masterpiece Taliesin burned down three times. Each time he rebuilt it bigger and grander. His biographer, Meryle Secrest (1993) wrote, "No one could have stopped him from becoming a success because he refused to be discouraged."

What is the Derivation of Tenacity?

Tenacity comes from the soul, a Nietzschean will to power, a Promethean spirit, all those things that separate winners from losers. It is not a head thing. It is a heart thing. The only time the mind becomes involved is to make sure there is a positive goal clearly in focus and that nothing interferes with that target or goal. Madonna is the consummate example of a young girl with minimum talent but a clear goal and an indomitable will. She found herself in Manhattan in 1980 without any means of support. She actually ate food from garbage cans during those dark days. That was a pretty tough act considering the Material Girl was a dedicated vegetarian. She refused to capitulate. The woman who would come to be known as the Bimbo of Babylon could have accepted her father's support and returned to Detroit, but she stayed in Manhattan and pursued a career in entertainment.

That internal will to win was never more apparent than in Paul Robeson. Robeson learned from his father and brothers never to capitulate to bullies or bigots. He was one of the most courageous and persevering subjects in this work. After high school Robeson decided to attend Rutgers University where he could play football. But no black man had ever played for Rutgers in the World War I era. When he showed up for practice the first day the team got together and decided to get him to quit. Their plan was to put him in the hospital or hurt him so bad he wouldn't be able to continue. Their plan almost worked. After the first day of practice he ended in the infirmary with a broken nose, abrasions, and other injuries from the beating he took, but it was the emotional trauma that hurt worst. Robeson returned home and told his father he was going to quit. His father, an escaped slave who was a self-made man, told him, "Robesons don't quit." The next day at practice Robeson decided that it would be up to him to determine his future, not some bigoted football players. The *New York Times* description of that day is pure Horatio Alger. "On the first play from scrimmage," Robeson said, "I made a tackle and was on the ground . . . when a boy came over and stepped hard on my hand. He meant to break the bones. The bones held, but his cleats took every one of the fingernails off my right hand. That's when I knew rage!" (Gilliam 1976, 16). At seventeen Paul was six foot, three inches and 230 pounds of pure muscle and in that era he was huge. He spoke of the rage he felt in his autobiography and the adrenaline that must have been surging through his body.

On the very next play from scrimmage Robeson saw that the whole team was coming at him. This play would determine his future. As the first battering ram of football players neared he extended a huge arm and with Herculean strength dropped three of them to the ground. He pushed aside the interference, grabbed hold of Kelly, the ball carrier who was also the captain and ringleader, and with a superhuman effort, Robeson grabbed hold of his nemesis when the coach interceded. Robeson said, "I got Kelly in my two hands and I got him up over my head. . . . I was going to smash him so hard to the ground that I would break him right into two, and I could have done it." Just then the coach saw disaster in the offing and yelled, "Robey, you're on the varsity."

That day Robeson earned the respect of those white guys. They would become lifetime friends and together went on to great success. Robeson was the first black to make the Walter Camp All-American football squad and the first All-American in Rutgers history. On graduating with a Phi Beta Kappa key the school paper predicted this tenacious man would become the future governor of New Jersey. How's that for using grit and guts to turn around a situation?

Karl Marx is another example of a man who could have easily capitulated to the establishment but refused. This Young Hegelian was a radical in college and the power elite decided to teach him a lesson by refusing him a teaching position after he completed his doctorate. Teaching was his career of choice but the conservatives succeeded in their quest and he never taught, however, they had created a Frankenstein who would spend the rest of his life using his prosaic pen to vent his revenge on the establishment. The result was the *Communist Manifesto* (1848) and then *Das Kapital* (1867), which would haunt the Prussian leaders although it would take another fifty years to do so. Marxism was really the byproduct of a tenacious man who refused to capitulate to those in power. Marx paid a horrible price as he became a man without a country and lived in austere poverty for the greater part of his adult life. Sometimes you have to die to become immortal. That was the case for Karl Marx.

Subjects with the Most Tenacity

The individuals who best personify tenacity refused to give up even though they had been devastated prior to their great success. Catherine the Great, the Empress of Russia, had to wait many years and suffer horrible indignities before wresting the throne from an idiot husband. Dame Agatha Christie's first book was written because of a bet with her older sister and it would take six publishers and four years for her to get published. Walt Disney flirted with bankruptcy for thirty straight years before finally getting the success and adulation he deserved. Soichiro Honda was a broken man just after World War II. His factory had been destroyed by American bombers and he found himself broke and without any means of livelihood but persevered to build one of Japan's preeminent automotive firms. Nelson Mandela spent twenty-seven years of his adult life in prison for his dream of destroying Apartheid. His sacrifice paid dividends but not until he was well into his seventies. James Michener spent many years teaching school before he finally realized his childhood dream of becoming an author. He persevered and finally at age forty his dream came true. "Rejection slips permeated my life" says Stephen King. He tells of his father walking out for a pack of cigarettes when he was two and never returning. In 1972 he was living in a trailer with two kids, no phone, no car, and a basket full of rejection slips from every publisher. That was when he threw the beginning of the manuscript *Carrie* into the trash and asked himself "Am I chasing a fool's dream?" But he persisted to become America's most successful author for the past two decades.

Catherine the Great

Catherine the Great is still the longest reigning empress of Mother Russia. She was christened Sophie Fredericke Anhalt-Zerbst but by age thirteen was committed to marry the grandson of Peter the Great, the future ruler of Russia. She never underestimated her role as a female who was there to produce an heir to the Russian throne. She and her mother moved to Moscow when she was fourteen and she spent the next eighteen years in isolation and bitter loneliness. Catherine knew she was but a pawn in the larger scheme of things but she never saw herself in that light. She wrote in her memoirs, "There was something within me which never allowed me to doubt for a single moment that I should one day succeed in becoming the Empress of Russia." It was that resolve that kept her sane during the long desperate years when she often felt she would not survive.

Catherine was German and never spoke anything but broken Russian. After producing a successor to the throne, even though her son, Grand Duke Paul was illegitimate by her lover Grigory Orlov, Catherine was expendable and she knew it. Her son was taken from her at birth to be a ward of the state and she saw him sparingly and therefore never bonded with him. Catherine was forced to tolerate a dominant mother-in-law, an imbecile husband, and a hostile court for many years. But she waited and planned, often bribing members of the court for the simplest privileges. She wrote in her memoirs, "I was sustained by ambition alone. . . . I lived a life for eighteen years from which ten others would have gone crazy and twenty in my place would have died of melancholy" (Alexander 1989, 39).

On Elizabeth's death, her son, Peter III, acceded to the throne and Catherine knew she would be imprisoned or killed within weeks since it was widely known that he planned to make his mistress, rather than his wife, queen. In his words, "she would perish by prison or poison." On June 28, 1762, this tenacious visionary mounted her white stallion, Brilliant, before the Imperial Guard, which her lover's brother led, and declared herself Empress of all the Russias. This intrepid woman told the soldiers, "Any man who wants to shoot your Empress, now is your time. FIRE!" No one fired. They dropped their arms and joined her as their reigning queen. Catherine told them "I go now to secure my throne." Within two weeks Peter was dead and Catherine was reigning empress.

Had Catherine not taken matters into her lovely hands she would have surely ended up in a convent, prison, or grave. With a force of 15,000 men she was prepared to engage Peter in battle but he feared her and renounced his claim to the throne. She had him imprisoned and two weeks later he was dead, causing Frederick the Great of Prussia to comment, "Peter III let himself be driven from the throne as a child is sent to bed." The psychological implications of Catherine's power play was pure Hollywood. Assuming a male-like role, this delicate female donned a colonel's uniform—the same rank as Peter had taken—and with saber in hand assumed the role of commander-in-chief, an unprecedented event. She even mounted her steed full-stride, an unheard of style for ladies of the time since they were supposed to ride sidesaddle. This was the woman who would rule Russia with an iron hand for the next thirty-four years. British Ambassador Harris described her unique style as a " masculine force of mind wanting the more manly virtues."

Biographers have described Catherine's reign as that of an autocratrix, a sovereign mistress who combined corpulence, elegance, and majesty in ruling over one-seventh of the world. She was a political genius who vastly expanded Russia's southern borders opening up a southern port via the Black Sea. She had fought the Ottoman Empire and wrested Crimea from them. Catherine's rule was an enlightened one. She established the first school for girls and opened the first medical college for peasants. The Empress was an erudite ruler who financed the first encyclopedia by Diderot and counted as her friends such men as Potemkin and Voltaire. She has been called a tyrant, political genius, adulteress, imperial wizard, murderer, nymphomaniac, and more but most of all she was a tenacious and enlightened leader.

Agatha Christie

The most famous and most prolific mystery writer in history, Agatha Christie, described herself as a "sausage machine" grinding out detective stories. She wrote, "Perhaps one day they will find me out and realize that I can't really write at all." For someone who couldn't write she did okay. Christie began writing her first book in 1916 but it took until 1920 to get published. The book began as a bet that her sister Madge couldn't decipher whodunit. *The Mysterious Affair at Styles* was rejected by six different publishing houses but it was Christie's start. It originally sold only 2,000 copies and Christie earned £26, but she has since sold over one billion books in 103 languages earning a fortune of $50 million at her death.

Dame Christie wrote a short play titled *Three Blind Mice* for Queen Mary's eightieth birthday in 1947. Five years later she adapted it to a full-length play called *The Mousetrap*. It started a run in London in 1952 and has become the longest running play in history of the legitimate theater. This home-educated writer (Christie was self-taught, with a Paris finishing school her only formal education) produced one book a year for fifty-seven straight years and ended with seventy-eight crime novels, seven romances, one poem, one children's book, twenty-six plays, and 150 short stories. The irony of her success is that she admitted to never meeting a real murderer and knew nothing of guns or other weapons and so chose poisons to dispatch her victims. She had been a nurse and dispenser of drugs in both world wars and therefore had some knowledge of arsenic and other such devices that she used to kill off her victims.

The greatest mystery of all was Christie's own bizarre disappearance on December 3, 1926. Her car was found abandoned near a lake and the police fully expected suicide since her dashing husband had told her he had fallen in love with a young lady named Neele. Beset by depression and a recluse by nature Christie was found on December 15 alone in a Northern England hotel and spa under the assumed name Mrs. Teresa Neele. She claimed amnesia but the facts indicate otherwise and it has been the longest lasting unsolved mystery in her life. Speculation indicates the Duchess of Death was attempting to cast her unfaithful husband, Colonel Archie Christie as the arch-villain. The police did suspect foul play and Colonel Christie became their number one suspect in a nation-wide search for his wife's body. The Queen of Crime and Mystery had orchestrated the events far more successfully than she wanted and spent the rest of her life attempting to avoid any reference to the whole episode.

Agatha Christie was a highly intuitive introvert who created two of the most famous protagonists in literary history—Hercule Poirot and Jane Marple. This Queen of Crime created her characters as a parlor game-type thriller. It was her cathartic release of her keen inner observations that had little outlet due to her extreme shyness. Her most famous works were *The Murder of Roger Akroyd* (1926), *Murder on the Orient Express* (1934), *Death on the Nile* (1937), *The Mousetrap* (1952), *Witness for the Prosecution* (1953), and *The Spider's Web* (1954). She had an unprecedented three plays running simultaneously on the London stage during the mid-1950s.

Walt Disney

"Uncle Walt" Disney refused to give up. He filed bankruptcy at age twenty-one and then flirted with it until he was in his mid-fifties. The father of animation was ridiculed by his brother, Roy; the board of directors; Hollywood film experts; and many of his employees, but he refused to buckle under the criticism. He survived eight nervous breakdowns and the theft of his earliest animated success, Oswald the Rabbit. Disney liked to say, "I do not make films primarily for children. I make them for the child in all of us."

One of Disney's innovations that is often lost on all but Disney financial executives is the way he was able to create mythical adventures that suspended all elements of time. In fact, they were timeless, as he purposely designed them to have no sign of the era in which they were produced. Disney knew his creations would depreciate in value if they became dated and "one-timers" in the vernacular of the industry. That is why the Disney Company has become a cash cow. Each one of his original works like *Snow White* (1937) *Pinocchio* (1940), *Bambi* (1942), *Dumbo* (1941) and *Fantasia* (1940) can be released every five to eight years to hit a new generation of children because they do not become dated. They can also be released in video for home play.

Walt flirted with bankruptcy his whole life. At twenty-six he was cheated out of his winning character, Oswald the Rabbit, by an unscrupulous distributor and was virtually out of business. At age twenty-seven he came back with Mickey Mouse but was forced to sell his car to save the firm. At twenty-nine another distributor cheated him out of $150,000, causing the first of eight nervous breakdowns and a failed suicide attempt. At thirty-one he went through a second nervous breakdown when the cost of color in movies almost bankrupted the firm. At thirty-two his brother, Roy, accused him of "Trying to ruin us," with *Snow White,* which became known as "Disney's Folly." At thirty-five Walt was close to bankruptcy once again and needed $5 million to complete *Snow White.* During the middle of the debacle Disney suffered another nervous breakdown but was revived when he won an Oscar for *Snow White* and he made the cover of *Time.* At thirty-eight the firm was nearly bankrupt when Roy came to the rescue with a public offering that saved the company, but by age forty Disney suffered another breakdown when his workers went on strike. He was close to suicide and a European vacation revived him. The United States Navy confiscated his studio during the World War II and almost put him out of business. Three more times while in his forties Disney Studios came close to bankruptcy and it was not until Disneyland opened, coupled with *Walt Disney Presents* on ABC, that the firm finally become solvent.

If the above flirtations with financial disaster were not enough, every one of Disney's ideas, including *Snow White* and Disneyland, were denigrated by his brother and industry experts. Disney persevered and refused to allow others to undermine him. While *Fantasia* was in production, Frank Lloyd Wright happened by the studio and Roy asked him to comment on Walt's newest production. The architectural visionary called it "absurd." Then Roy commissioned Howard Hughes, one of Walt's long time friends and a distributor of his films through RKO, to comment on *Seal Island.* Hughes predicted it would be "a commercial disaster." Disney ignored their advice in both instances. *Fantasia* has been called a "revolutionary marriage of music and animation"; *Seal Island* won the 1948 Oscar for Best Short Subject.

The final ridicule came when Disney came up with the idea for Disneyland and Roy called his idea a "carny" concept. When Walt attempted to explain that his park would be different, Roy exclaimed, "It's a fantasy and won't work." Once again Walt listened to his own internal messenger and ignored all the experts, including the Stanford Research Institute, who also demeaned his idea and advised the board of directors of Disney to not invest one cent in the concept. It is interesting to note that all the reasons these experts gave for the park's failure turned out to be the very reasons for the park's great success—one entrance and one price, year round operation, walk-around characters, and Space Mountain. Walt was forced to sell his Palm Springs home and borrow on his insurance policy to get the money to buy the land in Anaheim, California. Then he sold his soul to his mortal enemy television for the $15 million necessary to build the park. Ironically, it was ABC, which Disney Studios acquired in 1995 for $19 billion, that came up with the money in exchange for the *Walt Disney Presents* TV show. Disney refused to listen to the experts, including his brother and the board of directors. If he had listened to them, the world would be a worse place to live and enjoy.

Soichiro Honda

Soichiro Honda, the founder of Honda Motors, told a Michigan graduating class, "To me success can be achieved only through repeated failure and introspection. In fact, my success represents the 1 percent of the work that resulted from the 99 percent that was called failure." This is the trait that made him great that is often lost on less introspective types. He and Edison were inventors, but they were really masters of experimentation. They used what educators call heuristic learning techniques—trial and error to the point of exhaustion. Another way of describing Honda and heuristic learning is obsessive persistence.

Writer and economist George Gilder called Soichiro Honda "the world's greatest engineer since Henry Ford." That is something, considering Honda didn't make it past the eighth grade in school. In the 1980s the *British Sunday Times* auto critic wrote, "The precision of Honda's engineering, almost like a jeweled watch, has astonished every engineer I have spoken to." Honda's success was instrumental in having him become the first Japanese executive to have ever been elected into the American Automobile Hall of Fame.

Honda's election comes from his having solved the problem of the catalytic engine that had eluded the highly educated Detroit engineers. He also had created the most awesome dominance of the motorcycle market with over 60 percent market share worldwide in the 1970s and 1980s. All of this from a man who was broke and destitute in 1946 after American bombers and then an earthquake had destroyed his auto parts plant. The tenacious Honda refused to be defeated. He had no transportation since gas was off-limits in postwar Tokyo. The innovative Honda took a discarded GI engine and attached it to his bicycle for transportation. A friend saw the "motorbike" and asked Honda to build him one also. Honda built it for cost plus some food money. Then another friend wanted one, then another, and another, and thus was born the Honda Motorcycle empire. Honda was forced to hock his wife's jewelry to buy parts in those early days when he opened his first factory in 1948. That is the true definition of perseverance.

Estée Lauder

"I was single-minded in the pursuit of my dream." Those were the words of Estée Lauder, the founder of America's largest cosmetic firm, who followed them with "I was a woman on a mission." Lauder became the Queen of Cosmetics through many years of hard work which saw her mixing her concoctions at night and working all day to put them on the shelves and in the homes of her customers. Lauder launched her international beauty empire on street corners, in subways, in the homes of friends and clients, hotel rooms, and beauty salons. No venue was out of bounds for this tenacious woman. She wrote in her autobiography, "One summer after another, I pushed myself, lauding cremes, making up women, selling beauty. In the winters I'd visit these ladies at their homes" (1985, 249).

Estée Lauder was raised in a Queens, New York, ghetto but never admitted to her heritage. She wanted to be more, and in the end became what she wanted to be. It was pure persistence of purpose and a refusal to be defeated. It would take some years but Lauder grew her cosmetic dynasty into a multibillion dollar enterprise and a personal net worth of $5 billion. When asked about her secrets of success she said they are, "quality—perfection—drive—persistence." She also described her success as an obsessed dedication "to create beauty." Lauder believed "the most insidious myth" that instant success was possible. She had lived the heartaches and knew there was no such thing as a free lunch when it came to building a business empire. Lauder wrote in her memoirs, "I cried more than I ate. There was constant work, constant attention to detail, loss of sleep, worries, heartaches."

The Queen of Cosmetics believed in the Gandhian principle that would prove to be one her most successful promotions: "Whatever we give away, God will give back to us." This caused her to start her promotion of the "free gift with purchase." Prior to Lauder all monies spent in the cosmetics industry was spent in media advertising. Lauder changed all that with her eminently successful campaign that became one of the most successful promotion programs in the cosmetic industry. It differentiated her from the others and to this day is the hallmark of every Estée Lauder cosmetic center in the world. When she launched this promotion, Charles of the Ritz, a mortal enemy, said, "She'll never get ahead. She's giving away the whole business." Charles is history and Estée is still the queen.

Lauder learned early not to listen to experts like Charles of the Ritz or Charles Revson, the head of Revlon. Both had promised to "destroy her." When she was getting started, a lawyer told her, "Don't do it. The mortality rate in the cosmetic business is high and you'll rue the day you invested your savings and your time into this impossible business." Fortunately she ignored that professional advice and built a multibillion dollar empire.

Nelson Mandela

Former President of South Africa Nelson Mandela never gave up through twenty-seven deplorable years behind bars. He had dedicated his life to the end of Apartheid in his homeland of South Africa. He admitted in his auto-biography that he had little hope of success in his lifetime but felt his sacrifice would pay dividends for future generations. That is a very admirable quality to sacrifice your life for a dream that you have little chance of realizing.

Mandela was quite prophetic in saying "Struggle is my life." He had many opportunities to escape to freedom during those years when he was hunted like a dog while underground. He became known as the Black Pimpernel and used the name David as a pseudonym. Mandela had many offers to leave his homeland but turned them down, saying "I will not leave South Africa, nor will I surrender." A man trained to practice law, Mandela was more philosopher than attorney. He was a maverick political activist but not quite as nonviolent as Martin Luther King Jr. Testimony to his commitment came in the mid-1980s when international pressure on the white government forced his conditional release from prison.

Mandela had already spent much of his adult life behind bars and must have wanted desperately to spend the end of his days enjoying some sense of solitude. When the all-white government was about to come down they offered him a conditional release on their terms. After twenty-two years in prison he decided to stay rather than to capitulate to his mortal enemies. In his letter to President P. W. Botha he said, "I can't sell my birthright. What freedom am I being offered? Only free men can negotiate. I cannot. I will return." The tenacious leader of black freedom remained incarcerated for another five tortuous years until he was finally released on his terms at age seventy-three. That is the true definition of tenacity. Mandela was now the hero for underdogs everywhere and the model for persistence with a purpose. His life was one of waiting and winning.

When Mandela was a young boy he was raised in a tribal environment and learned from the chiefs how to negotiate with integrity. He was in college when the tribal chief insisted that he drop out and marry one of the women in the tribe. Mandela had to decide if he would live his life by the rules of others or follow his own path. He chose the latter, and lived up to his tribal name, Rolihlahla—a Xhosa name meaning "troublemaker." He left the tribe forever. It would take Mandela another ten years to complete his college education and thirteen to earn his law degree. Testimony to this man's persistence was the award (in 1990) of the Nobel Prize for Peace. A year later he was unanimously elected president of his beloved nation that was now free but in turmoil. When Mandela was finally released from prison he had screamed out "Amandla!" the Xhosa term for power. The people knew he was the man for the job and he was inducted into office on May 9, 1994, to international acclaim.

James Michener

The world's most prolific writer of historical novels was a man who was dedicated to finding the essence behind cultures and cities. Michener spent his life searching for identity, his and that of the many diverse cultures he researched for his historical novels. He died in 1997 after having produced forty-three books, mostly epic novels, in less than fifty years of writing. His autobiography, *The World is My Home* (1991) is a fitting tribute to his global lifestyle and vagabond nature. His dedication to the historical novel was based on his educational background and need to find the source of his own heritage. He was a foundling who never quite got over the fact that he had no roots.

Michener searched for the heritage of many things including religion in *The Source* (1965). He admitted, "I never had a childhood. It influenced all I would write." Although he would say, "I am an incorrigible optimist," Michener was also the rebel. "I had been thrown out of every school I had ever attended from grade school to college." Michener persistently searched for "whys" of the world and the source of things. This search led him to many cities and nations where he took residence while writing the history of their existence. If he couldn't know his own history, he wanted to know others', making him a vagabond who changed residences like most people change clothes. He took up residence in Israel, Poland, Hawaii, Spain, Alaska, Texas, Colorado, Maryland, and Hawaii while writing about those places. He decided to live his life in five-year increments and moved to Denver for *Colorado* (1974), Maryland for *Chesapeake* (1978), to *Poland* in 1980, Austin for *Texas* (1985), Miami for *Caribbean* (1989), and *Mexico* in 1992.

Michener was persistent and methodical. It took him three years to research and write a book but researched a new one while writing another. His tenacity came from his childhood desire to become a writer. He was never quite ready to write and devoured other authors like Balzac, Dostoevsky, Tolstoy, Theodore Dreiser, and Hemingway. He was forty years old before a near-death experience brought him face to face with his mortality and catapulted him into a writing career. He described this metamorphosis as a "theophany." It occurred when a plane he was on crash-landed on the South Pacific Island of New Caledonia while he was serving as a military correspondent with the navy. Michener said he went immediately back to his quarters, sat down and wrote, "I'm going to live the rest of my life as if I were a great man. . . . I'm going to concentrate my life on the biggest ideals and ideas I can handle." The next day he began work on his most famous book, movie, and Pulitzer Prize–winning play *South Pacific*. He was forty years old, but his perseverance had paid off. The book's success as a movie and play allowed him to quit teaching and to begin writing full time.

Stephen King

The King of Horror, Stephen King, knew rejection as a kid since he loved the occult and the weird and that set him apart. He escaped into weird books and movies to cope. Later he would write, "We make up horrors to help us cope with the real ones." In 1972 King had begun to drink as the rejection letters piled up in his trailer, he couldn't afford to get his car repaired, and the phone company had removed his phone, denying him the call that might come on one of his manuscripts. King had written as a teenager, all through high school and through four years of college and submission after submission had resulted in the same response. One editor wrote him in 1970 on his submission of *Sword in the Darkness*, "I can't even like it when I'm drunk." Two more novels earned similar responses.

Fate intervened when King started writing a Cinderella story with a supernatural twist for his fourth attempt at fiction. He had been published in *Cavalier* and a few other nondescript magazines and had always written horror. It had never occurred to him to write such a novel. After he had begun his first horror novel, he threw away the first few pages, but his wife, Tabitha, retrieved them and encouraged him to continue with the story, which depicted a girl with telekinetic powers. King continued, but when he was finished he said, "I had written the world's all-time loser." In traditional form, he submitted it to Doubleday anyhow. In January 1973 Doubleday picked up *Carrie* and paid King $400. Within six months it had been sold to a paperback publisher for $200,000 and then became the top film of 1976. Tenacity had paid off big time for the Titan of Terror. He immediately put in a phone, bought a car, and moved out of his trailer home.

Eight of King's first twelve books were made into movies and he sold 25 million books. He was the first writer to have three books on the *New York Times* Best Seller List at the same time—*Firestarter*, *Dead Zone*, and *The Shining*. By age forty King was earning $5 million per book, $10 million a year, and had just signed a four-book deal with Viking Press for $40 million. In the 1980s he was the most successful writer in the world with seven of the top twenty-five fiction books on the Best Seller List. This caused the head of the American Booksellers Association to label King "America's Horror Laureate." He has received little critical acclaim except as an "entertainment phenomenon" and as a "one person entertainment industry." His strength is storytelling, which he accomplishes with an innate sense of psychic fear and horror. King allows people to escape into their worst nightmares and fantasies, making the supernatural believable. King describes his talent as a function of his need for "cathartic release" from those demons lurking within his psyche. "If I weren't writing, I might be a mass murderer." On style he says, "I try to terrorize the reader, then I attempt to horrify, and only then to the gross-out." Whatever, he has persevered.

The Down Side of Tenacity

Those who never give up tend to be prone to anxiety attacks as in the case of many discussed here. All of these individuals tended to work until they dropped and when the dropped they were incapacitated for weeks at a time. Darwin was actually debilitated for the greater part of his adult life. Marx was also the victim of his own persistence and Napoleon, Mao Tse-tung, Howard Hughes, and Babe Didrickson Zaharias died without a friend who cared for them. Only a couple of people showed up at Babe's funeral, which seems strange for a woman who was the greatest female athlete who ever lived.

Roy Disney saw the signs in his brother, nervous tics, exhaustion, and impatience, and would send Walt off to Europe for an extended vacation until he recovered. The emotional collapses have been dealt with in different chapters but suffice it to say that all the greats paid a horrible price for their tenacity. Despite remaining healthier than most physically, it was their emotional health that proved their undoing. Marie Curie was sent to a rest home just after receiving her second Nobel Prize and spent much of her life as a lonely recluse. She was a dynamo compared to the hermit Agatha Christie and the antisocial Howard Hughes. Even when young Hughes would often disappear when life became too intolerable. Twice he was gone for months without anyone knowing his whereabouts. One time he was found in a Shreveport, Louisiana, jail. In another bizarre instance he was found walking in Manhattan in tennis shoes and carrying a dentist's bag with a douche bag and sundry other eclectic paraphernalia. Such is the price for refusing to give up.

Gender Implications of Persistence

Females are often forced to deal with male chauvinism on their way to the top. They have a real problem since it is just one more added adversity to overcome beyond those males face. One sure way to operate in a male-dominated environment is to be just as competitive, aggressive, risk-taking, and self-confident. Androgyny is one of the ways to fight such a battle. A number of these women were seen as aggressive and intransigent. Certainly those in the political arena were—namely Catherine the Great, Golda Meir, and Margaret Thatcher, consequently all three were treated as equals more than other women.

When Marie Curie discovered radium and its radioactive components she was actually working on her doctoral dissertation. Since no Frenchman would believe a woman capable of such a thing she had to share the Nobel Prize with her husband, Pierre. Her husband was then given a professorship at the Sorbonne with Maria as his assistant. Only at his death in 1906 did the French acknowledge her role at the university and elevate her to the post that had been held by Pierre but they still would not make her a full professor. She was allowed to take his post as lecturer and head of the laboratory but not as a chair of the department. No woman had ever held such a position, and she was the first woman even allowed to lecture at the prestigious institution. In 1908 she was finally appointed a full professor. Such is the speed of change for a woman in a man's world. But persistence does win out in the end, even though most biographical journals still give Pierre equal credit for the Curies' discoveries although even he said she did most of the research.

Maria Montessori was an indomitable spirit who refused to be categorized for any reason, least of all her gender. She needed her iron will to overcome the stereotypical belief systems in turn-of-the-century Italy. Montessori would ultimately be known as the Prophet of Pedagogy even though she refused to enter education as a child. Maria attended a "boys" school, then a technical high school and an engineering college. When she decided to become a medical doctor she had been on the path to such a career for some time, but even her father believed her to be impertinent and told her so. Refusing to accept a stereotypical role Montessori barged into the office of the University of Rome Medical School and told the head of the school, Guido Baccelli, that she wanted to become a medical doctor. Baccelli was stunned by her audacity and, admonishing her, said, "It is not only unprecedented, but unthinkable." The irrepressible Montessori walked out, leaving him with her caustic ultimatum, "I will become a doctor of medicine." The indomitable spirit then petitioned the pope, who interceded in her behalf. But she paid the price of violating tradition. The all-male student body made her life miserable through taunts and practical jokes aimed at making her quit. Then they forced her to take anatomy classes alone in the middle of the night, cutting up cadavers without anyone around. Montessori soon became distraught and walked out with the idea of quitting. She wrote of the experience saying, "My God, what have I done to suffer in this way? Why me alone in the midst of all this death?" However, she persevered and became the first female medical doctor in Italy on July 10, 1896.

Summary

Tenacity, perseverance, and persistence are the necessary ingredients of success. Great people must have a dream, not just any dream, but one that is so strong it makes you forget everything else and dominates your life. Once you have that dream well entrenched it is then imperative you pursue it and refuse to capitulate to any of the roadblocks on the journey. The most important trait to achieve tenacity is the confidence to ignore all those who will demean your trip. Many will call you crazy but those words need to empower rather than debilitate you.

Trauma is often an asset for those struggling to achieve a goal. These subjects are certainly excellent examples of facing failure and never giving up. Disney attempted suicide a number of times as did Napoleon, Twain, Balzac, Hitler, Curie, Hughes, and Hemingway, who finally succeeded. But, if nothing else, reaching the very bottom often conditions one for the top by instilling an intransigent will to succeed despite all adversity. Staring mortality in the mirror often conditions a person to take the big risks and to overcome the difficult obstacles.

Frank Lloyd Wright was insolvent at age sixty after producing a lifetime of great masterpieces, but he continued to work and produced one-third of his life's work after age eighty. Twain was bankrupt at age fifty and Edison at age fifty-three. Balzac and Dostoevsky were constantly fleeing debtors intent on interring them in a debtor's prison. Disney was insolvent for thirty straight years. But it is telling that none of these men quit and because of that most died quite wealthy. These superstars never gave up and that is why they ended up with the gold. It is the defining characteristic in the truly eminent personality. If you never give up you can never be defeated.

CHAPTER 9

Success imprints of Greatness

SUCCESS IS LEARNED, NOT INHERITED!

"Research now indicates that creative people are made not born."
Science Digest (1996)

Nature versus Nurture

Most psychologists now agree that about 50 percent of our personality, intelligence, and other characteristics are acquired, not inherited. We become what we are on the journey through life and even though we don't fall too far from the tree we are still molded by our myriad of experiences, traumas, and interactions. If less than half of what we become is inherited then it is imperative we place ourselves in environments conducive to success, not failure.

What this tells us is that our aggressive or submissive behaviors, our ability to see the trees or the forest, our laziness or ambition, are all merely extensions of how we see the world and how we are preprogrammed to deal with it. We like peanut butter not because of some conscious need for protein, but because of some preprogramming in our unconscious mind. The same is true of our preference for tall, dark, trim males or tiny, blonde, blue-eyed females.

It is imperative that we understand that our future is cast in putty, not concrete, after matriculating into adulthood. Freud and many of his disciples believed we were cast in concrete after adolescence. Psychologist Erik Erickson and others, including myself, disagree. We have been programmed with *success imprints* and *failure imprints* and our future successes and failures are a function of those inner belief systems. What is important is that we understand what makes us tick so that we can maintain that course or modify it. Changing is not easy, but I believe we can alter our paths throughout life, even into old age.

Is it easy to change what we are? No! The more programmed we are the tougher it is to change, but change is possible if we understand how we got the way we are. One way we change is through traumatic events. It is in this state that we can experience *superlearning* where instant changes and growth can transpire. In military parlance this is known as brainwashing. Psychologists label it a "hypnagogic state"—the theta or twilight state that occurs between waking and sleeping. Thomas Budzynski of the University of Colorado Medical Center says in this trancelike state "a lot of work gets done very quickly." When are you in this state? When you have an emotional or physical trauma like an automobile accident, a parent's unexpected death, or other such crisis. It can also happen when you unexpectedly perform far beyond your ability and are praised for it. The media often call it being in shock. What has happened is that you have turned off your conscious and lapsed into a theta state—that state you are in just prior to sleep. Brain waves are very slow and you find yourself in a dreamlike or mysterious state of consciousness. In such a condition your unconscious is very open to new ideas and you can be imprinted with new information. That is why behavior modification gurus ask you to listen to their tapes just prior to going to sleep.

When you find yourself in a trauma or crisis you are also placed in a position to benefit or be hurt by what has occurred. Dr. Ilya Prigogine has called this a state of "dissipitative structures" where you hit a *bifurcation point* and either reemerge stronger for the experience or you die—emotionally, physically, or mentally. Many of these subjects hit this wall and used the trauma to succeed. Michener's near-death experience in New Caledonia led to his writing *South Pacific*, Picasso's sister's tragic death led him to vent his inner rage in art, Oprah Winfrey's getting fired in Baltimore and her attempted suicide launched her into a talk-show career, the cancellation of Fred Smith's contract with the Federal Reserve led to his Federal Express empire, and Maya Angelou's rape led to a successful career in poetry. Without the traumatic nervous breakdowns experienced by Twain, Dostoevsky, Tesla, Curie, Hughes, and Disney it is almost certain they wouldn't have experienced such success.

Wilhelm Reich was a controversial but visionary psychologist who believed our experiences become "anchored" in our unconscious and they become a kind of "armor" against outside threats. This is what happened to these wunderkinds. They became imprinted with critical traits to success in their formative years and these success imprints molded their temperaments and personalities, allowing them to overcome adversity. It is not an accident that many of these renegade innovators had fathers who were con men and mothers who were doting. It was quite interesting to find so many similarities in so many eminent people.

Reprogramming Our Inner Tapes

I am convinced these eminent successes were all programmed, many later in life, to become successful. The older we get the more difficult it is too reprogram ourselves. Once we are deeply entrenched in our beliefs, operating in concert to those early imprints, it is much more difficult to change. An example is changing from an extroverted to an introverted type personality. That is very difficult for a forty-year-old but not impossible. Metaphorically speaking, our personality is equivalent to a huge container of red droplets. Attempting to change their color by adding an equal amount of blue droplets only succeeds in modifying the color to a mix, in this case purple. Using this example to change from an extrovert to an introvert you must change those internal tapes that demand that you be energized externally through interaction with other people to some imprints that make you more capable of internal energizing. That is, you must alter the need for external stimulation (other people) to a more introspective or internal satisfaction with being alone.

If early environmental, traumatic, and parental influences help shape our personality then it should only be necessary to alter those programs in the same fashion as they were formed. If we can do this then we can program ourselves with the optimum personality traits that are conducive to success. Taking this to an extreme, the personality becomes the critical component of whether we become prime minister or prostitute, titan of industry or wino, Pulitzer Prize–winning author or derelict, athletic hero or druggie. The only difference lies in how the two entities perceive the world. One group has bought into their success imprints, and the other their failure imprints. Our inner tapes and imprints determine our destiny: Our boardrooms are filled with people who have bought into their success imprints. Our prisons are full of those who identify with their failure imprints.

Further validation of this hypothesis comes from the American Psychological Association, which published a book called *Can Personality Change?* (1994) by Todd Heatherton and Joel Weinberger. The authors said, "If personality is nothing but behavior, then personality manifestly changes throughout life." Harvard research psychologist Jerome Kern confirms this with his comment, "No human quality is beyond change." One French study found that "the home environment can produce as much as a 20 point IQ improvement."

The subjects studied here appeared to be able to buy into their success imprints better than most people. These visionaries did not have some genetic predisposition to greatness like Mozart's musical precocity. What they had was a personality that conditioned them to deal with life so that they achieved success in their particular field of endeavor. A few, like Bill Gates, Martin Luther King Jr., Ayn Rand, Sigmund Freud, and Nikola Tesla, were exceptionally bright but most were quite average in cognitive ability. But the brightest subjects didn't make it to the top because of a superior intellect. They made it to the top because they were better able to communicate, take risks, compete, intuit new concepts, and persevere. It was their approach to life that made them great.

This would indicate that personality is the key difference in success and failure. This is a highly controversial statement and not easy to validate. But the data on these visionaries would suggest that their behaviors had much more to do with their success than any genetic predisposition. It also suggests that greatness is a function of an objective introspection rather than due to any subjective cause. Concentration on fundamentals is the key to greatness whether you are an athlete, businesswoman, artist, actress, scientist, politician, or author. In other words, anyone with the right temperament can make it to the very top. And what's more, it is never too late to be great based on the findings of these subjects. Frank Lloyd Wright produced one-third of his life's work after age eighty, Dostoevsky published his greatest novel, *The Brothers Karamazov* at fifty-nine, Michener wrote daily until ninety-two, Helena Rubinstein ran her company with an iron fist until she succumbed to father time at age ninety-four, Freud wrote *Civilization and Its Discontents* at seventy-three, and Montessori published *An Absorbent Mind* at seventy-eight.

Success and Failure Imprints

We are all a byproduct of our past experiences. I believe dysfunctional people are those who bought into their failure imprints. A young child who is told "you are a loser and will end up a hood" too often lives to fulfill that prediction. A stepfather suggesting "you are lazy and will end up on welfare" too often programs a young girl to live on the dole. Whether spoken in jest or not, such inane statements can become indelibly imprinted on the hearers' inner tapes, determining their destiny. Children often live their lives as others see them. That is good when the images are positive and bad when negative. Each can become self-fulfilling prophecies. This was true of Freud and Mead who both were told they were "special" as children and "destined for greatness." Both lived out those early predictions.

These visionaries spent their lives fulfilling positive internal dreams acquired early in life. That doesn't mean they never questioned their ability or potential or were not insecure at times. Most were very insecure and those insecurities drove them to overachieve. Ted Turner often said his success was due to the "insecurities" beaten into him by an alcoholic father. But most overachieved due to an internal vision that told them they were special. Isadora Duncan said in her memoirs "I was born under the star of Aphrodite. . . . At birth my mother said 'this child will not be normal. . . . This child is a maniac.'" Isadora lived out her mother's prophecy and became a renegade founder of modern dance who refuted god, marriage, and the establishment. She wrote, "I am a rebel and revolutionist." By age ten this iconoclast had the audacity to quit school and open her own dance studio, explaining her internal vision of greatness by saying, "My art is just an effort to express my Being. . . . An inner self is the driving force of my life."

Born versus Bred

Researchers now know that over half of our intelligence is acquired, not inherited, and the majority of our behavioral characteristics are picked up on the trek through life. Some of the astute subjects in this book knew this intuitively. Ayn Rand believes man to be the master of his fate and wrote "No one is born with any kind of talent and therefore, every skill has to be acquired. Writers are made, not born. To be exact, writers are self-made." Stephen King also told reporters he believed writers were made not born. Nelson Mandela believed man was a function of his experiences, not his genetic heritage. He said, "I maintain that nurture, rather than nature, is the primary molder of personality." Renowned Harvard pediatrician Dr. T. Barry Brazleton corroborates this based on his work with newborns. He said, "They learned *success* and *greatness*" while still in the crib (emphasis added). Brazleton could see "success" and "failure" on the faces of the babies. They would look like they were thinking, "See, I'm great" or "I'm no good. See, I've failed" (Goleman 1995, 193).

Madonna is a classic example of someone with mediocre talent who made it to the top of her profession. The Material Girl is an average dancer, worse singer, and was voted the world's worst actress in 1993. Despite such handicaps she broke every one of the Beatles' number one hit records in her rise to the top and in the process accumulated a net worth of $150 million. How does someone become so successful without talent? Because talent has little, or maybe nothing, to do with success in almost any discipline. Something else is going on, and that something is what this whole book is about. In Madonna's case it was a drive to be somebody, to overcome the loss of her mother at age five, to seek her father's attention, and to pursue her own self-actualization no matter the cost. If innate talent had been the defining attribute for success, Madonna wouldn't have made it out of the starting gate.

Jung's Collective Unconscious

Freud's disciple Carl Jung concocted an elaborate system of personality based on archetypes that he believed were innate and instinctual and handed down from previously imprinted generations of ancestors. Jung believed these archetypes predetermine behavior. For example, he believed a woman's emotional or feeling approach to decision-making, her reticence to take risks like men, and her nurturing nature were a function of millions of years of conditioning to secure the household against outside forces. Jung labeled these archetypes the anima (the feminine component of a personality) and animus (the masculine component of a personality). He said these two forces come together in a syzygy—the confluence of the masculine and feminine in all of us, and the secret of success in a social world.

Jung wrote, "In the unconscious of every woman there is hidden a male personality, and in the unconscious of every man there is hidden a female personality." Tapping into those opposites—the animus for females, the anima for males—is the secret of success for the integrated personality. In the book *Profiles of Female Genius*, I mistakenly wrote, "These women acted like men." What was really taking place was that Catherine the Great, Margaret Thatcher, Ayn Rand, and Madonna were successfully tapping into their animus (inner maleness) and that allowed them to be more of a totality, especially when forced to compete in a male-dominated world.

Further confirmation of Jung's syzygy hypothesis comes from *Fortune* magazine (August 8, 1994): "Women entrepreneurs are more like men entrepreneurs than they are like other women." Columbia University researcher Anke Erhardt wrote, "Women who showed more tomboy behavior in youth actually had higher IQ's" (quoted in Branden 1994). Psychologist Nathaniel Branden (1994) confirms this with his statement, "Most creative individuals are those who can integrate both male and female aspects of personality." University of Chicago researcher Mihalyi Csikszentmihalyi told *Psychology Today* (July 1996), "Creative and talented girls are more dominant and tough than other girls, and creative boys are more sensitive and less aggressive than their male peers."

Researchers at UCLA, Berkeley, and the University of Southern California add credence to the environmental influence on behavior. They found that enriched or embellished environments (those which included positive motivating items like swings and few negative items like electric shocks) materially impacted the way rats performed. Those bred in enriched environments had higher IQs than those bred in impoverished environments. The impact on thinking and learning was a function of how they were reared. Rats raised in an embellished atmosphere were more successful than those raised in impoverished one. University of Illinois psychologist

Gary W. Ladd found, "Rejection during childhood is one of the best predic-tors of later-life difficulty. . . . The anguish never really goes away." Success does beget success based on this new research.

intelligence Quotient

Yale psychologist Robert Sternberg in *Successful Intelligence* (1996), said, "IQ may predict people's grades in college but they are not a measure of their intelligence." What he was saying is that Ted Turner may have an IQ of 122, but even though he would be rejected by MENSA, which requires a min-imum IQ of 140 or the top 2 percent of scores, Ted was still an entrepre-neurial genius who dramatically changed the world with CNN. The majority of the subjects included here would not have been eligible for MENSA, and therefore would not have qualified for what some writers have called the "cognitive elite" who supposedly are destined to become the world's leaders in the twenty-first century.

Most of these visionaries were bright but not brilliant. In fact, according to biographer Frank Sulloway (1996), Darwin was "surprisingly average," in the opinion of his father and teachers. A number of writers have called Thomas Edison an extremely average intellect. His other qualities were any-thing but average but his cognitive talents were certainly nothing to brag about. Edison told reporters, "I wouldn't have amounted to anything if I had gone to school. University trained scientists only see what they are taught and thus miss the great secrets of nature."

Walt Disney did not make it through high school and only lasted one week as a cartoonist due to his ineptitude. Picasso was considered dull by his teachers and barely made it through grammar school. Honda was a horrible student who frequently failed tests and could never qualify for engineering school. Even Einstein failed a Swiss entrance exam to electrical engineering college. Hitler failed the entrance tests for art school not once but twice. Helena Rubinstein flunked out of high school and Babe Didrickson Zaharias could hardly write a sentence. None of these would have passed the SAT minimums for most colleges.

I am convinced that cognitive ability, beyond a bare minimum, has little to do with greatness even though some educators still tout it as the guarantee of success. The only success with which IQ is correlated is school grades and SAT scores, and not always with those. Being smart can get you invited to MENSA meetings but it cannot get you to the top of anything except maybe the honor roll. And many who are too smart think that will get them by in the world and when they can't find it they often crawl into a bottle and end up on skid row.

Bill Gates is very bright but it was his drive, work ethic, and other skills like risk-taking propensity that made him the wealthiest man in the world. It was not his IQ. Frank Barron researched intelligence and other personality characteristics at the Institute of Personality Research (IPAR) at Berkeley. He found "For certain intrinsically creative activities a specific minimum IQ is probably necessary to engage in the activity at all, but beyond that minimum, which is surprisingly low, creativity has little correlation with scores on IQ tests." Psychologist Robert Sternberg says, "IQ is a pretty miserable predictor of life achievement."

Harvard professor Howard Gardner has isolated eight intelligence types that he labels word smart, logic smart, picture smart, body smart, music smart, people smart, self smart, and environment smart. These categories and the intelligence they describe are better predictors than IQ for people like Disney, Picasso, Honda, Lauder, and Turner. Psychologist Daniel Goleman believes emotions, not IQ, are the true measure of human intelligence. He wrote "genes alone do not determine behavior; our environment, especially what we experience as we grow, shapes how a temperamental predisposition expresses itself as life unfolds" (1995, 224).

Socio-Economic Influence

Being raised in a country club environment will certainly help your golf handicap and social skills, but it is a poor predictor of success in the real world. The visionaries described in this book represent a fairly normal distribution with seven (14 percent) from affluent or privileged backgrounds and six or (12) percent from poverty or the lower classes, leaving the majority, thirty-seven, from the middle class.

Research would suggest that having it too easy too early is counter to success. Swanee, the outspoken daughter of billionaire H. L. Hunt, told reporters, "Inherited wealth does more harm than good." She went on to describe how money had proved to be a terrible detriment to her personally and predicted that any child who was given too much was being set up to fail. I agree. Success requires a person to overcome obstacles and those success imprints will go a long way to building internal belief systems that will ultimately lead to greater and greater successes. Even the subjects in this work who came from money had to overcome huge adversity in their trek to the top. Eminent individuals such as Catherine the Great, Charles Darwin, Rupert Murdoch, Bill Gates, Fred Smith, and Howard Hughes all were faced with great insecurities, trauma, and other problems which contributed to their later success. Often these adversities were the main reason they made it to the top and the ability to win those inner wars with themselves is what made them successful.

Formal Education and Success

A pedigree from a prestigious university will open many important doors but once inside it will be those other factors discussed in this book that will determine success or failure. We often believe that the world owes us a living because we succeeded in school but that is not true. Getting a degree is only a preliminary to the main event. Example of this axiom comes from Karl Marx, who struggled to get a Ph.D. in philosophy but made his mark in the world in political science. Darwin had a degree in divinity but was successful in biology and anthropology. Freud had a medical degree but made his mark in psychology. Robeson had a law degree but his success was as an entertainer. Maria Montessori had a medical degree but her great contribution to society came in the field of education.

It is telling that only 48 percent of the females and 37 percent of the males in this book finished college. Only two graduated from Ivy League schools. Why? Because too often graduates of these schools fully expect to start their careers in the middle or upper-middle of any organization and that is not where great success is born. Creative genius is born and bred in the trenches but unfortunately the gutter is not the preferred playground for the cognitive elite. Do you think Thomas Edison, Walt Disney, Howard Hughes, or Amelia Earhart would have attended an Ivy League school even if they had been invited? No chance! Earhart told reporters, "Experimentation is better than any college education." She and the other greats in this work knew that success was not to be found in a classroom.

There is one area where a formal education is critical to success and that is in the world of science or technology, and in some cases, politics. The ultimate truth is Bill Gates, who would not have changed the world of the personal computer nor would he be the richest man in the world had he graduated from Harvard. He would now probably be a prominent attorney in his father's law firm or be teaching math at some prestigious university.

Birth Order as a Key to Greatness

Being born first is not critical to becoming a great success in the world, but often where you are born influences the way you are treated by your parents and other family members. That is what is critical to success in later life because first or only children are given a special responsibility to carry on the family name, and are often imbued with a strong sense of self that correlates well with leadership.

Fifty-four percent of these subjects were first born and another 12 percent were the first-born of their gender. It appears birth order is more important for males than females due to the 10 percent difference between genders. Marx, Tesla, Hemingway, Murdoch, and Gates all had older sisters but were considered the head of family after the parents. Another factor making non–first-borns more like one was the loss of a sibling. Nikola Tesla lost his older brother at age six, elevating him to the role of oldest child. Others, like Margaret Thatcher, were raised as if they were first-born. Thatcher's father looked at her in the cradle and vowed that she would be his son since she would be his last child and he desperately wanted a son to nurture as a leader.

One of the stronger arguments for birth order as a causal agent for leadership comes from science and politics. The first seventeen astronauts were first-born males, as were World War II ally and axis leaders Winston Churchill, Franklin Roosevelt, Joseph Stalin, Adolph Hitler, Benito Mussolini, Mao Tse-tung, and Hirohito. Is being born first important? No! What is important is being told by proud parents that you are a born leader, important in the scheme of things as the one to carry the mantle of the family name, and future head of the family. The way first-borns are treated and doted on is what separates them from others.

Harvard researcher Frank Sulloway has written volumes attempting to show that later-borns are more rebellious and therefore more prone to creativity. In his book *Born to Rebel* (1996) he admits that first-borns of both sexes "tend to be Alpha males" (Darwin's term for the largest and strongest male in any anthropological group) and consequently more prone to become dominant leaders in politics and technology. Sulloway confirms my contention that originality among scientists and technologists is "indisputable in first borns." He says, "it lies in their clever puzzle solving" (1996, 356). Examples of this are rampant in history. Newton, Galileo, Martin Luther, Marat and Robespierre, Einstein, Freud, Jonas Salk, Linus Pauling, and Watson and Crick were all first borns. Sulloway goes on to say, "the influence of birth order on personality is typically 5 to 10 times greater than it is on IQ" (Sulloway 1996, 357). This gives credence to my thesis that personality is learned rather than acquired.

Parental Influence—Doting and Permissiveness

The male subjects in this work had very strong mothers who proved to be the most important influence in their lives. Conversely, the females had very strong fathers who tended to be their greatest role model. Margaret Thatcher, Madonna, and Oprah Winfrey all said, "I owe everything to my father." The only picture found in Hitler's bunker was that of his mother. The Führer's mother spoiled him to a fault. She bought him a piano that he never played, then she paid for his education in a Vienna art school that he never attended. Others indulged by the mother they idolized included Napoleon, Freud, and Picasso, to name just a few.

Doting

The parent is the first and most important role model for a child and the greatest influence on how the child sees the world. This was poignantly evident in these eminent individuals. Parental influence was the differentiating ingredient in the formation of their personality. Frank Lloyd Wright's mother told him he was the reincarnation of the Welsh god Taliesin, something she truly believed. That treatment proved to be one of the most overriding influences on the great architect—he grew up believing he was not subject to the laws of society or architecture, leading to unbelievable arrogance. Wright's mother gave him the middle name Lincoln, after the great emancipator, since she fully expected him to become as influential. Later he changed it to her maiden name, Lloyd, to give some indication of her enormous influence on him.

Sigmund Freud also had a doting mother. She gave the father of psychoanalysis his own room and special eating privileges as a child while relegating his younger brother and sister into an inferior role within the family. When his sister Anna's piano playing bothered young Freud, his doting mother sold the piano. Both parents believed a psychic who had advised them that the boy was special and told him "You are destined for greatness."

Isadora Duncan gave her permissive mother credit for having groomed her for greatness by allowing her freedom to roam the streets of San Francisco. "I could wander alone by the sea and follow my own fantasies." The freedom spawned a young entrepreneur who opened her first dance studio at age ten. She said, "My brothers and I were free to follow our own vagabond impulses. It is certainly to this wild untrammeled life of my childhood that I owe the inspiration of the dance that I created, which was but the expression of freedom. I was never subjected to the continual don'ts of other children " (Duncan 1927, 11).

Agatha Christie spoke of a similar freedom, saying in her autobiography, "My mother allowed me to run wild as much as possible as if I were a boy." In the infancy of planes her mother bought her a ticket for a ride that was considered quite dangerous and frivolous during the early days of the century when planes had open cockpits. Anne Rice's mother, Katherine, was permissive to the point of eccentricity. Anne and her sister were permitted to use any wall in the house as their personal coloring book. Very little was off limits for Anne when she was growing up and consequently she is an off-the-wall iconoclastic writer of supernatural novels. Her unconventional childhood created a maverick adult with few inhibitions. Babe Didrickson Zaharias was another southern girl allowed to roam about the streets of Beaumont, Texas, with abandon. She wrote that she only came home to eat and sometimes didn't even do that. Her free spirit took her to Los Angeles at age fourteen, where she took a shot at joining the circus. She left home permanently when she was in high school to join an industrial basketball team.

Picasso was raised as a messiah in a household full of adoring women. Their idolatry molded him into an arrogant, self-centered titan who believed he could do anything to anyone, especially females. His mother told him as a child, "If you become a soldier, you'll end up a general. If you become a monk, you'll end up pope." The early homage formed an indomitable self-esteem that would not be denied. The visionary Nikola Tesla also felt that his mother's influence had groomed him to become innovative. He wrote in his memoirs, "My mother was an innovator of the first order. I inherited my photographic memory and inventive genius from her." Margaret Mead con-firmed the part played by her father, saying, "My father defined for me my place in the world." And Napoleon wrote, "I was very well brought up by my mother. I owe her a great deal." That was something coming from the Little Corsican who admitted to having not a friend in the world, including his brothers and sisters.

Game Playing

Bill Gates is an example of how competing in games at a very young age can groom one to be more aggressive while learning to win and lose gracefully. Games were a ritual each night after dinner in the Gates home, and ranged from ping-pong and cards to jigsaw puzzles. Playing to win was deeply ingrained in his young psyche and has made him the competitor he is today. The founder of Domino's, Tom Monaghan, had a similar early experience with game playing. He wrote in *Pizza Tiger* (1986), "I was the best jigsaw puzzle solver, the best ping-pong player, the best marble shooter."

Most of these visionaries grew up competing which left them with a predilection for winning, whether the game was marbles, puzzles, pool, or building blocks. Frank Lloyd Wright's mother invested in Froebel Blocks, which had been designed in Europe as an educational tool for abstract problem solving. Babe Didrickson Zaharias won a marble contest at age six and it set her on a road of competitive drive that never abated. The Babe was unable to go fishing with friends without betting on who would catch the biggest fish. Michael Jordan began competing in Little League and never stopped until he became Air Jordan.

Overprotective Mothers—The Bane of Creativity!

The mothers who never allow their children to skin their knees or get a bloody nose are, in fact, depriving their offspring of important learning as a child. By locking their children in any protective environment they are pro-tecting them but at the same time are impeding their emotional development. Security becomes a goal rather than a defense. No one ever gets to the top if security is his or her number one objective.

Most of the subjects in this work were permitted to risk and err without remorse, and encouraged to fight their own battles, win or lose. The best example of this comes from Richard Branson's mother. Branson was a high school dropout who became Great Britain's most famous risk-taking billionaire prior to age forty. The founder of Virgin Records and Virgin Atlantic Airlines was not trained for his ventures. So when his mother was asked how someone with so little training could accomplish so much she responded, "Well, I was very inclined to teach him independence. At age eight I drove Richard across London, dropped him off in a field, and drove off, challenging him to find his way home." She was a master at instilling independence and chutzpah, but how many mothers would have that kind of temerity? Most American mothers are reticent to allow their kid to walk alone to the school bus or to the grocery store.

Self-Employed Parents

Ninety-three percent of these subjects had self-employed parents (see table 4) with the males having a slight edge on the females. It appears that growing up and seeing your prime role model in life not punching a time clock, not depending on others for earning a living, and not doing the 9:00 to 5:00 routine is critical to instilling independence. Three of these subjects had fathers who were medical doctors—Darwin, Dostoevsky, and Hemingway. Six had parents who were entrepreneurs—Christie, Disney, Hughes, Gordy, Turner, and Smith. Two had parents who were lawyers—Gates and Marx. Five had parents who were sales agents—Einstein, Rubinstein, Freud, Campbell and Mother Teresa. Duncan and Picasso had parents who were artists, and Tesla, Robeson, Wright, and King had parents who were preachers. Some of the other subjects had parents who were itinerant contractors, pharmacists, farmers, mariners, or educators.

What does a self-employed parent have to do with creativity and innovation? A lot! The child learns to look up at his or her primary role model in life and see someone who has not had to buy into a corporate womb or seek success outside his or her own control. They learned early in life that one could control his or her own destiny and not be dependent on others for success. Such early impressions molded them with independence, self-reliance, self-sufficiency, resilience, and a strong sense of self. These subjects learned early to be self-reliant and to be responsible for making their way in life. In other words, they viewed success as a function of a personal and internal, not impersonal and external, occurrence.

Transiency and Travel

Most of these visionaries moved constantly as children and the early experience seems to have preconditioned them to continue their vagabond life as adults. Frank Lloyd Wright had lived in ten states before he was ten years old, Mead had lived in sixty homes by age eleven, and Michener had hitchhiked his way through all but a few states by age fifteen. Just as telling, Walt Disney and Amelia Earhart each attended four different high schools in three different states. Stephen King lived in six states prior to age six and Chairman Mao ran away from home at age ten, returned, but moved three more times before he left on his own at eighteen. James Michener's hitchhiking escapades are a study in a young boy attempting to find roots. He speaks of visiting all but two states by age eighteen in his memoirs, *The World is My Home* (1992). He wrote, "I had worked in 130 sovereign nations by age 40."

What is the meaning of all this moving and traveling at such an early age? It forces the child to cope with the new, the unknown, and the foreign. Children must learn to make new friends, understand new cultures, learn new languages or new dialects. They must find comfort with ambiguity. These are the very things they will face as entrepreneurs and innovators. When you learn self-sufficiency and independence at an early age it is much easier to deal with discontinuities as an adult. Entrepreneurs and change masters are constantly faced with the new and unknown and must learn to be fleet of foot. These subjects learned to cope with unknown environments quite early in life. Consequently, the new and different did not frighten them as adults. In fact, it appears to have groomed them to view the unknown as a positive not a negative, just the opposite of those raised in more secure environments.

When Wright attended ten different schools in ten states he learned early to cope with new friends, teachers, towns, and cultures—he was experiencing many of the same challenges he would face as a maverick architect. Margaret Mead learned to deal with the new by living in so many different homes as a young girl. She began to thrive on the new and see it as a challenge rather than a threat and part of progress in a dynamic world. This held her in good stead as a single young female exploring the jungles of New Guinea and Samoa. She discussed this at length in her autobiography *Blackberry Winter—My Early Years* (1972).

Amelia Earhart reflected back on her early transiency and viewed it as a learning experience. She said, "I grew up like a rolling stone. . . . I've had 28 jobs in my life and I hope I have 228 more." Maya Angelou and Paul Robeson had similar experiences. Angelou was born in Los Angeles, reared in Arkansas, St. Louis, Los Angeles, and San Francisco with other stops on the way. Her early transiency groomed her with a vagabond spirit that allowed her to perform *Porgy & Bess* in seven different languages, all of which were self-taught. Paul Robeson performed *Othello* in twenty-seven languages for much the same reasons since he had lived in four cities before attending high school in New Jersey. Einstein attended schools in three different nations: Germany, Switzerland, and Italy. Napoleon, Balzac, Darwin, Dostoevsky, Turner, Smith, and Tesla were raised in boarding schools. Picasso lived in four different cities before he was a teenager. These stories of dislocation at an early age add credence to change being a positive influence on leadership and creativity. It does not change across disciplines since all of these subjects moved often and traveled extensively at an early age. It appears their early transiency helped them deal with being out in front of the pack.

Mythical Mentors and Heroes from Books

Balzac concocted a theory he called "mythomania" to describe his hero worship of Napoleon and Attila the Hun. Karl Marx had a lifelong idolatry of the Greek god Prometheus who stole fire from the gods and purportedly brought science to mankind. Chairman Mao spent much of his youth studying the great warriors and through books came to idolize Napoleon, Peter the Great, Catherine the Great, and many European writers. At age twenty he buried himself in a library and stayed there for six months doing nothing but reading about great heroes from the past. Joseph Campbell did the same but for one year, and he chose to read about the classics.

Such passion for books and their fantasy heroes instills an internal hero-worship that remains for life. I am convinced these early stories and fables can kindle an internal drive that is instrumental in the greatness these visionaries achieve later in life. Identifying with fantasy heroes who are larger than life tends to remove all personal limitations for greatness. Napoleon conquered Egypt because his childhood hero, Alexander the Great, had done the same some 2,000 years earlier. He and Tesla were both enamored of the superhuman machinations of Goethe's *Faust*. Turner and Balzac both idolized Napoleon as children. Gates and Joseph Campbell idolized Leonardo Da Vinci. Hitler became caught up in Nietzsche's Overman as the quintessential man. These heroes were adopted after the visionaries had read about them in books. Books often became the escape into a fantasy where life is wonderful and the powerful conquer the weak. A few of the subjects, Agatha Christie and Walt Disney, were enraptured by fables and fairy tales. Stephen King became caught up in horror fiction books and movies. He wrote, "I lived and died with Dr. Jekyll and Mr. Hyde," but his obsession was with the weird and occult he found in comic books and H. P. Lovecraft and Ray Bradbury. He said, "Supernatural horror opened the way for me. I loved *Weird Science, Tales from the Crypt, Creature from the Black Lagoon,* and *Mars is Heaven.*"

Edison said, "I didn't read a few books. I read the library." He told a reporter, "I began at A and read half way through the Detroit library." Joseph Campbell attempted the same, as did Bill Gates. The protagonists they came to identify with appear to have had a strong influence on how they perceived the world. Books were their escape and their inspiration. Many adopted the fantasy heroes as their role models and mentors. When children adopt a hero or idol who moves them emotionally that character becomes ingrained in their unconscious and becomes mystical and supernatural. Escaping into such a surreal world alters the child's psyche, arming him or her with an omniscient belief system. Such children grow up with fewer internal limitations as to what they may accomplish as adults. They suspend disbelief more than other children, thus opening up vast vistas of potential, at least in their heads and hearts.

Oprah told an audience at the national bookseller's convention in Miami Beach, "I owe everything to books." She spoke of using books to escape into a happier fantasy world. She read voraciously while attempting to escape the reality of the degradation of a Milwaukee ghetto. Reading imprinted her with a belief that there was some magic world out there beyond what she knew and it gave her hope. That is what books can do. Berry Gordy Jr. spoke extensively about his fantasy love affair with Joe Louis at age eight. He wrote in his memoirs, "Joe Louis is the greatest hero in the universe. In that moment (when he won the heavyweight boxing championship) a fire started deep inside me, a burning desire to be special, to win, to be somebody. Joe Louis was the first person who made me know what the word hero meant" (1994, 11). Then as a teen Gordy discovered Kipling's inspirational poem "If." He would reprint the poem in full fifty years later in his autobiography, and said, "I learned this poem by heart, picking apart each verse and finding ways to apply its philosophies to my own life."

A similar hero worship occurred in the early lives of both Joseph Campbell and Bill Gates. Both adopted Leonardo Da Vinci as their childhood hero after reading of the Renaissance man's great exploits. The early impression was so telling that Gates spent millions to buy the great inventor's notebook. Isadora Duncan escaped in books in San Francisco, New York, London, Paris, Berlin, and Athens, and she would write in her memoirs, "I was possessed of the dream of Promethean creation." She came to believe that she had become transformed spiritually and wrote, "I am indeed the spiritual daughter of Walt Whitman and Aphrodite," and she actually relocated to Greece and opened a school of dance in Athens.

Dostoevsky said, "I read like a fiend" while he was incarcerated in a Siberian prison that stripped him of his self-worth and dignity. Books were his escape into a fantasy world of hope. He found intellectual and emotional solace in the Bible, allowing him to escape from the nihilism that was his physical existence. This experience armed him with the experience to become one of the world's great existential writers producing *Notes from the Underground* (1864), *Crime and Punishment* (1866), and *The Brothers Kara-mazov* (1880). Dostoevsky spent the rest of his life searching for the meaning of man's inhumanity to man. He wrote his brother saying, "I won't even tell you what transformations were undergone by my soul, my faith [reading the Bible], my mind [books], and my heart in that four years. . . . The escape into myself from bitter reality, did bear its fruit" (Gide 1923, 63).

The eerie mysticism of Charles Dickens's *A Christmas Carol* and super-natural qualities of Scrooge had "obsessed" Anne Rice since she read this classic as a young girl. She escaped into the ethereal world of the occult and supernatural where immortality lived. This has since become the essence of her own obsession with the occult and mysterious. She wrote,

> I was very influenced by Nathaniel Hawthorne and Edgar Allen Poe and at age five I escaped into a fantasy world of imagination. I've adopted Charles Dickens as my guardian angel and mentor. I've always been obsessed with *A Christmas Carol*. I've watched the English film version of it probably more than anyone in history, read and reread the story. I wanted to go into the supernatural per-sona of Scrooge. (Riley 1996)

It is quite easy to see where she got her urge to pursue the supernatural plots and vampires. It all came from her early imprints.

Ayn Rand had a similar hero worship, focusing on Catherine the Great; Cyrus, a conquering Ottoman hero; and Hugo's *Les Misérables*. Michael Jackson, the Peter Pan of Pop, so identified with his mythical role model he once jumped out of a second story window in a futile attempt to fly like Peter Pan. It is also telling that he named his California ranch Neverland. He became so caught up in this fantasy he told reporters as a teen, "We can fly, you know. We just don't know how to think the right thoughts and levitate ourselves off the ground" (Jackson 1988). The fantasy heroes and mythical mentors of various subjects are listed in table 10.

Joseph Campbell spent his life researching myths and their influence on the great. He is considered the preeminent scholar on mythology and his work gives confirmation to my own belief that mythical hero mentors are merely internal manifestations of our own need to self-actualize or become as great as we can be—to strive for perfection, superiority, and success. Most fan-tasy heroes are merely protagonists out of books that catch the fancy of lonely young people searching for a fictional role model with whom to identify.

Some of these subjects didn't use books to find their heroes. Michener became enamored of great operas. Wright found solace in Aladdin and his magic lamp, Madonna admired screen stars Jean Harlow and Marilyn Monroe, Stephen King looked to horror movies and comic books, Christie and Disney to fairy tales, and Mao to warrior-heroes. Paul Robeson spoke of the influence soul music had on his development: "Folk songs are in fact a

Table 10
Mythical Mentors and Success Imprints
"All myths make heroes out of those who heed them. . . .
Myths are models for understanding your life" (J. Campbell)

Maya Angelo	*"Crime and Punishment* changed my life"; "I act like my hero/shero would act."
Honoré de Balzac	Coined the term "Mythomania" to describe his theory of hero worship of Napoleon and Attila the Hun
Napoleon	Idolized Alexander the Great, Rousseau, and Goethe; carried their books to battle
Joseph Campbell	New York's Museum of Natural History and Indian books with totems altered life"; Reading about Leonardo Da Vinci changed my life." [see quote above]
Agatha Christie	Influenced by Charles Dickens and Arthur Conan Doyle's Sherlock Holmes
Charles Darwin	Read Thomas Malthus for entertainment and it influenced his theories of evolution
Fyodor Dostoevsky	"I read like a fiend." Balzac and the Book of Job inspired him to write
Isadora Duncan	"I am indeed the spiritual daughter of Walt Whitman and Aphrodite."
Thomas Edison	"I didn't read a few books, I read the library."
Albert Einstein	"I had read Kant and Darwin by age twelve."
Bill Gates	"My favorite hobby is reading"; Leonardo da Vinci enormous influence
Berry Gordy Jr.	"Joe Louis is my hero. He changed my life. When he became champion I was 8, a fire started deep inside me, a burning desire to be special." Loved "If" by Kipling
Ernest Hemingway	Read Walpole's *Dark Forest* at 18; hero inspired enlistment as ambulance driver
Adolph Hitler	Carried Schopenhauer to battle; based his Master Race thesis on Nietzsche's Superman
Stephen King	"Lovecraft's books struck me with such force. He opened the way for me. I lived and died with Dr. Jekyll and Mr. Hyde. My books are visual movies in my head."
Karl Marx	Dedicated thesis to Prometheus and lived life in his image in radical revolt
James Michener	"I read 40 volumes of Balzac's *Pere Goriot* by age 12."
Mao Tse-tung	A hero worshipper who spent six months at age twenty reading about great heroes
Maria Montessori	"I carried books to the theater"; Influenced by Seguin, Piaget, and Erickson
Anne Rice	"I'm obsessed with Dickens, *A Christmas Carol* had a profound influence on me."
Ayn Rand	Admired Ottoman hero Cyrus, Catherine the Great, Victor Hugo's novels, and Aristotle
Nikola Tesla	Reciting *Faust* during creation of alternating current; "Mark Twain changed my life."
Mark Twain	At age 15 Joan of Arc was his hero; "I read Kipling's *Kim* every year."
Ted Turner	Alexander the Great, Attila the Hun, Gandhi, and General George Patton
Frank L. Wright	*Aladdin and His Magic Lamp* story; taught he was Welsh God Taliesin

poetic expression of people's innermost nature. This is utterly and completely true for the song culture of my people." Nelson Mandela had a similar experience with African fables. He wrote, "These childhood fables enchanted me and fired my imagination for these African warriors" (Mandela 1994). On meeting an African poet he said, "This man instilled pride in my heritage. I felt like one of the chosen people."

Myths as Masks

The godfather of mythology, Joseph Campbell, is the best example of the mythical hero mentor. It is indeed interesting that he spent his whole life pursuing a subject that he encountered at age six and eight. When he was six his father took Campbell to see a wild west show in New York City and he immediately fell in love with Buffalo Bill and the Indians. Then at eight he was taken to visit the New York Museum of Natural History. These two events, along with books on Leonardo Da Vinci, changed his life. After going to the movies and watching Douglas Fairbanks Jr., the great actor became his hero, and Campbell actually grew to look like the famous actor, dressing just as he did.

Campbell wrote, "The material of myths is the material of our life." The totem poles, masks, and legends he saw in the museum were the mythical symbols of our nation that he decided to study. Campbell would spend the rest of his life chasing myths from the Far West to India, and Indonesia to New Zealand. As a teen he became enamored with books and read *Decline of the West*, *Outline of History*, *The Light of Asia*, and *Finnegans Wake*, and began a love affair with the myth of Black Elk, a Sioux indian medicine man. As an adult he traveled the world and learned to speak Sanskrit and Japanese in order to better understand other cultures and their myths.

Those caring to look further into Campbell will find most of his philosophy in two defining works, *The Hero with a Thousand Faces* (1949) which he wrote at age forty-five, and *The Power of Myth* (1988) based on his PBS television series with Bill Moyers. Campbell said, "Our imagination evolves out of life experiences," and that is the essence of this work. When he said, "myths are spontaneous productions of the psyche—imprinted archetypes buried in the unconscious," he was validating the hypothesis of a fantasy mentor for success.

But what does a mythical hero mentor mean for each of us? It means that reading books as a child and identifying the heroes, even if they are comic books where Batman, Robin Hood, and Wonder Woman are the heroes, will imprint us with the will to power and success. Larger-than-life heroes like Alexander the Great, Napoleon, or Superman allow us to see life as a place where anything can be accomplished. That is what happened to

Michael Jackson when he discovered Peter Pan, Wright with Aladdin, Isadora Aphrodite, and Gates his hero Leonardo.

How does fantasizing make you successful? It doesn't, but the internalization of an omniscient belief system is a positive influence on future self-belief. If Alexander the Great could conquer the world by age thirty-three why couldn't Napoleon? He made it at thirty-five. And why couldn't Turner win the America's Cup and conquer something mundane like cable TV? These were nothing in relation to his hero mentor conquering the world. If Aladdin and his magic lamp could create something out of nothing why couldn't Frank Lloyd Wright defy the architectural gods in America and marry form with ecological function? What had happened with these individuals? It appears they internalized their real-life fantasy dreams to such a degree they came to believe, at least inside, that virtually anything was possible, thereby removing the internal doubts that tend to limit or inhibit our ability to self-actualize.

As a teenager, I was told frivolous books like Captain Marvel, Batman, Robin Hood, Superman, and Mickey Spillane suspense novels had no redeeming value. My high school teachers denigrated such reading. Joseph Campbell's thesis has vindicated me. Finally after a lifetime spent searching for truth and vision Campbell found it. He told his audiences "Follow your bliss." He encouraged his followers to listen to their souls and follow their dreams.

Crisis—The Mother of Creativity

Seventy-five percent of these subjects lost a sibling or parent prior to coming of age. That is a telling statistic. Even those who didn't experience such a loss were faced with some life-threatening illness or other calamity. Based on the findings it is apparent that getting to the top necessitates a visit to the bottom and living through that dilemma.

Darwin and Mother Teresa both lost a parent when they were eight. Robeson watched his mother burn to death when he was four. Two of the entrepreneurs, Fred Smith and Tom Monaghan, tragically lost their fathers when they were only four. Smith had a double whammy having been born with a degenerative hip disease that caused him to walk on crutches until high school. Monaghan spent his youth in an orphanage due to his father's death. Michener was born out of wedlock and lived his life in search of an identity. Authors Agatha Christie and Stephen King both lost their fathers quite early and Mao Tse-tung lost his father when he was fourteen and later witnessed the execution of his wife and brother.

Mark Twain lost his sister, brother, and father before he was twelve and Karl Marx lost his father as a teenager. Marie Curie lost her sister and mother at nine and ten respectively. Freud lost a brother when he was two and felt that it was an unconscious influence on his driven need to overachieve. Tesla's older brother died purportedly at Tesla's own hand as he fell down the steps of the family home and it left the inventor with a lifetime of guilt and the need to overachieve. Margaret Mead was allowed to pick the name of her little sister, Katherine, and when Katherine died at age two Margaret was devastated. It is not surprising she named her own daughter Katherine thirty years later. Hughes lost both parents during his teens. When they died he was alone in the world and took it upon himself to become master of his fate, buying out his relatives in a power play that would prove pure genius. His later success can be drawn right back to that time when he was transformed from a frivolous teen to a driving entrepreneur. Crisis armors the psyche to perform far beyond that of others. Four subjects, Dostoevsky, Picasso, Michener, and Rice, each give credence to this claim.

Fyodor Dostoevsky—Crisis and Creativity

Fyodor Dostoevsky's personal traumas were far greater than those who just lost parents or siblings. That is why the father of the psychological novel was able to touch the heartstrings of his readers. He had suffered most of the traumas of which he wrote; his emotionally intense scenes were drawn from within a ravaged psyche. Writing of man's condition was easy for an epileptic, manic-depressive, alcoholic, and compulsive gambler. He had lost everything emotionally, spiritually, and physically, beginning with his mother's premature death when he was fifteen to his father's brutal castration and murder when he was seventeen. Not many people could match his flirtation with death and five-year Siberian imprisonment. Dostoevsky hit Prigogine's bifurcation point (that crises point where one dies—figuratively and literally—or reemerges stronger than before), bounced back, hit it again, bounced back, and then became almost self-destructive as he gambled away all chance for a respectable or normal existence.

Freud believed Dostoevsky's traumas were caused by unconscious guilt over his father's murder. It is interesting to note that Freud was highly influenced by Dostoevsky's intensely emotional writing and chose to diagnose the derivation of his dysfunctions. As a young struggling writer with great potential Dostoevsky was arrested for sedition and sentenced to die before a firing squad. On the designated morning the guards walked him, blindfolded, to the courtyard and he listened as the guns were cocked, awaiting the sting of death. At the eleventh hour the czar gallantly walked out and commuted the sentence to five years in Siberia. Many of the "mystic terrors" besieging Dostoevsky began at this time.

The tragic characters and realistic nihilism of the *House of the Dead* (1860), *Notes from the Underground* (1864), and *Crime and Punishment* (1866) could have only been born of the pen of someone who lived such personal denigration. The ever-present existentialism in *Notes from the Underground*, *The Possessed* (1872), and *The Brothers Karamazov* (1880) could only have been fathered by a person who had stared mortality in the face and survived the experience. Dostoevsky's intransigent willpower influenced Nietzsche's philosophy, Freud's psychology, and the tragic existentialism of writers like Camus and Sartre. Nietzsche said, "Dostoevsky is the only person who has taught me anything about psychology." After Dostoevsky lost his mother he became mute and Freud believed his epileptic fits were the result of guilt over wishing for his father's death. After surviving the degradation of Siberia, Dostoevsky wrote to his brother about his renaissance, saying, "Prison has destroyed many things in me and created the new."

Dostoevsky was so self-destructive it was as if he had a death wish. One would think he was sadomasochistic, the way he opted for the absolute worst kinds of solace. He once sold the rights to all of his work and then gambled the money away in one night on the turn of a roulette wheel. Then he sat down and wrote *The Gambler* in just twenty-five days in an attempt to stay out of debtor's prison. It was his flirtation with death, disaster, ruin, and behavioral dysfunction that allowed him to write so realistically about nihilism.

Picasso—The Birth of Cubism

When Pablo Picasso's sister contracted diphtheria, her older brother made a Faustian pact with God to save her from suffering—if she lived, he would lay aside his brushes and never paint again. The teen didn't understand how a merciful god could be so cruel and he internalized the rage of her horrific and painful death. His ambiguity over wanting to paint and have his sister live became internalized and released ten years later in his exorcisms against religion, god, women, and society. The birth of cubism and Picasso's surrealism were as much a by-product of his sister's death as anything. It was his way of releasing the ambiguous guilt and assuaging his inner rage. Most of Picasso's inner torment was released in his art and subliminally directed against mankind and a system that could allow such trauma. He viewed himself as an agent of death, and cubism and his surrealistic art were born of that nihilistic vision. *Les Demoiselles d'Avignon* and *Guernica* are testimonies to his internal need to assuage the guilt and torment of his sister Conchita's death.

James Michener—Crises Led to Writing Career

James Michener, the master of the historical novel, was in a plane attempting to land on New Caledonia in the South Pacific when he faced his trauma. He was forty years old and had never written anything except academic papers. When the plane he was in attempted to land in bad weather three different times he and the crew saw the end. They finally crash-landed, and welcoming another chance at life, Michener went back to his quarters, sat down and wrote, "I'm going to live the rest of my life as if I were a great man." The next day he began writing *South Pacific*, which would win the Pulitzer Prize for literature in 1948. Michener's brush with death had become his motivation to do what he had wanted to do since he was a small boy. In his autobiography, Michener described his epiphany; "I passed from callow youth to manhood. I was as good a man as I would ever be the moment after that decision on the airstrip."

Anne Rice—Trauma Produced Vampire Book

Anne Rice's experience was even more traumatic than most of the other subjects. She was first devastated when she lost her grandmother and mother when she was eight and fifteen, respectively. With these traumatic events still lingering in her unconscious she attempted to write but was unsuccessful. By her mid-thirties she was working diligently on many projects, including pornography, but was unable to break through. Then tragedy struck in 1972, when her five-year old daughter, Michelle, died of leukemia. Anne quit her job, started drinking heavily—three six-packs of beer daily— but more importantly, began writing *Interview with the Vampire* in a cathartic attempt to exorcise her loss.

Interview was finished in 1974 and published in 1976. Rice describes this pivotal work as the "cathartic release of her daughter's death" and the final purging of the deaths of her mother and grandmother. She wrote, "The book is symbolically to grant Michelle immortality," and added, "The destructive nature of the vampire was evident in what alcohol had done in the death my mother, what leukemia had done to Michelle, and what Michelle's death had done to me." Rice's great crisis transformed her from a housewife with a penchant for writing to a world-famous novelist. It has made her rich and famous even though she would not agree that the causal relationship was not a good trade-off. But it is telling that she chose vampires—the living dead, immortality, the supernatural, and mysticism as a means of keeping her loved ones alive, at least in the world of fiction. It is not a coincidence that she is obsessed with death and immortality and vampires are the vehicle by which she can accomplish what she couldn't in real life.

Nervous Breakdowns

Over one-third of the subjects experienced a nervous breakdown sometime during their career. Walt Disney experienced eight and attempted suicide at least three times. Nikola Tesla experienced at least five nervous collapses and Howard Hughes three. Other data is more fragmentary but Marie Curie had a nervous breakdown at age fifteen and another at forty-three. Napoleon went through a number of emotional collapses in which he attempted suicide. Balzac, Christie, Darwin, Dostoevsky, Marx, Montessori, Hemingway, Robeson, and Twain all experienced emotional traumas that were debilitating. Even Sigmund Freud went through such an experience in 1895 after he lost his partner and was struggling for recognition for his controversial work.

A surprising number of these subjects were in a state of emotional collapse or inner rage when they produced their most innovative work. Tesla was in the throes of a nervous breakdown when he discovered the secrets of alternating current and the induction motor. John O'Neill quoted Tesla's description of the experience in *Prodigal Genius* (1968): "I was at the point of breaking down. I knew I would perish if I failed." Walt Disney had eight nervous breakdowns, each occurring as he succeeded with Mickey Mouse, Snow White, *Fantasia*, and Pinocchio. His brother, Roy, learned to read the signs indicating an imminent breakdown and would send Walt off for a rest cure. Paul Robeson finally collapsed from exhaustion in Russia after the McCarthyite politicians destroyed his career and then him.

Prigogine's Dissipative Structures Theory

What do crises have to do with success? A lot! Staring mortality in the face has a remarkable impact on the psyche. It forces you to reevaluate loves, hates, values, and problems. What was once important suddenly appears trivial. And most important, we tend to alter our sense of what is risky and what is not. There is not much to fear after we have overcome the worst life has to offer. At that critical moment that Prigogine defines as the bifurcation point you either die or reemerge better than before the trauma. Such a transformation can be likened to breaking a bone in your arm. Once the bone is healed it is virtually impossible to break it in the same spot because it heals stronger than before the break. Ilya Prigogine, a biologist, won the Nobel Prize in 1977 for biological chemistry for his theory of dissipative structures, which addressed the derivation of these metamorphoses and demonstrated how this also works for the emotional system as well as biologically.

When a person faces disaster, he or she hits Prigogine's bifurcation point and must come to grips with the condition or pay the ultimate price. Either fear or tenacity will win out. Some people facing such a transition point crawl into a bottle or worse. Others go off the deep end and strike out against society. Others, like Walt Disney, use the shock to create and innovate. When Disney lost his character Oswald the Rabbit to an unsavory competitor, the trauma was personally debilitating and he suffered a nervous breakdown and contemplated suicide. But he did not allow it to defeat him and he drew Mickey Mouse on the train back to California. Had the crisis not occurred Mickey would never have been borne. There are hundreds of similar stories in this book.

Prigogine began his work as a means of combating the nihilistic Second Law of Thermodynamics that says all things burn up in a kind of heat death. His strategy was to demonstrate scientifically that biological systems are not so negative, and could be a positive force. He concocted the hypothesis that entropy—breakdown and *disorder*—ultimately leads to this bifurcation point where a system will die or reemerge better than before the crisis. He said that negentropy—breakthrough and *order*—automatically emerge out of chaos if sufficiently energized. In his work *Order Out of Chaos* (1980), Prigogine concluded, "Every artistic or scientific creation implies a transition from disorder to order." He said, "Life emerges out of entropy [chaos] not despite it. . . . It is out of chaos, turmoil, and disorder that higher levels of order and wisdom emerge, thus if the creative thinkers have less mental stability . . . they also experience higher levels of mental connectedness, complexity, evolution" (Hutchison 1990, 263). In other words, the traumas experienced by our subjects were in fact the catalyst for their later success.

Prigogine's system has application for machines, individuals, nations, and climatic events like volcanoes, typhoons, and floods. Are all of these examples of entropy? Volcanoes kill but without them we would not have the magnificent Polynesian Islands. Floods irrigate the soil for future food growth. Hurricanes and typhoons blow away bad air and nourish the land. Even nations at war in true dialectic form create a superior synthesis out of their crises. Would Japan and Germany be the most dominant industrial powers in the world today had they not been destroyed in World War II? I don't think so. They are only powerful because they were destroyed and their cities were in ashes. China is presently on a similar track to greatness.

What does Prigogine's theory of dissipative structures mean for us? It means that it is imperative to see crises as a potential for new opportunity and growth. It isn't what happens to us that is important but how we deal with it. These subjects experienced catastrophic traumas in their personal and professional lives, but without those crises they probably would not have become so successful. Their visit to the bottom led them to the top. From this research it almost appears that it is "good" to have something bad happen in order to instill the drive and motivation necessary for success. Intensity comes out of adversity or in Prigogine's words, "negentropy emerges out of entropy." When we hit the wall, what Prigogine calls the bifurcation point, we either become less or reemerge better than before. Our jails are full of those who allowed the crises to win, but our boardrooms are filled with those who refused to be defeated. This book is full of those who found empowerment in crisis.

Success Imprints of the Super Successful

Most of these visionaries were imprinted by some earth-shattering experience that appears to have led them to success. Space limits the examples of these metamorphoses to the most glaring examples. Ten examples follow on "success imprints" from crises and the resulting transformation into a self-actualized person.

Napoleon Bonaparte

It was at the battle of Lodi in Italy that the Little Colonel was transformed from a young general into the world's greatest military genius. Napoleon was just twenty-four when he went into a battle he was supposed to lose. He wrote of his epiphany years later in St. Helena and said this battle was the beginning of his rise to fame and fortune: "It was only after Lodi that I realized I was a *superior being* and conceived the ambition of performing great things" (Markham 1996, 42; emphasis added).

In April 1796 Napoleon went into battle with 30,000 men against the combined forces of 70,000 Italian and Austrian soldiers. Outnumbered and expected to be soundly defeated, the irrepressible Napoleon defied all traditional military tactics and raced around the field spurring his troops on to superhuman effort. He won a decisive victory and although he was not visibly changed, he was a different man inside. Napoleon suddenly believed himself to be superior and invulnerable to mere mortals and began acting the part. His attitude and talent proved unbeatable in French politics and on the battlefield, motivating his archenemy the Duke of Wellington to declare, "The force of the Little Corsican on the field of battle is equivalent to 40,000 men." Within three years Napoleon was crowned First Consul of France, even though he was of Italian ancestry, not French. Five years later he was proclaimed emperor, and five years after that he had defeated all of the European powers.

Honoré de Balzac

The father of the modern novel, Honoré de Balzac, wrote *Cromwell*, his first novel, which was rejected as unacceptable. The book was ridiculed by the critics and it appeared he would not be a writer. He said, "I condemned myself to oblivion after the public proved to me with some brutality that I was a mediocrity. I therefore took the public's side in the matter and dismissed the man of letters, replacing him with the man of metal letters" (i.e., he became a printer and publisher). He embarked on a career of documenting French society that culminated in his *La Comédie Humaine* (The

Human Comedy), an epic series of ninety-two novels that ultimately made him famous as the father of the realistic novel. Modern critics describe him as the chronicler of nineteenth-century French society. His biographer Graham Robb describes him as "the first writer to make bureaucracy the subject of serious fiction." (1994, 106). Had he not failed miserably at what he wanted to be—a writer of nonfiction—he would never have changed the world of literature through his own unique innovation in novels. He was introspective enough to have recognized his weaknesses and altered his career to one at which he was able to achieve great success.

Mao Tse-tung

At age seventeen Mao Tse-tung became immersed in a freedom fight that changed his life. It was during this period that he saw a newspaper for the very first time and cherished the printed word as a window to posterity. He was so moved he impulsively sat down and wrote his own editorial that was "my first expression of political opinion, it was somewhat muddled, making me part reformist and part revolutionary" (Terrill 1980, 216).

The experience proved to be a major transformation in his young life. Mao was so stirred by revolutionary fervor he joined the Hunan Revolutionary army Changsha, China. From that point forward Mao altered his way of life and aimed himself body and soul at becoming an intellectual revolutionary. He became a self-proclaimed radical philosopher impressing his soldier friends. Mao said, "I could write and they (the soldiers) respected my great learning." He also was becoming self-centered and wrote "I am the universe." This early experience changed his path and he would soon start reading the works of intellectual radicals who would become his heroes: Marx, Engels, Lenin, and Darwin. He saw himself as a cult leader and future military strategist.

Amelia Earhart

Amelia Earhart, the world's most famous aviatrix, experienced a metamorphosis when she was five. She was belly-flopping onto a sled, like the boys near the family home, refusing to sit up like a proper little lady. Earhart came flying down the hill on her stomach. She suddenly saw a horse and carriage in her path but was going far too fast to stop or change direction. The irrepressible Earhart put her head down and went under the carriage and came out the other side unscathed. Earhart was a renegade even early in life but this incident transformed her from a tomboy into a lifelong risk-taker who preferred to act like a man.

Had Earhart been sitting up like a girl she would have been decapitated or otherwise severely injured. She remembered this event years later and wrote about it to explain her risk-taking personality. Earhart always challenged men to beat her air speed records and never wanted to act submissively, as women were expected to. Thrill-seeking and defying the odds were her forte and she would spend the rest of her life living on the edge. The riskier the act the more she was energized. When Wiley Post advised her not to attempt a speed record across the Gulf of Mexico because "It is too dangerous," she had to do it and went out and broke the record. It is not surprising Earhart became one of America's first androgynous sex symbols, wearing short hair and long pants in complete defiance of societal standards for the time. Death-defying ventures were her life and they all began with that sled ride as a very young girl.

Maria Montessori

The Messiah of Education, Maria Montessori, was transformed from a medical doctor into an innovative educator when she was given a roomful of "idiot" and "noneducable" children by a medical system that refused to accept her as an equal. Not to be defeated, Montessori took on the challenge and had the children reading and writing at normal rates within months. She was so empowered by the experience she quit her job, returned to school, and starting creating the Montessori method of education that would ultimately revolutionize the learning process. One of her great insights, "Education is social engineering," is the very essence of what this book is about. She had discovered much of what this study has found—that greatness is learned through hard work and diligence, it is not inherited.

James Michener

A near fatal airplane crash on New Caledonia Island in the South Pacific transformed Michener from a struggling teacher into a best selling author. Michener had dreamed of becoming a writer since childhood but was never able to make the leap from schoolteacher to writer until he saw his life about to end in that plane. Surviving, he looked within himself to find solace and reasoned that life is short and he had better get on with it before it was too late. Almost immediately after the crash he began writing his Pulitzer Prize winning novel, *South Pacific*. A year later when he submitted his manuscript he was told it wasn't acceptable and he would not be able to become a writer. His publisher told him he could not write. Even his agent quit, saying, "you have no future as a writer." Michener persevered and had the work published. He was awarded the Pulitzer Prize for literature in 1948 and the man who couldn't write produced forty-three best selling books and many movies.

Maya Angelou

World-renowned poet and author Maya Angelou was raped when she was seven and became mute for the next six years because she thought her testimony in court had been responsible for the death of her assailant. (He had been brutally murdered by her uncles.) Angelou had internalized the guilt and never spoke until a teacher rescued her from her silence at age eleven. The teacher tricked her into reciting poems by Shakespeare, Poe, and other writers to get her to speak. Books, especially classics and poetry, became the catalyst for Angelou's return to normalcy. Poets and great writers had brought her out of her trauma and it is truly ironic that she would become a great writer and poet herself many years later despite never having gone to college. Books had rescued Angelou from her self-proscribed world of silence, spawning a lifetime love affair with books and poetry. This early experience was a prime moving force in her literary career. This self-made author, poet, screenwriter, and professor delivered the memorable poem "On the Pulse of the Morning" at President Clinton's 1993 inauguration.

Joseph Campbell

The father of mythology, Joseph Campbell, often spoke of his epiphany as the day he first walked into the New York Museum of Natural History and saw the totems and masks. He spent the rest of his life looking for the source of the myths (which he saw as a motivating force to success) those items represented. From that first day Campbell was enthralled with books that explained how the world works, such as *Decline of the West* (by Oswald Spengler), *Outline of History* (H. G. Wells), *The Light of Asia* (Edwin Arnold), and *Finnegans Wake* (James Joyce). He knew and visited with Carl Jung and other notables such as the human consciousness guru Krishnamurti in search for life's great secrets. That search led him to write *The Hero with a Thousand Faces* (1949) that would influence the George Lucas *Star Wars* movies.

As an adult he wrote, "Each individual must find the *myth*, which is fundamental to his internalized needs. Only a myth can help one live a systematic life with meaning" (emphasis added). Campbell believed that our mythological representations and other experiences are merely symbols of a larger meaning in our life. Campbell believed that the ritual and rites from eons ago were the rites of passage, particularly for males. He said boys are turned into men by learning courage. He wrote, "All of our images are masks and myths are metaphorical," adding, "We must undergo death and resurrection rituals. To kill our dependent infancy to be reborn in maturity as self-responsible, active, protecting males" (Moyers 1989).

Campbell's life was spent pursuing the truths of nature and man. He was probably the most erudite individual in this book, and he admonished us all to find our self-actualization and to "follow our bliss wherever it leads." He followed his bliss to the ends of the earth. The truth of his research and metamorphosis was that "myths make heroes out of those who heed them and are models for understanding . . . life." That is extremely profound and exactly what these visionaries spent their life doing.

Berry Gordy Jr.

As an impressionable boy of eight Berry Gordy Jr. became empowered to live a better life while listening to the blow by blow description of his hero, Joe Louis, knocking out Hitler's embodiment of the Master Race, Max Schmelling. When Louis won the heavyweight championship of the world Berry was transformed from a black kid in a Detroit ghetto into someone with hope. Louis gave Berry hope just as the world was about to enter into World War II. He wrote extensively of the impact this had on him, changing him from a boy with no chance to one with a goal. Gordy was so energized he became a boxer in his teens and delayed his entry into the world of music, his first love. He would have fifteen professional fights before he returned to music and became the Magic Man of Soul. The competitive drive resulting from those fights left him with a resolve to make Motown Records into the preeminent label in the music industry, but his transformation had taken place many years earlier next to a radio that said, "The Brown Bomber is champion of the world."

Michael Jordan

Michael Jordan had become disenchanted with college basketball during his freshman year at the University of North Carolina. He wanted to quit and actually went home once but was brought back by an assistant coach. His life was transformed in one game at the end of that season during the 1982 NCAA finals against Georgetown University. In the final seconds of that final game the score was tied and Jordan found himself with the ball. He took the shot that was destined to change his life and it hit nothing but net. That shot won the national championship for North Carolina. The student body started chanting "superman, superman" at Jordan.

Ever since, Air Jordan has insisted on having the ball in his hands when the game was on the line because he knew deep down that he could make it. He never *thought* he could, he *knew* he could. In Nietzsche's immortal words, "power accedes to he who takes it," and Michael took it whenever he laced up his sneakers. That was what made him into the most exciting basketball player who ever lived. Jordan became an icon because of that college shot and once told a reporter, "I was fearless after that shot."

Summary

Daniel Goleman, author of *Emotional Intelligence*, says "emotional learning is lifelong and is just as important as logical intelligence" (1995, 221). Goleman defines emotional intelligence as self-awareness, management of feelings, motivation, empathy, and social skills. Whether learning is emotional, as Goleman believes, or cognitive, as most educators believe, or one of Howard Gardener's eight intelligences, I believe it emerges from life experiences. The journey decides our destiny, not our heritage.

This book is about greatness being acquired, not inherited. Greatness is not a function of IQ, socioeconomic status, money, or even formal education. It is a function of *success imprints* that become so ingrained into our psyche we live to fulfill them. The key elements are birth order, transiency, doting parents, self-employed fathers, books and fantasy hero mentors, and life crises. The key factors in the development of the key traits are:

- Birth order: First born is best, because it instills a mantle of responsibility and leadership.
- Transiency: Excessive travel and moving instill self-sufficiency, resilience, and independence.
- Doting parents: Indulgent and permissive parents instill confidence and self-esteem.
- Self-employed father: Time clocks impede independence, and running one's own business demonstrates self-sufficiency.
- Fantasy hero mentors: Books and their heroes are important, they arm the psyche with heroic role model imagery.
- Crises and trauma: Mortality imprints creative drive. Reaching the bottom grooms one for the top.

CHAPTER 10

Creative Genius and Greatness

"Life is a comedy for those who think, and a tragedy for those who feel!"
Horace Walpole

Did They Achieve Greatness?

Professionally, the subjects studied here certainly achieved greatness, but personally, they did not. All achieved critical acclaim in their field of expertise and most made it to the very top of their discipline in their lifetimes. They changed the world more than most people do, and even a despot like Napoleon left some positive legacy, such as the Napoleonic Code that was important to the legal future of Europe. Freud's contribution has been questioned in recent years, but it is virtually impossible to read a newspaper without some reference to a Freudian slip or talk about the ego or unconscious. And one must only travel around the world once to get a feel for the contribution of Turner's ubiquitous CNN. Hitler certainly changed the world, although not for the good. He left forty million dead in his wake of power for the sake of a Master Race. Michael Jordan changed the way basketball was played in the NBA and Margaret Thatcher created Thatcherism. Catherine the Great expanded Mother Russia and Berry Gordy Jr. married soul with pop while Stephen King made horror acceptable.

But Were They Successful?

Determining if they were successful depends on a person's definition of success. If you value fame and fortune, most of these people were phenomenally successful. If you place a high value on having a balanced life of work, family, and friends, then they were miserable failures. Most did contribute to the progress of their given field. Einstein gave us further insights into space, time, and energy, and life wouldn't be quite so good without Disneyland and Mickey Mouse. Edison's light bulb lights our homes and factories and Tesla's power generators drive the engines of the world. We must not forget that much of these successes had a down side. Einstein's theory of relativity gave us cheap atomic energy and the potential to annihilate mankind. Edison's light bulb lit our homes and destroyed the gas lamp industry just as Tesla's generators destroyed Edison's direct current stations. Nothing comes without a price and success must always be evaluated by the cost paid.

The one constant is that most "followed their bliss," to use Joseph Campbell's aphorism. And they did so with such passion most had little time to think about those parts of their life that were lacking—like a family life, relaxation, and fun. Most would have admitted they were not the best choice of a mate or boss. They were so driven they even scared themselves. But if nothing else, they did meet their inner needs for overachieving and self-actualization, despite sacrificing family, friends, health, and relationships. Inner passion defined them and was the fuel that drove their manic engines. Had they stopped to think about what they were doing to themselves and those around them they would have been shocked at what they found.

Fame, Fortune, and Behavior

All were successful beyond their wildest dreams and most died rich and famous. But what is the definition of success? Is it money and notoriety? A 1997 survey found that only 25 percent of the people surveyed ranked money at the top. They ranked being satisfied with your life as number one indicator of success, and being in control of your life number two with three having a good marriage and relationship. The subjects studied here fared quite well on number one and two, but most failed miserably on number three. But that is the price of reaching the very top. A person cannot serve two masters and overachieving, self-actualizing personalities must decide early in life if they are willing to pay the price of being the very best in their field. These fifty all paid some price for their success, and the cost was higher for some than for others. For example, Howard Hughes became such a control freak he was unable to control his own self despite being the richest man in the world. Karl Marx had to die to become famous and his life was a living hell while he pursued his dream of a political revolution.

Renegades All

The one constant that ties these subjects together is that they were different. All marched to a different drummer and refused to conform. Those who get to the top are unique personalities. Their uniqueness is strangely similar, although the similarities are behavioral rather than genetic. This study uncovered few similarities in physical size, socioeconomic status, family backgrounds, pedigrees, or formal education. What was strangely similar was the manner in which the subjects viewed the world and their methodology in dealing with it. Most viewed the world through a filter that saw opportunities and possibilities, not fear and security.

Visionaries Ignore Experts and Don't Sweat the Details

Great entrepreneurs and innovative leaders seldom worry about the little stuff, preferring to concentrate their vast energies on the big picture. In his first job as a store manager at J. C. Penney's, Sam Walton was told by his boss that he wouldn't make it in retailing. Why? Because of his inept handling of paperwork. Despite his refusal to worry about the paperwork, Walton went on to build Wal-Mart into the largest retail chain in the world.

Walt Disney was fired from his first job as a cartoonist by a Kansas City newspaper due his incompetence in art, but he went on to create the most famous cartoon characters in the world in Mickey Mouse, Pluto, Donald Duck, and Goofy. Walt knew that *art* had nothing to do with success in cartoons, animation, or creativity, and therefore refused to allow the word "art" to be used at Disney Studios. The *whole* or *essence* of the cartoon was the only thing that counted and Disney refused to allow the traditionalists to divert him from that goal. Einstein was queried about the distance to the moon by a reporter and promptly told him, "Look I know where to find such trivial information if I need it. I have too many important things to think about to clog up my mind with stuff I can find elsewhere."

Mao Tse-tung told Indian leader Jawaharlal Nehru, "The atom bomb is not to be feared. The death of 10 or 20 million or even 300 million can be tolerated since they can be replaced. Lives have to be sacrificed for the cause of the revolution." The uneducated, but well read Mao understood that the whole was more important than any of its parts. The Chinese dictator reveled in his unpredictability as a leader. He never took the same path twice when he walked and was always in search of the new and untested—a classic trait of the Promethean personality. Ted Turner never wrote a business plan for launching CNN and Frank Lloyd Wright was infamous for refusing to worry about the details in the creation of his architectural masterpieces.

Synthesize to Success

Every dimension of personality lies on a continuum, one that is seldom visited by the average person, but which is visited often by the multi-dimensional and creatively adaptable who successfully transcend their personality limits when the situation demands. Holistic people optimize their opportunities by daring what they hate and becoming what they are not, by adapting to what Carl Jung labeled a state of syzygy—tapping into the opposite gender.

If you optimize your strengths you can be good but to be great you must defeat your weakness. This sounds trite, but it is true, because our strengths take care of themselves but our weaknesses are capable of destroying us. Master your weaknesses and you will transcend the single-dimension nature of the average person and the world can be your oyster. All personality lies on a continuum between excess and insufficiency. Therefore, it isn't what you are, such as in extroversion or introversion, or Type A or Type B behaviors. It is where you lie on those scales. It is how much of an introvert or extrovert or how much of a Type A control freak you are. A person's normal propensity is to operate somewhere between pathological shyness (extreme introversion, like Howard Hughes) and brazen loquaciousness (extreme extroversion, like Margaret Mead). Other dimensions, like decision making, fall somewhere between emotional decisions (extreme feeling types like Mother Teresa) and strictly rational ones (extreme thinking types like Bill Gates). The "greats" were able to vacillate between the two when required and that is the quality of genius. The average person tends to be stuck in his or her preference; the creative geniuses are adaptable. The pathologically shy Hughes was an incredible speaker in front of Congress and defeated his enemies by daring to do what he hated. Margaret Mead was a people person but made her mark in the world by leaving society and living alone in the wilds of New Guinea. By adapting, the greats functioned at a higher level than those mired in a single dimension.

Marrying what we are and what we are not can be the true key to greatness and it can be accomplished by moving adroitly along the continuum to that place where the needs meet the situation. This tends to be an oversimplification since it is easier to say than do. Extroverts are energized externally, which is why they are empowered when around other people and it is difficult for them to hibernate in a library to do research, but that is just what the extroverted Joseph Campbell did when he dropped out and spent four years alone in the mountains reading the Greek classics. It was not easy for the shy and introverted Hitler to stand in front of millions to speak, but that is what allowed him to take over Germany. For an introvert to stand in front of a strange audience and make a speech is difficult but research shows introverts are often the best lecturers as was the case with Karl Marx, Howard Hughes, Ayn Rand, and Mother Teresa.

Syzygy

Examples abound of those who could flip-flop between different dimensions of personality, gender, and even ideologies. Sophocles described the effects of this quite eloquently when he said, "When woman becomes the equal of man she becomes superior." He was saying that adding masculine qualities to a woman's feminine powers would arm her for superior battle in either arena. Carl Jung said that such a woman would be tapping into an archetype he called the animus, a place in the unconscious where "all of woman's ancestral experiences of man exist." He described the female archetype in men as the anima where "all men's ancestral experiences of woman could be found." He wrote, "In the unconscious of every woman there is a hidden male personality, and in the unconscious of every man there is a hidden female personality.

Exceptional people are able to tap into their syzygy or synthesize to success. They are capable of tapping into their opposite gender on command, can operate at various points on the personality continuum, and attack their greatest weakness when needed. When one can defeat his or her worst fear everything else is a piece of cake. Let's look at some examples in history who rose to the top by attacking their greatest fears and tapped into their opposite gender when needed. Napoleon, Hitler, and Mao Tse-tung wrote poetry despite being destructive beasts who killed without remorse. They were Machiavellian killing machines while on the battlefield, but once in the drawing room they were able to write highly sensitive poetry. Even the diabolical Picasso and the electronics visionary Tesla spent much of their spare time writing sonnets. The result was all of these men possessed a magnetic attraction to women. Balzac, Tesla, Frank Lloyd Wright, and Martin Luther King Jr. dressed in sartorial splendor that would have done women proud. They were often the envy of the women they met and their attire could have aroused jealousy in the most flamboyant female couturier. Balzac's mistress described him as "more female than male." Joseph Campbell, Freud, Martin Luther King Jr., and Howard Hughes all flip-flopped between their feminine and masculine sides.

Most of the women had a similar talent; they were able to tap into their maleness on command and did so without hesitation. Catherine the Great wrote, "I have the most reckless audacity." When about to be imprisoned by her imbecile husband she donned a colonel's uniform complete with sword and mounted her steed like a man in an era when no self-respecting woman would dare straddle a horse for all kinds of psychological and sexual reasons.

But Catherine knew that no male would follow a "typical" female to engage the enemy. Catherine was extremely feminine and had many lovers, but her duality of behavior removed the single dimension stereotype that would have stymied her attempt to wrest power from her husband. Any woman operating in a male-dominated environment must be prepared to follow Catherine's lead, or Margaret Thatcher's, whose steadfastness earned her the name The Iron Lady. Thatcher had learned early from her father that leaders must be different and became the captain of her hockey team. Once in office she was such an indomitable spirit President Ronald Reagan said, "Margaret Thatcher is the best man in England." Later a London newspaper said, "Thatcher does not have one feminine cell in her body." Golda Meir had a similar propensity for dual gender roles. Early in her career she was a femme fatale but when it came to taking risks she was braver than any of Israel's male elite. No man dared cross the desert to meet with king Abdullah. Meir did. David Ben Gurion told the media, "Golda is the only man in my cabinet. "What was he saying? That Meir was a female, but the only one, male or female, who had the temerity and guts to fight for the State of Israel's existence.

Edison, Tesla, Wright, and Howard Hughes were pathologically shy, but were famous for ostentatious press conferences aimed at promoting themselves and their products. Hughes was the most reclusive but the true master of hype. The billionaire recluse had not been seen in public for over a year in 1947 when Senator Ralph Owen Brewster decided to use Hughes's Spruce Goose boondoggle for his own political advantage. Brewster called for a congressional hearing, fully expecting Hughes to be a no-show. He said, "Hughes's flying boat cannot fly," and implied that Hughes had cheated the government out of $20 million in design monies. The normally reticent Hughes, refusing to be intimidated, called a press conference and told them, "If the plane is judged a failure I will probably leave the country and never come back." He had no such intentions and in fact had known from its inception the plane would never fly and that it made no practical sense. He wowed congress and returned to Los Angeles and flew the plane to a media blitz that forever made this self-proclaimed hermit the famous billionaire. Years later he came out of hiding to challenge the authenticity of Clifford Irving's fraudulent biography on his life.

Fortune magazine (August 8, 1994) said, "Women are more like men entrepreneurs than they are like other women." *Psychology Today* wrote, "Creative and talented girls are more dominant and tough than other girls" (Csikszentmihalyi 1996). And psychologist Nathaniel Branden wrote, "The most creative individuals are those who can integrate both male and female aspects of personality. What does this mean? That females should tap into their so-called maleness when operating in a male-dominated environment and males should tap into their "femaleness" when faced with a nurturing environment or one dominated by females. To be successful, introverts should *extrovert*, extroverts should *introspect*, the cautious need to take *risk*, and the myopic number-crunchers need to envision *new opportunities*. Feeling types should learn to *think*, hard-core rationalists must learn *sensitivity*. If you operate in the forest of life you must learn to deal with the *trees*. Mihalyi Csikszentmihalyi of the University of Chicago studied ninety-one creative geniuses and found a similar duality of roles. He said "Creative individuals are more likely to have not only the strengths of their own gender but those of the other." He also wrote:

> Perhaps the most important duality that the creative persons are able to integrate is being open and receptive on one hand an hard-driving on the other. . . . When an extrovert learns to experience the world as an introvert it is as if he or she discovered a whole new missing dimension of the world and we double and double again the amount of life. Keep exploring what it takes to be the opposite of who you are. (1996, 360–62).

Androgyny

Csikszentmihalyi commented, "Creative individuals escape rigid gender role stereotyping and tend to androgyny." Androgyny has been found to be pervasive in many famous women, especially those in this book. Amelia Earhart was probably the most androgynous of any woman since she disdained dresses, wore no makeup and short hair, and dared to go where few men would. Anthropologist Margaret Mead, entrepreneur Helena Rubenstein, educator Maria Montessori, dancer Isadora Duncan, and super athlete Babe Didrickson Zaharias were equally able to tap into their male side and because of it rise to the top of male-dominated disciplines. All of these women were fearless, more aggressive and competitive, and had the drive of most men, if not more. Mead ran off alone to remote jungles when she was in her early twenties. Earhart told the world, "I just want to go where no one has ever gone." And Montessori did go where few women ever had, as she was the only girl enrolled in a high school science program, majored in engineering in college, and graduated as the first female doctor in Italy. Every one of them refused to be secluded in a household environment or the security of one place and became vagabond warrior with the world their stage. They traversed the world, usually alone, with Duncan setting up dance schools in Berlin, Athens, St. Petersburg, and London; Mead wandering through Indonesian jungles; Rubenstein opening a beauty empire on three continents; and Montessori spreading her message from the United States to India and becoming famous as the "Vagabond Pedagogue."

What Made Them Tick?

As discussed in chapter 9 these subjects were imprinted with a unique set of drives, egos, wills, and behavioral characteristics that were both intrinsic (internal) and extrinsic (external). These early imprints armed most with an intransigent and indomitable personality that would not be denied. They created a person programmed for greatness. They weren't the only ones so programmed, but they had those qualities needed for their time and goals and it is amazing how truly similar the subjects were in terms of their need to take divergent paths with confidence, charm, tenacity, competitive drive, and a risk-taking propensity that knew no limit. Timing was on their side, but they still had to be willing to seek the opportunity and go for the gold when others said it was fool's gold. What am I saying? That eminent success in life comes down to eight key traits that we call personality. Let's look at the intrinsic source of that personality and the extrinsic manifestation as seen by the world.

Inter-Disciplinary Differences

These subjects were selected from six different professional disciplines subdivided into nine categories. A summary of the birth order, parental influence, education, religious orientation, and other personality factors can be found in table 11. Ninety-three percent of the subjects had self-employed fathers and were high risk-takers; 88 percent were hyperactive. An equal amount were Type A personalities and 75 percent had lost a sibling or parent prior to their twenty-first birthday. Only 38 percent worshipped regularly and 46 percent graduated from college.

Notice the artists and politicians were the most prone to hyperactivity with the business types having the most Type A personalities. It is not surprising that the humanitarians like Montessori, Mead, Mother Teresa, and Martin Luther King Jr. were the most spiritual. The politicians were the most likely to have experienced some major crises early in life—the death of a sibling or parent. Sports only had two subjects but these two were neither first born, religious, or bereft from an early tragedy. But they were manic Type A's with a strong risk-taking propensity. The males were most likely to have experienced some trauma or crisis in their life and were more prone to risk-taking, mania, and Type A behavior. Females were more likely to be extroverted and religious.

Being the first born was only important for those from the humanities and was a slight advantage for those in business and science. The two surprises were in the importance of college education and religion. These two

Table 11
Behavioral Data on Eminent Visionaries
Source: doctoral dissertation plus five published books

Discipline	1st Born	Slf-Emp. Parent	Coll.Grad.	Extroverted	Type A Person	Hi Risk-Taker	Hypomanic	Relig./Spirit.	Crisis/Death
Arts–12	7–58%	11–92%	7–56%	5–42%	8–67%	9–75%	11–92%	7–58%	11–85%
8 Males	4	8	5	5	6	7	7	5	8
4 Females	3	3	2	0	2	2	4	2	3
Business–8	5–63%	8–100%	1–13%	4–50%	8–100%	8–100%	7–88%	2–25%	6–75%
7 Males	4	7	1	3	7	7	7	2	6
1 Female	1	1	0	1	1	1	0	0	0
Humanities–5	3–80%	5–100%	3–60%	4–80%	4–80%	5–100%	4–80%	4–80%	3–60%
1 Male	1	1	1	1	1	1	1	1	1
4 Females	2	4	2	3	3	4	3	3	2
Politics–6	4–67%	5–83%	3–50%	3–50%	5–83%	6–100%	6–100%	1–14%	5–83%
4 Males	3	3	2	1	4	4	4	0	4
2 Females	1	2	1	2	1	2	2	1	1
Science–7	4–57%	7–100%	4–57%	3–43%	5–71%	7–100%	5–71%	0–0%	5–71%
6 Males	4	6	3	3	4	6	4	0	4
1 Female	0	1	1	0	1	1	1	0	1
Sports–2	0–0%	1–50%	1–50%	2–100%	2–100%	2–100%	2–100%	0–0%	0–0%
1 Male	0	0	1	1	1	1	1	0	0
1 Female	0	1	0	1	1	1	1	0	0
Totals	23–58%	37–93%	19–48%	21–53%	34–85%	37–93%	35–88%	14–35%	30–75%
27 Males	18–59%	26–96%	13–48%	15–56%	23–85%	26–96%	24–89%	9–33%	23–85%
13 Females	7–54%	11–85%	6–46%	8–62%	9–69%	11–85%	11–85%	5–38%	7–54%

differ quite a bit from the average population. One surprise was the 20 percent who didn't even graduate from high school, namely Thomas Edison, Frank Lloyd Wright, Agatha Christie, Walt Disney, Adolph Hitler, Isadora Duncan, Howard Hughes, and Soichiro Honda. They were all highly learned in their particular disciplines but detested the rigors of formal education.

Political Orientation

Most of the subjects were apolitical except those who made their mark in the political arena like Catherine the Great, Napoleon, Karl Marx, Hitler, Mao, Nelson Mandela, and Margaret Thatcher. A large number were rabid pacifists, including Nikola Tesla, Frank Lloyd Wright, Isadora Duncan, Albert Einstein, Maria Montessori, Paul Robeson, Ayn Rand, Walt Disney, Joseph Campbell, and Mother Teresa.

A number of the subjects were card-carrying members of the Communist party. Their leader was Karl Marx, who originated the ideology of dialectical materialism in his treatise the *Communist Manifesto*. The others who espoused Communism at some point in their life were Isadora Duncan, Mao, Robeson, and Mandela. Mandela was highly sympathetic to Marxism, as he was drawn to the central theme of workers of the world uniting in a common cause to discard the shackles of the ruling classes. Lenin was one of his early heroes. Both Duncan and Robeson moved to Russia and were advocates of Communism.

Libido and Success

Libidinal drive is an absolute factor in success, as documented by Napoleon Hill and others. Libido is an important subset of drive—one of the eight keys to greatness—and therefore it is important to examine this aspect of the subjects' lives. Research on the libido of these subjects was based on secondary data, sources such as biographies, biographical studies, and periodical research. Due to the sensitivity of information on sexual preferences, no conclusions were drawn on the sexual proclivities of the subjects unless they were verified by three different sources. In most cases, the information came right out of the subjects' own autobiographies, as was the case for Duncan, Christie, Tesla, Mead, and Robeson or from the biographies of their wives, doctors, or lovers as in the case of Mao, Hughes, Gordy, and Rice. Most of the information was gleaned from various periodicals and other sources.

It appears from this research that great leaders have some genetic predisposition to chase and seduce. Most of these certainly led an abnormally active sex life with sex pervading either their personal lives or work. Incest, rape, and other sexual themes pervaded the fiction of the placid and sedate writer Agatha Christie. Others whose writings or lives were obsessed with sex were Catherine the Great, Balzac, Freud, Mao, Duncan, Mead, Hughes, Robeson, Hemingway, and Rice. It is ironic that Freud and Rice appear to have led spartan lives yet they attached sex to everything they wrote about. Hughes produced many movies that according to his biographers were nothing but masturbatory devices aimed at his own titillation. Authors Balzac, Hemingway, and Christie used their writing to subliminally release their libidinal drives.

Balzac wrote, "My orgies take the form of books." He believed that physical sexual activity was detrimental to productivity and led a restrained sex life and didn't marry until age fifty. Biographer Robb, however, described the father of the realistic novel as having a "rabid participation in real orgies" during his healthy years as an eligible bachelor in Paris. It is psychologically significant that Balzac wrote most of his most noteworthy novels while attired in monastic robes. Robb believed he wore the robes as a means of self-restraint so as not to be tempted to waste his pent-up energies on passions of the flesh instead of passions of the pen.

Anne Rice wrote a number of pornographic novels under a pseudonym. The mistress of the occult says, "I've had sexual fantasies since I was very little." She confirms a strong predilection for sex saying, "I go through life seeing everything as highly sensuous and erotic" (Riley 1996, 63). Hemingway's son wrote a biography about his father and said, "Papa felt too much intercourse was counter-productive to good literature." This did not seem to deter him from marrying four different women and being unfaithful to each, leading F. Scott Fitzgerald to say that Hemingway needed a great love affair to produce another great book. Hemingway was a womanizer as was Napoleon, Balzac, Mao, Honda, Robeson, Gordy, and Turner. That is not unusual for leaders.

In *Think and Grow Rich*, Napoleon Hill wrote, "Sex energy is the creative energy of all geniuses. There never has been and never will be a great leader, builder, or artist lacking in this driving force of sex" (1960, 84). I agree, although there are always exceptions to every rule, and in this book those exceptions were Darwin, Freud, Tesla, Campbell, and Disney. These men believed that libidinal emissions were contrary to creative productions. Tesla felt women and creativity were bitter enemies and refused to even consider having a date let alone marriage or sex. He did capitulate and have dinner with a few women, but his phobias with earrings and other jewelry was a distraction that made his celibacy easy. The most asexual women included Montessori, Rubinstein, Mother Teresa, Thatcher, and Zaharias. And it is apparent that these women sublimated their sexual energy, redirecting it into work, just as Freud said all people do.

Freud himself can be used as an example of this sublimation, according to biographer Anthony Storr, who believed Freud ceased having sexual relations with his wife when he was forty. (According to Joseph Campbell, however, Carl Jung believed Freud was intimate with his sister-in-law [1971, xvi].) Freud may have believed his own axiom that a fully sated person can achieve nothing worthwhile in life. In his words:

> What motive would induce a man to put his sexual energy to other uses if by any disposal of it he could obtain fully satisfying pleasure? He would never let go of this pleasure and would make no further progress.

Most of the subjects—80 percent—had raging libidos. Hughes seduced an alarming number of Hollywood starlets and Mao purportedly had 3,000 concubines available for his every whim, which tended to orgiastic liaisons. Berry Gordy Jr. had eight children by five different women, only two of whom he married. He had a penchant for blondes and according to one ex-wife, Raynoma, he spent his honeymoon with one of the blondes at Motown. About one-third of the male subjects could be labeled as having satyriasis—pathological sex drive—and some of the women, like Catherine the Great and Duncan, were nymphomaniacs. Ten of the subjects, or 25 percent, were insatiable.

Even some of the so-called average subjects were quite provocative in their approach to sex. One example is Ayn Rand, who decided to have an affair with a young protégé, Nathaniel Branden, who was twenty-five years her junior. The inimitable Rand, who believed in a rational approach to all things in life, called a meeting among Barbara Branden; Branden's husband, Nathaniel; Rand's understanding husband, Frank O'Connor; and herself to discuss an objective approach to this liaison. She saw it as a purely physical need that should be approached within the confines of physical needs and apart from any emotional or financial considerations. She deemed divorce illogical both emotionally and financially. She was able to convince all parties to an arrangement that included a once-weekly *affaire d'amour* while her husband took a walk in the park. Her young lover would come to her Manhattan home and O'Connor would leave while the two lovers explored the depths of each other's libidinal needs. This liaison lasted almost fifteen years, at which point Branden took up with a younger woman who became his second wife. Writers have suggested that Rand was fantasizing herself to be Dagny Taggart, the feminine protagonist out of *Atlas Shrugged*, and that her lover was John Galt (see Brandon 1989 and Branden 1986).

Religious Orientation

Only 35 percent of these subjects belonged to an organized faith and adhered to one doctrine or dogma. The females tended to be more spiritual than the males, although Joseph Campbell and Paul Robeson were quite spiritual. Only four subjects were devoutly religious: Dostoevsky, Montessori, Mother Teresa, and Martin Luther King Jr.

Atheists

Fifteen percent of the subjects, Marx, Darwin, Marie Curie, Freud, Duncan, and Rand, were card-carrying atheists. Marx and Rand were the most vocal on their absolute beliefs that there was no superior being. Marx's famous aphorism, "Religion is the opiate of the masses" became a rallying call for Communism and atheists. Rand became an atheist at age eleven despite having very religious parents and she spent her adult life as the enemy of organized religion. Freud was also raised to be religious, but described religion as "illusory." Marie Curie was also the product of devout parents but wrote, "I would like to believe but I cannot." Darwin's lack of faith was the most amazing, considering he was educated at Christ Church College to become a man of the cloth and went on the *Beagle* while awaiting assignment to a church to "become a country clergyman," as he said in his autobiography. He wrote:

> I gradually came to disbelieve in Christianity as a divine revelation. Disbelief crept over me at a very slow rate but was at last complete . . . and I have never since doubted even for a single second that my conclusion was correct—I can indeed hardly see how anyone ought to wish Christianity to be true. (Darwin 1958, 87)

Agnostics

Agnostics represent the single largest group of subjects, with 30 percent believing that no one knows the existence of a superior being. Those with such beliefs were Napoleon, Twain, Edison, Freud, Einstein, Hitler, Honda, Earhart, Turner, Rice, and Gates. Bill Gates's Roman Catholic wife told reporters, "Bill just doesn't have time for such things." She described his philosophy on the subject of religion: "Just in terms of allocation of time resources, religion is not very efficient. There's a lot more I could be doing on a Sunday morning."

Devout Believers

Forty-five percent of the subjects believed in a higher being with the majority of those being Christians. Mao, Honda, Campbell, and Tesla believed in Buddhism, which views God as lying within and not some external force pulling the strings of the world. Michener was raised a Quaker but was more Buddhist than anything. Robeson, Disney, and Hughes were fundamentalists. Agatha Christie and Margaret Thatcher were devoted members of the Church of England and Stephen King is a strong Methodist. Mother Teresa was a Roman Catholic, and of course she and Martin Luther King Jr. dedicated their life's work to religion.

Margaret Mead is interesting in that she was raised by two agnostic parents but decided at age eleven to adopt religion as part of her life. She then married a minister. Einstein was involved in a deep-seated religious struggle for a new Jewish nation, but he was never a dogmatic believer in the Old Testament. Napoleon professed to be Catholic since he was ruler of a highly religious nation, but finally admitted to being an agnostic while exiled on St. Helena.

They Were Successful, but Were They Happy?

From the perspective of how society values success, these subjects may have been successful, but they were not believed to be happy. The top three success values in America according to a 1997 poll found only 25 percent of the people reported that having lots of money was number one in importance. Had fame and fortune been the requisite for success then these people would be right up there on top of the list.

These subjects were highly driven to overachieve and consequently attained their goals and dreams. Most said they had exceeded their wildest dreams, but they paid a very high price for their success in terms of family and personal lifestyle.

Lonely Recluses

Michael Jackson wrote in his autobiography, Moonwalk (1988), "I am one of the loneliest people in the world." This comes from a man who at the time was being pursued and idolized by millions of adoring fans. Similarly, Michael Jordan often eats Thanksgiving and Christmas dinners alone in a hotel room rather than risk the media assaults and fan fury by going out. Consequently, both of these pop icons lead lonely, reclusive lives similar to Babe Ruth, Elvis, and the Beatles.

Napoleon wrote about his loneliness:

> Always alone in the midst of men, I come to my room to dream by myself, to abandon myself to my melancholy in all its sharpness. In which direction does it lead today? Toward death. . . . What fury drives me to my own distraction? Indeed what am I to do in this world? Since die I must, is it not just as well to kill myself? . . . Since nothing is pleasure to me, why should I bear days that nothing turns to profit? (Herold 1955, 34)

Balzac, Dostoevsky, Curie, Tesla, Mao, Christie, Hughes, Michener, Smith, Disney, Hitler, Rice, and Stephen King were recluses. They adamantly refused to socialize, and in severe cases like Hughes locked themselves in rooms so as not to have to deal with society. Balzac would closet himself in a remote hideaway in order to finish an important book. He spoke of his manic nature and unhappiness as "Genius is the only alternative to death. . . . I am wearing myself out in a horrible fashion." Dostoevsky wrote, "I have the reputation of an uncommunicative, reserved, unsociable person." He was even disgusted with his own work, saying, "My dissatisfaction with my novel [*The Idiot*] amounts to disgust." Mao had "no friends, no loved ones, not even his wives or children" according to his personal physician.

These visionaries paid a horrific price for their success. Babe Zaharias died alone with virtually no one attending her funeral. Earhart paid with her life for her need "to go where no one else has been." Darwin was physically incapacitated for a large percentage of his adult life with psychosomatic symptoms resulting from his heretical theories that opposed those of his wife, family, and friends. Marie Curie's biographer quoted her friend Rutherford as saying, "She is very pathetic." Hemingway was at constant war with himself and finally succeeded in killing himself. Frederick Engels summed up the life of his friend Karl Marx at Marx's funeral with the words, "He was the best hated and most calumniated man of his time." Without Engels's help, Marx and his family would have starved to death. Despite that help the father of communism paid a dear price for his political activism and lived his whole life in dire poverty.

Self-Destructive Natures

These subjects were their own worst enemies. Most operated with a kind of death-wish mentality. Napoleon was quite introspective, writing, "What fury drives me to my own destruction?" Balzac, Twain, Edison, Tesla, Wright, Duncan, Hughes, Gordy, and Turner invested in wild new ventures when they should have been spending their money and energies saving existing ones. Dostoevsky, Tesla, Smith, and Gordy should not have gambled away their life's work but all did so, not once, but many times. In many respects, their live-on-the-edge mentality is what contributed to their great success, but often contributed to their self-destruction. Mao would swim in waters that jeopardized his safety and infuriated his Chinese associates.

At the time of her second Nobel Prize, Marie Curie was so distraught by her husband's untimely death, her notorious headline affair with a young assistant, plus the debilitating affects of radiation, she attempted suicide. She killed herself through continual exposure to the deadly radiation poisoning caused by her work on radium. No one could convince her that she was slowly killing herself, but the rush from working on her dream drove her to the edge.

Howard Hughes and Amelia Earhart had a number of serious automobile and airplane crashes, most of which could have been avoided. Many of the crashes were the result of running out of gas due to overzealousness. Others were due to some inane operator error that was the by product of their daredevil natures. Mother Teresa earned the epithet "Saint of the Gutters" by working with those dying with leprosy and other contagious diseases. Michael Jordan often gets cited for driving his Maseratti 175 mph down the Eisenhower Expressway in Chicago. Wright, Honda, and Gordy had near-fatal head-on crashes. Howard Hughes almost died while filming *Hell's Angels* when he impulsively jumped in the cockpit of a World War I fighter plane without the vaguest idea of how the plane flew or how to operate the controls. His problems later in life were all a byproduct of a plane crash that could have clearly been avoided. He insisted on flying over Katharine Hepburn's house in West Hollywood and ran out of gas and crashed into a house. Hughes became physically and emotionally incapacitated after that July 7, 1947, crash.

Tesla was known as the "Electrical Sorcerer" due to his penchant for allowing one million volts of electrical current pass through his body for the amusement of his friends and associates and to demonstrate the safety of his alternating current invention. Golda Meir smuggled hand grenades in her bra in Jerusalem during the Palestine wars. Amelia Earhart was a daredevil who venerated thrill seeking. She was energized by the threat of death that others experience only through fantasy in a movie theater. Amelia created her own adventures. Cora Skinner, the woman who taught her to fly, said "She used to scare me to death." Fast cars, boats, and airplanes were her favorite toys.

Earhart told her husband, "When I go, I'd like to go in my plane. Quickly." She was granted her wish when she attempted the impossible—landing on a tiny pacific atoll named Howland Island, which was located in the middle of the Pacific Ocean. She would have survived had she taken along the most basic communications equipment. Her good friends Franklin and Eleanor Roosevelt had half the navy ready to help her but she was unable to communicate with them since she had left the gear in order to save weight.

Every time Walt Disney became solvent he would jump into a new creative venture that would jeopardize the life of Disney Studios. Each time the price was a career-threatening nervous collapse. He lived his life in the throes of financial and emotional breakdowns and actually died from a three-pack-a-day cigarette habit and an excessive use of alcohol. Edison, Hughes, Smith, and Turner made business decisions as if they had a death-wish. They only seemed to like opportunities if the risks were capable of burying them. Betting beyond their limits was their hot button and it is what ultimately made them rich and famous. As soon as things became too safe they were off on another acquisition that could wipe them out. Leverage was their god and they used it like most use a checking account. A family friend of Turner said, "Ted will always throw the dice for something bigger, bigger, bigger."

Age and Greatness

The average age of success for the females in this study was thirty-eight. The average age for the males was thirty-five. Athletes Jordan and Zarharias were the youngest to make their mark in the world—both were just nineteen. Nelson Mandela was the oldest who earned the Nobel Prize at age seventy-four. Golda Meir was not much younger when she was elected prime minister of Israel at age seventy. Mother Teresa was fifty-five before the pope authorized her Sisters of Charity Mission as a papal autocracy.

Looking at age relative to discipline shows that those in the athletic field were the youngest although there were only two—Jordan and Zaharias. Those in the field of the arts were the next youngest with an average age of thirty-one. The oldest were the politicians, with an average age of fifty-one. The entrepreneurs averaged thirty-six, scientists thirty-two, and those in the humanities thirty-seven.

Even though they became successful earlier many were able to produce masterpieces quite late in life. The most amazing was Frank Lloyd Wright, who produced one-third of his life's work after he was eighty. He created the Guggenheim Museum and the Marin County Civic Center buildings after he was ninety. Picasso painted into his nineties and produced *The Peeing Woman* at eighty-four. One of his great masterpieces, *Guernica*, was done when he was fifty-six. Disney didn't open Disneyland until he was in his mid-fifties and Dostoevsky didn't complete his greatest work, *The Brothers Karamazov*, until he was fifty-nine, the same age Marx was when he completed his *Das Kapital*. Michener wrote until he died at age ninety. Table 12 is a list of the subjects, their great successes, and the age at which they accomplished them.

Living a long life is the goal of most people. This study illustrates that longevity can be the result of extreme diligence to a goal. It is not the enemy, like most believe, of a risk-taking lifestyle, a driven personality, or a traumatic past. Long life appears to be correlated to extreme diligence and hard work, even high risk. Frank Lloyd Wright lived a frenetic life, but worked every day until he was nearly ninety-three. Helena Rubinstein globe-trotted the world until she was in her nineties and worked every day until her death at age ninety-four. Even Picasso, who lived on the edge much of his life, painted daily until well into his nineties.

Prophetic Visionaries

Philosophy permeated the thoughts of these visionaries as they saw the world as something to analyze and conquer. Most would have qualified as self-actu-

Table 12
Fifty Greats and Age of First Success

19 Females: average age of success—38.1 years
31 Males: average age at success of 35 years

Superstar	Success	Age of Success
Maya Angelou	I Know Why the Caged Bird Sings (1970)	42
Mary Kay Ash	Mary Kay MLM Launch (1962)	52
Honoré de Balzac	The Human Comedy—La Peau de Chagrin (1831)	32
Napoleon Bonaparte	Battle of Lodi (1893); Dictator of France (1899)	24/30
Joseph Campbell	The Hero with a Thousand Faces (1949)	45
Catherine the Great	Empress of All the Russias (1762)	33
Marie Curie	Discovery of Radium, Nobel Prize, and Ph.D. (1903)	36
Charles Darwin	Origin of the Species (1859); Descent of Man (1871)	50/62
Walt Disney	Mickey Mouse (1928); Disneyland (1955)	27/54
Isadora Duncan	Parisian, London, and Berlin concerts (1902)	24
Fyodor Dostoevsky	Poor Folk (1846); The Brothers Karamazov (1880)	25/45
Amelia Earhart	Trans-Atlantic flight (1928)	31
Thomas Edison	Invention of light bulb (1879)	32
Albert Einstein	Special Theory of Relativity (1905)	26
Sigmund Freud	The Interpretation of Dreams (1899)	43
Bill Gates	Personal computer software deal with IBM (1981)	26
Berry Gordy Jr.	The Supremes' big hits (1964)	36
Ernest Hemingway	A Farewell to Arms (1929); Old Man and the Sea (1953)	30/54
Adolph Hitler	Chancellor of Germany (1933)	44
Soichiro Honda	Super Cub Motorcycle development (1958)	52
Howard Hughes	Academy Award for Hell's Angels (1931)	26
Michael Jackson	Thriller, "Billy Jean," the Moonwalk (1984)	26
Michael Jordan	All-American and University of North Carolina NCAA Championship (1982)	19
Bill Lear	First car radio invention (1924); Lear jet (1963)	22/60
Martin Luther King Jr.	Formation of SCLC (1957); Nobel Peace Prize (1960)	33/35
Estée Lauder	National launch of Estée Lauder cosmetics empire (1947)	52
Madonna	Warner record deal (1983)	25
Nelson Mandela	Nobel Prize (1993); President of South Africa (1994)	74/75
Karl Marx	Das Kapital (1869)	59
Margaret Mead	Coming of Age in Samoa (1928)	29
Golda Meir	Prime Minister of Israel (1969)	70
James Michener	Tales of the South Pacific (1947)	40
Tom Monaghan	Domino's Pizza national home delivery system launched (1980)	43

Table 12. Fifty Greats and Age of First Success (continued)

Superstar	Success	Age of Success
Maria Montessori	Children's House Project—Montessori Method (1907)	37
Rupert Murdoch	Launched *Australian* newspaper (1964)	33
Pablo Picasso	*Les Demoilles d'Avignon* (1907)	26
Ayn Rand	*The Fountainhead* (1943); *Atlas Shrugged* (1957)	38/52
Anne Rice	*Interview with the Vampire* (1976)	35
Helena Rubinstein	Australian beauty empire (1908)	36
Paul Robeson	Broadway star in Eugene O'Neill's *Emperor Jones* (1924)	26
Fred Smith	Federal Express launch (1973)	29
Nikola Tesla	Westinghouse contract for alternating current power stations (1886)	30
Margaret Thatcher	Elected Prime Minister of Great Britain (1979)	54
Mother Teresa	Sisters of Charity Mission (1965)	55
Ted Turner	WTBS Superstation (1976); CNN (1980)	38/42
Mark Twain	*The Celebrated Jumping Frog of Calaveras County and Other Tales* (1867); *Huckleberry Finn* (1884)	28/50
Oprah Winfrey	*Oprah Winfrey Show* (1983)	29
Frank Lloyd Wright	Taliesin (1911); Guggenheim Museum (1961)	42/92
Babe D. Zaharias	All-American basketball player (1929); Olympic records (1932)	19/22

alized individuals who saw life through a unique filter. This approach to life appears to have armed them with a philosophic sense of humor rather than the hostile sarcasm that is so destructive to the bureaucratic personalities.

Picasso is one example of the philosopher-humorist. He described himself in an epitaph written when he turned fifty: "I have the revelation of the inner voice. I see things as they really are, past, present, and future. . . . The encyclopedias will write Picasso—Spanish poet who dabbled in painting, drawing, and sculpture" (Huffington 1988, 300). This turned out to be prophetic, as Picasso is often described as having documented the psyche of the twentieth century through his work—his philosophy is foremost, and his artistic works are merely the media used to depict the concepts. Rage permeated all of Picasso's work but he saw it as a nihilistic, if not an existential, force that fueled his ability to create cubist and surrealistic art. His vision of his role was effective in casting him as a perverse illustrator of the twentieth-century psyche. "A picture," he said, "lives only through the one who looks at it—and what they see is the legend surrounding the picture." Thus when people said Picasso's portrait of Gertrude Stein did not resemble her, he responded with "But it will," since he was painting her unconscious being, not her physical being.

Catherine the Great had the vision of a philosopher. She financed the first encyclopedia, by Denis Diderot, to advance knowledge, but the work was eerily precognitive. Catherine predicted the French Revolution and the arrival of Napoleon in terms that were surreal in 1788:

> When will this Caesar come? Oh! Come he will, make no doubt about it! . . .
> If revolution takes hold in Europe, there will come another Ghengis . . . to
> bring her to her senses. That will be her fate. You can depend on it. If France
> survives she will be stronger than she has ever been. . . . All she needs is a supe-
> rior man, greater than his contemporaries, greater perhaps than an entire age.
> Has he already been born? Will he come? Everything depends on that! (Troyat
> 1980, 243)

Napoleon had already been born in Corsica in 1769 and was nineteen years old and attending military school in Paris by the time Catherine wrote this. The future emperor of France was also quite the visionary for a military officer, writing, "In the siege of fortresses; concentrate fire on a single point; when the breach is made the equilibrium is broken; all the rest becomes use-less and the fortress is taken."

Dostoevsky was quite prophetic, speaking of the Russian Revolution fifty years prior to its occurrence. He wrote, "There's going to be an upset as the world has never seen before. . . . Russia will be overwhelmed with dark-ness, the earth will weep for its old gods." Before it took place, he had pre-dicted the Communist Revolution, including the atheist ideology that would be at the seat of its government.

Joseph Campbell told Bill Moyers on a PBS special aired in August 1995, "None of us live the life of the *intended*. It [life] just evolves and mate-rializes in some magic order that is controlled by the will." He added, "Each of us must find the myth which is fundamental to our internalized needs. Only a myth can help one live a systematic life with meaning." He con-cluded with the admonition, "Follow your bliss wherever it takes you because each of us are only mythological representations of our inner truth, and our jobs and other mundane experiences are merely symbols of a larger mythological meaning in our lives." That is truly prophetic since it validates the fantasy hero-worship discussed earlier in this book even though he saw it forty years ago.

Summary

In conclusion, these wunderkinds were unique individuals who reached the very pinnacle of success by following their inner dreams. They were unique personalities but it was their wills that separated them from the pack. All became either rich or famous by ignoring tradition and following an inner vision to their destiny. Most were politically incorrect, allowing a perverse nature to guide them to an innovative vision. Many sacrificed their families, marriage, and friends for the realization of their dreams.

The great have an unusual facility for introspection. They are often able to tap into their opposite gender while maintaining their own. Examples include women like Catherine the Great, Marie Curie, Maria Montessori, and Margaret Thatcher, all of whom were able to maintain a strong femininity while adopting an assertive, almost male competitiveness and a penchant for risk-taking more normally associated with male stereotypes. Conversely, many of the males like Napoleon, Tesla, Mao, and Joseph Campbell were quite feminine in many ways, including a very feminine ability to tap into their inner feelings, intuition, compassion, and nurturing natures.

Most of the subjects were considered megalomaniacs who sacrificed their personal health, money, and family for a place in history. They did so to such a degree that society saw them as self-destructive and sociopathic. Despite this, they changed the world and left it better than they found it. The majority gave more than they got and left their disciplines with more than they found. That appears to be the destiny of visionary and entrepreneurial genius that is the label best suited to these eminent innovators.

Most—Greatest—Best

Bill Gates was the richest. His net worth reached $48 billion in the spring of 1998. He also ranked as the smartest. Estée Lauder was the wealthiest female with a $5 billion nest egg accumulated from her cosmetic empire. The poorest subjects were Karl Marx, Fyodor Dostoevsky, and Mother Teresa, who took vows of poverty when she entered religious life. The most powerful were Napoleon, Mao Tse-tung, and Catherine the Great.

Karl Marx, Charles Darwin, and Ayn Rand were the most influential. Each of these spawned a system of thought or ideology that has outlived them. Marxism is the result of Marx's *Communist Manifesto*, the theories of evolution and natural selection are the result of Darwin's *Origin of the Species*, and Rand's philosophy of objectivism spawned the Libertarian party.

Napoleon, Hitler, and Mother Teresa were easily the most charismatic, although most of these greats had the ability to charm and communicate. By far the most competitive were Michael Jordan and Babe Didrickson Zaharias. Balzac and Madonna were the most driven. Einstein, Tesla, Freud, and Curie were the most intuitive. The subjects who lived closest to the edge were Nikola Tesla, Howard Hughes, Berry Gordy Jr., and Amelia Earhart, although most of the subjects took such great risks friends and family thought they had a death-wish.

Mark Twain, Nikola Tesla, and Frank Lloyd Wright were known for their sartorial splendor and Estée Lauder was elegant in her Parisian gowns.

The most eccentric were Nikola Tesla, whose obsessive-compulsive behaviors were bizarre, and Anne Rice, who said if she had one wish it would be to be a man. The most hated in the twentieth century was easily Adolph Hitler, due to his role in causing World War II and his Final Solution, which wiped out 6 million Jews in his death camps. Ironically, Mao Tse-tung was one of the most admired, but purportedly he killed many more of his own people than Hitler did. In the nineteenth century Karl Marx was the most detested. Babe Didrickson Zaharias and Ayn Rand were the most disliked females; both had a way of infuriating anyone they encountered on their trek to the top. The most confident were Frank Lloyd Wright and Margaret Mead. Both were arrogant.

In my opinion, the most admired were Martin Luther King Jr. and Mother Teresa, and the most radical were Karl Marx and Isadora Duncan. The unhappiest were Mao Tse-tung and Agatha Christie. All of these classifications can be found in table 13.

Propensity for Greatness?

From the previous data it would appear that greatness is learned, not inherited and given the right conditions, anyone with an iron will can reach the very top of most any discipline. In other words, greatness is more attitude than innate talent, more self-esteem than any genetic superiority, more overcompensation of inferiorities than IQ, more drive than inheritance, more tenacity than an Ivy League education, and more willingness to live on the edge than being raised with money. In essence it is more about behavior than about any genetic predisposition for greatness.

Do You Have the Right Disposition for Greatness?

Only about 2 percent of the population are inclined to greatness not due to any lack of ability, but due to a fairly rare inner need to overachieve and a personality inclined to change the world. In other words, the world's eminent innovators tend to see the world through a unique filter that separates them from the general population. The following self-assessment offers some insight into your own, or your offspring's, propensity for greatness. It is not a guarantee, but will give you some indication as to your propensity for it by ranking you with others who have done the impossible and reached the very pinnacle of success.

Before completing the self-assessment it is imperative we define greatness. For the purpose of this exercise greatness is the propensity to reach the very top of any profession, stay there for a significant period, say ten years, and have some material impact on your profession or discipline. In other words, changing the world in some significant way. In some sense it is

Table 13
Most—Greatest—Best

Category	Male	Female
Richest	Bill Gates ($48 billion)	Estée Lauder ($5 billion)
Poorest	Karl Marx	Mother Teresa
Most Famous	Charles Darwin/Albert Einstein	Marie Curie
Most Powerful	Napoleon/Mao Tse-tung	Catherine the Great
Most Eccentric	Nikola Tesla	Anne Rice
Most Radical	Karl Marx/Paul Robeson	Isadora Duncan
Most Hated	Adolph Hitler/Karl Marx	Babe Zaharias/Ayn Rand
Most Admired	Martin Luther King Jr.	Mother Teresa
Best Dressed	Nikola Tesla	Estée Lauder
Highest Integrity	Mark Twain	Margaret Thatcher
Most Influential	Karl Marx/Charles Darwin	Ayn Rand
Most Devout	Martin Luther King Jr.	Mother Teresa
Longest Life	Frank Lloyd Wright (93)	Helena Rubinstein (94)
Most Charismatic	Adolph Hitler	Mother Teresa
Most Competitive	Michael Jordan	Babe Zaharias
Most Confident	Frank Lloyd Wright	Margaret Mead
Most Driven	Honoré de Balzac	Madonna
Most Erudite	Joseph Campbell	Isadora Duncan
Happiest	Sigmund Freud	Catherine the Great
Unhappiest/Loneliest	Mao Tse-tung	Agatha Christie
Most Intuitive	Albert Einstein/Nikola Tesla/ Sigmund Freud	Marie Curie
Greatest Risk-Takers	Nikola Tesla/Howard Hughes/ Berry Gordy Jr.	Amelia Earhart
Smartest	Bill Gates	Margaret Mead

ascending to Maslow's *self-actualization* state as a politician (e.g., Napoleon), as a humanitarian (e.g., Mother Teresa), author (Hemingway), or scientist (Einstein). Another way to reach such a pinnacle would be to become rich and famous as an entertainer (Oprah), athlete (Michael Jordan), or an entrepreneur (Bill Gates).

Rank yourself or your offspring on each of the observed traits. The ranking should be a 1 if you have a low likelihood for such behavior and a 5 if you have a high likelihood for such behavior. There are no right or wrong answers or high or low scores. This assessment will only show the propensity for an individual to be happy pursuing a life of innovation. Some people are so inclined, and are driven to change their world, others would rather spend their weekends fishing or playing golf.

Greatness Self-Assessment Test

*Derived from Landrum's research on eminent
entrepreneurs, artists, politicians, and scientists.*

Directions: Rank yourself on each observed trait between 1 and 5 and total. Scoring key is below.

Communications   1 2 3 4 5

1   Rich and fluent vocabulary
2   Excellent self-expression
3   Inspires others to follow your lead
4   A philosophic communication style
5   Voracious reader of nonfiction books

Views the World

1   Always sees the big picture or essence of situation
2   More interested in the qualitative than quantitative
3   Inquisitive
4   Seeks opportunities and possibilities—never the safe and secure
5   Has a long-term perspective on most things

Creativity

1   Has a vivid imagination
2   Short attention span when listening to proposals by others
3   Inveterate need to know—in constant search for new knowledge
4   Prefers math to accounting—the abstract to the routine
5   Intolerant of useless conformity

Lifestyle

1   Is a high risk-taker
2   Spontaneous adventurer
3   High in intellectual playfulness
4   Often called a renegade
5   Eats, talks, walks, and thinks fast—(for example, often receives speeding tickets)

Self-Image

1   Easily bored with routine tasks
2   Prefers to work independently
3   Comfortable with ambiguity
4   Enjoys juggling many tasks simultaneously
5   Belief in own ability to succeed at new tasks
6   Strong sense of self—uses "I" often
7   Optimism pervades thinking—very positive
8   Needs little confirmation to proceed on new adventures
9   Flexible in dynamic environments
10   Candid responses to controversial inquiries

Critical Thinking Style

1   Prefers being different to being perfect
2   Asks many questions
3   Compulsion to reduce the complex to the simple
4   Searches for similarities and differences in people
5   Impatient in lines and with incompetence

Self-Sufficiency

1   Needs little support in proceeding on novel ideas
2   Very achievement oriented
3   Has variety of interests
4   Grasps new concepts quickly
5   Gets things done without being told

*Greatness IQ: 175–200 = Sure Thing; 150–174 Good Chance;
120–149 = Some Chance; Below 120 = Enjoys Life*

Eminent Subjects by Profession

Arts—12 (30%)
[4 female—8 male]

Maya Angelou●—Poet/Author
Honoré de Balzac—Novelist
Joseph Campbell—Mythologist
Agatha Christie—Author
Fyodor Dostoevsky—Author
Isadora Duncan‡—Dancer
Ernest Hemingway—Author
Michael Jackson●—Entertainer
Stephen King—Author
Madonna†—Entertainer
James Michener—Author
Pablo Picasso‡—Artist
Ayn Rand†—Philosopher/Writer
Anne Rice—Author
Paul Robeson●—Entertainer
Mark Twain—Author
Oprah Winfrey†—Entertainer

Entrepreneur/Business—8 (20%)
[1 female—7 male]

Mary Kay Ash†—Cosmetics
Walt Disney‡—Cartoons
Bill Gates*—PC Software
Berry Gordy Jr.●—Motown Records
Soichiro Honda*—Automotive
Howard Hughes‡—Entrepreneur
Estée Lauder†—Cosmetics
Bill Lear*—Inventor/Entrepreneur
Tom Monaghan*—Domino's Pizza
Rupert Murdoch‡—Media
Helena Rubinstein‡—Cosmetics
Fred Smith*—Overnight Package Delivery
Ted Turner*—Cable Television

Footnoted subjects included in past books:
   *Profiles of Genius (1993)
   †Profiles of Female Genius (1994)
   ‡Profiles of Power and Success (1996)
   ●Profiles of Black Success (1997)

Science and Technology—7 (18%)
[1 female—6 males]

Marie Curie—Physics/Chemistry
Charles Darwin—Evolution
Thomas Edison—Inventor/Entrepreneur
Albert Einstein—Physics
Sigmund Freud—Psychology
Nikola Tesla‡—Energy
Frank Lloyd Wright—Architecture

Humanities—5 (13%)
[4 female—1 male]

Amelia Earhart‡—Aeronautics
Martin Luther King Jr.—Social Reform
Margaret Mead—Anthropology
Maria Montessori‡—Education
Mother Teresa—Social Reform

Politics—7 (18%)
[3 females—4 males]

Napoleon Bonaparte‡
Catherine the Great
Adolph Hitler‡
Mao Tse-tung
Karl Marx
Margaret Thatcher†

Sports—2 (.5%)
[1 female—1 male]

Michael Jordan•—Basketball
Babe Zaharias—Basketball, Golf, Track and
    Field, and others

References

General References

Adler, Alfred. (1979). *Superiority and Social Interest*. New York: Norton & Co.

Agor, Weston. (First Quarter 1991). "How Intuition Can Be Used to Enhance Creativity in Organizations." *Journal of Creative Behavior*, p. 11.

Amabile, Teresa. (1989). *Growing Up Creative—Nurturing a Lifetime of Creativity*. New York: Crown Publishing.

Andreas, Steve, and Charles Faulkner. (1994). *NLP—The New Technology of Achievement*. New York: William Morrow & Co.

"Are You Satisfied with Life?" (January 19, 1998). *USA Today*.

Barzun, Jacques. (Summer 1989). "The Paradoxes of Creativity." *American Scholar*, p. 337.

Baumeister, Roy, Laura Smart, and Margaret Boden. (March 1996) "Relation of Threatened Egotism to Violence and Aggression: The Dark Side of High Self-Esteem." *American Psychological Association, Psychological Review* 103: 5–29.

Begley, Sharon. (March 27, 1995). "Gray Matters." *Newsweek*, p. 48.

Boden, Margaret. (1990). *The Creative Mind*. New York: HarperCollins Publishing.

Boorstin, Daniel. (1992). *The Creators*. New York: Random House.

Branden, Nathaniel. (1994). *Six Pillars of Self Esteem*. New York: Bantam Books.

Branson, Richard. (1998). *Losing My Virginity*. New York: Random House.

Brigham, Deidre. (1994). *Imagery for Getting Well*. New York: Norton & Sons.

Brodie, James Mathew. (1987). *The Creative Personality: A Rankian Analysis of Ernest Hemingway*. Ann Arbor, Mich.: UMI Prress.

Buffington, Perry W. (September 1990). "Star Quality." *Sky Magazine*, pp. 101–103

Cantor, Dorothy, and Toni Bernay. (1992). *Women in Power—The Secrets of Leadership*. Boston: Houghton-Mifflin.

Capra, Fritjof. (1992). *The Turning Point*. New York: Simon & Schuster.

Cappon, Daniel. (May/June 1993). "The Anatomy of Intuition." *Psychology Today* 26, no 3: 40–49.

Clark, Barbara. (1988). *Growing Up Gifted*. Columbus, Ohio: Merrill Publishing.

Cohen, Roger. (August 12, 1990). "What Publishers Will Do for a Place on the Right List." *New York Times*.

Conger, Jay. (1989). *The Charismatic Leader*. San Francisco: Jossey-Bass Publishing.

Contemporary Authors. (Various years). Detroit: Gale Research Co.

Contemporary Literary Criticism. (Various years). Detroit: Gale Research Co.

Csikszentmihalyi, Mihaly. (1990). "The Creative Personality." In *Flow*. New York: HarperCollins.

———. (1993). *The Evolving Self*. New York: HarperCollins.

———. (July/August 1996). "The Creative Personality." *Psychology Today*, pp. 37–40.

———. (1996). *Creativity—Flow and the Psychology of Discovery and Invention*. New York: HarperCollins.

Current Biography. (Various years). Bronx, N.Y.: H. W. Wilson Co.

Denning, Linda Erikson. (April 26, 1992). "Helping Children Develop a Positive Self-Esteem." *Naples Daily News*, p. 11E.

Draper, P. Joseph. (1992). *World Literature Criticism*. Detroit: Gale Research Co.

Emery, Marcia. (November 26, 1996). "A Conscious Effort to Cultivate Intuition." *USA Today*, p. 9D.

Farley, Frank. (May 1986). "World of the Type T Personality." *Psychology Today*, pp. 46–52.

Farrell, W. (1986). *Why Men Are the Way They Are*. New York: McGraw-Hill.

Feldhusen, John. (Fourth Quarter 1995). "Creativity: A Knowledge Base, Metacognitive Skills, and Personality Factors." *Journal of Creative Behavior*, p. 255.

Ferguson, Marilyn. (1976). *The Aquarian Conspiracy*. Los Angeles: J. P. Tarcher.

Frankl, Victor. (1959). *In Search of Meaning*. New York: Pocket Books.

Franzini, Louis, and John Grossberg. (1995). *Eccentric and Bizarre Behaviors*. New York: John Wiley & Sons.

Fucini, Joseph, and Suzy Fucini. (1985). *Entrepreneurs—The Men and Women Behind Famous Brand Names and How They Made It*. Boston: G. K. Hall.

Gardner, Howard. (1983). *Framing Minds—The Theory of Multiple Intelligences*. New York: Basic Books.

———. (1993). *Creating Minds*. New York: Basic Books.

———. (1997). *Extraordinary Minds*. New York: Basic Books.

Garfield, Charles. (1986). *Peak Performance*. New York: Avon.

Geschwind, Norman. (August 1992). "Lefthandness: Association with Immune Disease." *Proceedings of the National Academy of Sciences*. Cited in *The Anatomy of Sex and Power*, by Michael Hutchinson. New York: Morrow, 1990.

Geschwind, Norman, and Peter Behan. (August 1982). "Lefthanders." *National Academy of Sciences*.

Ghislin, Brewster. (1952). *The Creative Process*. Berkeley, Calif.: Berkeley Press.

Gilder, George. (1980). *Wealth and Poverty*. New York: Simon & Schuster.

———. (1984). *Spirit of Enterprise*. New York: Simon & Schuster.

Gilligan, Carol. (1982). *In a Different Voice: Psychological Theory and Women's Development*. Cambridge, Mass.: Harvard University Press.

Goleman, Daniel. (1995). *Emotional Intelligence—Why It Can Matter More Than IQ*. New York: Bantam.

Goleman, Daniel, Paul Kaufman, and Ray Michael. (1992). *The Creative Spirit*. New York: Dutton.

Gornick, Vivian, and Barbara Moran. (1971). *Women in Sexist Society—Studies in Power and Powerlessness*. New York: New American Library.

Gray, John. (1993). *Men, Women, and Relationships*. Hillsboro, Ore.: Beyond Words Publishing.

Guiles, Fred L. (1969). *Norma Jean*. New York: Bantam.

Halamandaris, The Brothers. (1994). *Caring Quotes*. Washington, D.C.: Caring Publishing.

Hart, Michael. (1978). *The 100—A Ranking of the Most Influential Persons in History*. New York: Citadel Publishing.

Heatherton, Todd, and Joel Weinberger. (1993). *Can Personality Change?* Washington, D.C.: American Psychological Association.

Hershmann, D., and J. Lieb. (1988). *The Key to Genius—Manic Depression and the Creative Life*. Amherst, N.Y.: Prometheus Books.

———. (1994). *A Brotherhood of Tyrants—Manic Depression and Absolute Power*. Amherst, N.Y.: Prometheus Books.

Herzog, Brad. (1995). *The Sports 100*. New York: Macmillan & Co.

Hill, Napoleon. (1960). *Think and Grow Rich*. New York: Fawcett Crest.

Hirsh, Sandra, and Jean Kummerow. (1989). *Life Types*. New York: Warner.

Horn, Thelma. (1992). *Advances in Sport Psychology*. Miami: Human Kinetics Publishers.

Hunt, Morton. (1993). *The Story of Psychology*. New York: Doubleday.

Hutchison, Michael. (1990). *The Anatomy of Sex and Power*. New York: Morrow.

Jamison, Kay. (1994). *Touched with Fire—Manic Depressive Illness*. New York: Free Press.

———. (1995). *An Unquiet Mind—A Memoir of Moods and Madness*. New York: Alfred Knopf.

Johnson, Robert. (1986). *Inner Work—Using Dreams and Active Imagination for Personal Growth*. San Francisco: Harper.

Jung, Carl. (1976). *The Portable Jung*. New York: Penguin.

Kaufman, Walter. (1967). *Nietzsche's Genealogy of Morals*. New York: Viking Press.

Keirsey, David. (1987). *Portraits of Temperament—Personality Types*. Del Mar, Calif.: Prometheus Nemesis Book Co.

Keirsey, D., and M. Bates. (1984). *Please Understand Me*. Del Mar, Calif.: Prometheus Nemesis Book Co.

King, Neil. (April 22, 1998). "World Competitive Study—US #1." *Wall Street Journal*.

Klein, Burton. (1977). *Dynamic Economics*. Cambridge, Mass.: Harvard University Press.

Korda, Michael. (1975). *Power—How to Get It How to Keep It*. New York: Random House.

Kroeger, Otto, and Janet Thuesen. (1992). *Type Talk at Work*. New York: Delacorte Press.

Landrum, Gene. (1993). *Profiles of Genius*. Amherst, N.Y.: Prometheus Books.

———. (1994). *Profiles of Female Genius*. Amherst, N.Y.: Prometheus Books.

———. (1996). *Profiles of Power and Success*. Amherst, N.Y.: Prometheus Books.

———. (1997a). *Profiles of Black Success*. Amherst, N.Y.: Prometheus Books.

———. (1997b). *Promethean 2000: Truth—Vision—Power*. Naples, Fla.: Genie-Vision Press.

Lauder, Estée. (1985). *Estée—A Success Story*. New York: Random House.

Leman, Kenneth. (1985). *The Birth Order Book*. New York: Dell Publishing.

Lemann, Nicholas. (February 1994). "Is There a Science of Success?—An Analysis of David McClelland's Life Work on Motivation." *The Atlantic* 13: 82.

Leonard, Linda Schierse. (1993). *Meeting the Madwoman*. New York: Bantam Books.

Lever, Maurice. (1993). *Sade*. New York: Farrar, Straus, & Giroux.

Ludwig, Arnold. (1995). *The Price of Greatness*. New York: Guilford Press.

MacKinnon, David. (1965). "Personality and the Realization of Creative Potential." *American Psychologist*, pp. 273–81.

Mahar, Maggie. (October 1992). "No Bull Advice." *Working Woman*.

Martin, Ralph. (1988). *Golda*. New York: Scribner & Sons.

Maslow, Abraham. (1971). *The Farther Reaches of Human Nature*. New York: Viking Press.

McClelland, David. (1978). *Power—The Inner Science*. New York: John Wiley & Sons.

Mellou, Eleni. (Second Quarter 1996). "The Two Conditions View of Creativity." *Journal of Creative Behavior*, p. 126.

Mellow, James. (1993). *Hemingway: A Life without Consequences*. Boston: Addison-Wesley Publishing.

Monaghan, Tom. (1986). *Pizza Tiger*. New York: Random House.

Mudd, Samuel. (Fourth Quarter 1995). "Suggestive Parallels between Kirton's A-1 Theory of Creative Style and Koestler's Bisociative Theory of the Creative Act." *Journal of Creative Behavior*, p. 240.

Ornstein, Robert. (1972). *The Psychology of Consciousness*. New York: Penguin.

Pearsall, Paul. (1993). *Making Miracles*. New York: Avon Books.

Peters, Thomas J., and Robert H. Waterman Jr. (1982). *In Search of Excellence: Lessons from America's Best-Run Companies*. New York: Harper & Row.

Plomin, Robert, and Gerald E. McClearn. (1993). *Nature, Nurture and Psychology*. Washington, D.C.: American Psychological Association.

Pohlman, Livia. (First Quarter 1996). "Creativity, Gender and the Family: A Study of Creative Writers." *Journal of Creative Behavior*.

Prigogine, Ilya. (1980). *From Being to Becoming*. San Francisco: Freeman & Co.

Prigogine, Ilya, and Isabelle Stengers. (1984). *Order Out of Chaos*. New York: Bantam Books.

Rogers, C. R. (1980). *A Way of Being*. Columbus: Bell & Howell.

Rosenzweig, Mark. (1971). *The Biopsychology of Development*. New York: Academic Press.

Sagan, Carl. (December 4, 1994). "Scam or Miracle." *Parade Magazine*, pp. 8–9.

Schwab, Lynne. (Third Quarter 1991). "No Static in Your Attic: Tapping into Your Creative and Intuitive Abilities." *Journal of Creative Behavior*, p. 256.

Shallcross, Doris, and Dorothy Sisk. (1989). *Intuition—An Inner Way of Knowing*. Buffalo, N.Y.: Bearly Limited.

Silver, David. (1985). *Entrepreneurial Megabucks—The 100 Greatest Entrepreneurs of the Last 25 Years*. New York: John Wiley & Sons.

Simonton, Dean Keith. (1994). *Greatness*. New York: The Guilford Press.

Steinem, Gloria. (1992). *Revolution from Within—A Book of Self-Esteem*. Boston: Little, Brown & Co.

Sternberg, Robert. (1996). *Successful Intelligence*. New York: Simon & Schuster.

Stibbs, Anne. (1993). *A Woman's Place*. New York: Avon Books.

Storr, Anthony. (1983). *The Essential Jung*. New York: MJF Books.

———. (1987). *The Female (Animus) and Male (Anima) of Jung*. New York: MJF Books.

———. (1989). *Freud*. New York: Oxford University Press.

———. (1993). *The Dynamics of Creation*. New York: Ballantine Books.

———. (1996). *Feet of Clay: Saints, Sinners, and Madmen: A Study of Gurus*. New York: Free Press.

Sulloway, Frank. (1996). *Born to Rebel—Birth Order, Family Dynamics, and Creative Lives*. New York: Pantheon Books.

Talese, Gay. (1993). *Thy Neighbor's Wife*. New York: Ballantine Books.

Tarrobelli, Randy. (1989). *Call Her Miss Ross*. New York: Ballantine Books.

Taylor, I., and J. Gretzels, eds. (1975). *Perspectives in Creativity*. Chicago: Aldine Publishing Co.

Toffler, Alvin. (1990). *Power Shift*. New York: Bantam Books.

Wallace, Irving, Amy Wallace, Sylvia Wallace, and David Wallechinsky. (1993). *The Secret Sex Lives of Famous People*. New York: Dorset Press.

Walsh, Anthony, and Grace Walsh. (1993). *Vive la Difference—A Celebration of the Sexes*. Amherst, N.Y.: Prometheus Books.

Walton, Sam, with John Huey. (1992). *Sam Walton, Made in America: My Story*. New York: Doubleday.

Weeks, David, and Jamie James. (1995). *Eccentrics: A Study of Sanity and Strangeness*. New York: Villards.

Wilson, Anton. (1990). *Prometheus Rising*. Phoenix: Falcon Press.

Wolf, Naomi. (1991). *The Beauty Myth*. New York: Anchor Books, Doubleday.

World Competitiveness Yearbook. (1996). Lausanne, Switzerland: International Institute for Management Development.

Zubov, V. P. (1968). *Leonardo da Vinci*. New York: Barnes and Noble.

Subject References

Honoré de Balzac

Maurois, Andre. (1965). *Prometheus—The Life of Balzac*. New York: Harper & Row.
Robb, Graham. (1994). *Balzac: A Biography*. New York: W. W. Norton.
Zweig, Stefan. (1947). *Balzac*. New York: Viking Press.

Napoleon Bonaparte

Geyl, Pieter. (1949). *Napoleon For and Against*. New Haven, Conn.: Yale University Press.
Herold, J. Christopher. (1955). *The Mind of Napoleon*. New York: Columbia Press.
Markham, Felix. (1966). *Napoleon*. New York: Penguin Books.
Seward, Desmond. (1988). *Napoleon and Hitler: A Comparative Biography*. New York: Viking.

Joseph Campbell

Campbell, Joseph. (1949). *The Hero with a Thousand Faces*. New York: MJF Press.
———. (1986). *The Inner Reaches of Outer Space*. New York: A. van der Marck Editions.
———. (1988). *The Power of Myth*. New York: Doubleday.
———. (1990). *Transformations of Myth*. New York: Harper & Row.
Larsen, Stephen, and Robin Larsen. (1991). *A Fire in the Mind—The Life of Joseph Campbell*. New York: Doubleday.
Moyers, Bill. (1987). *The Power of Myth—Joseph Campbell's Theories of Life and Myth*. PBS TV series shown in four parts.
Segal, Robert. (1987). *Joseph Campbell—An Introduction*. New York: Mentor Books.
Toms, Michael. (1989). *An Open Life—In Conversation with Joseph Campbell*. New York: Harper & Row.

Catherine the Great

Alexander, John. (1989). *Catherine the Great*. New York: Oxford Press.
Troyat, Henry. (1980). *Catherine the Great*. New York: Berkley Books.
Zwingle, Erla. (September 1998). "Catherine the Great." *National Geographic*, pp. 92–117.

Agatha Christie

Christie, Agatha. (1977). *Agatha Christie—An Autobiography*. New York: Berkley Books.
Gerald, Michael. (April 14, 1994). "The Poisonous Pen of Agatha Christie." *New England Journal of Medicine*.
Gill, Gillian. (1990). *Agatha Christie—The Woman and Her Mysteries*. New York: Maxwell Macmillan.
Magill, Frank N. (1994). "Agatha Christie." *Great Women Writers*, pp. 94–97. New York: Henry Holt & Co.
Robyns, Gwen. (1978). *The Mystery of Agatha Christie—An Intimate Biography of the Duchess of Death*. New York: Penguin Books.
Shenker, Israel. (September 1990). "The Past Master of Mysteries, She Built a Better Mousetrap." *Smithsonian* 21, no. 6: 86–95.

Marie Curie

Curie, Eve. (1937). *Madam Curie*. New York: Pocket Books.
Reid, Robert. (1974). *Marie Curie*. New York: New American Library.

Charles Darwin

Bowlby, John. (1990). *Charles Darwin*. New York: W. W. Norton & Co.
Darwin, Charles. (1958). *The Autobiography of Charles Darwin*. New York: W. W. Norton.
Hyman, Stanley Edgar. (1963). *Darwin for Today*. New York: Viking Press.
Naik, Gautam. (April 28, 1998). "Darwin's Home Made Fit to Survive." *Wall Street Journal*, p. A16.

Walt Disney

Eliot, Marc. (1993). *Walt Disney—Hollywood's Dark Prince*. New York: Carol Publishing Co.
Hinman, Catherine. (April 24, 1994). "Disney Becomes a Movie Monarch." *Orlando Sentinel*, p. 1A.
Mosley, Leonard. (1986). *Disney*. New York: Stein & Day Publishing.
Thomas, Bob. (1994). *An American Original—Walt Disney*. New York: Hyperion.

Fyodor Dostoevsky

Dostoevsky, Fyodor. (1946). *The Gambler*. New York: Bantam Books.
———. (1950). *Crime and Punishment*. New York: Random House.
———. (1955). *The Insulted and Injured*. New York: Grove Press.
Frank, Joseph. (1976). *Dostoevsky—The Seeds of Revolt*. Princeton, N.J.: Princeton University Press.
———. (1990). *Dostoevsky—The Years of Ordeal*. Princeton, N.J.: Princeton University Press.
———. (1995). *Dostoevsky—The Miraculous Years*. Princeton, N.J.: Princeton University Press.
Gide, Andre. (1923). *Dostoevsky*. New York: A New Direction.
Morson, Gary Saul. (Winter 1995). "A Writer's Diary 1873–1876 by Fyodor Dostoevsky." *American Scholar*.

Isadora Duncan

"The Creators—Barefoot Contessas." (September 7, 1992). *U.S. News & World Report*, p. 101.
Desti, Mary. (1929). *The Life of Isadora Duncan*. New York: Horace Liveright.
Duncan, Isadora. (1927). *Isadora Duncan—My Life*. New York: Liveright.
Schneider, Ilya Ilyich. (1968). *Isadora Duncan: The Russian Years*. New York: De Capo Press.
Steegmuller, Francis. (1974). *Your Isadora: The Love Story of Isadora Duncan and Gordon Craig*. New York: Random House.

Amelia Earhart

Rich, Doris. (1989). *Amelia Earhart—A Biography*. New York: Dell.
Ware, Susan. (1993). *Still Missing—Amelia Earhart and the Search for Modern Feminism*. New York: W. W. Norton & Sons.

Thomas Edison

Friedel, Robert. (1994). "Great Inventions—New Light on Edison's Light." *Forbes*, p. 26.
Josepheson, Matthew. (1992). *Edison—A Biography*. New York: John Wiley & Sons.

Albert Einstein

Clark, Ronald W. (1972). *Einstein—The Life and Times*. New York: Avon Books.

Sigmund Freud

Campbell, Joseph. (1971). *The Portable Jung*. New York: Penguin Books.
Elson, John. (July 6, 1992). "Is Freud Finished?" *Time*, p. 60.
Freud, Sigmund. (1925). *On Creativity and the Unconscious*. New York: Harper.
Gay, Peter. (1993). *Freud—The Life for Our Time*. New York: Doubleday.
Hunt, Morton. (1993). "Freud." In *The Story of Psychology*. New York: Doubleday.
Jones, Ernest. (1957). *Sigmund Freud*. New York: Basic Books.
Storr, Anthony. (1989). *Freud*. New York: Oxford University Press.

Berry Gordy Jr.

Bagwell, L. S. (June 29, 1995). "Berry Gordy and Carol Publishing Suit." *Publishers Weekly*, p. 13.
Benjaminson, Peter. (1979). *The Story of Motown*. New York: Grove Press.
"Berry Gordy Files $250 Million Libel Suit against *New York Daily News*." (May 9, 1994). *Jet*, p. 53.
Gordy, Berry, Jr. (1994). *To Be Loved*. New York: Warner Books.
Waller, Don. (1985). *The Motown Story*. New York: Charles Scribner's Sons.

Ernest Hemingway

Brodie, James Matthew. (1987). *Dissertation: The Creative Personality: A Rankian Analysis of Ernest Hemingway*. Ann Arbor, Mich.: UMI Dissertation Services.
Hemingway, Ernest. (1926). *The Sun Also Rises*. New York: Macmillan Publishing.
Hemingway, Gregory. (1976). *Papa—Personal Memoir*. New York: Pocket Books.
Leff, Leonard. (1998). *Hemingway and His Conspirators*. New York: Scribners.
Lynn, Kenneth. (1987). *Hemingway*. New York: Fawcett Columbine.
Mellow, James. (1993). *Hemingway—A Life without Consequences*. Boston: Addison-Wesley Publishing.
Sanderson, Stewart. (1961). *Hemingway*. Edinburgh, Scotland: Oliver & Boyd.
Young, Thomas, and Ronald Fine. (1968). "Ernest Hemingway." *American Literature: A Critical Survey*, p. 315. New York: American Book Company.

Adolf Hitler

Bullock, Alan. (1971). *Hitler—A Study in Tyranny*. New York: Harper.
Gay, Peter. (1988). *Adolf Hitler*. New York: Anchor Books.
Martin, Gilbert. (1978). *Holocaust*. New York: ADL.
Petrova, Ada, and Peter Watson. (1995). *The Death of Hitler*. New York: Norton & Company.

Schwarzwaller, Wulf. (1989). *The Unknown Hitler*. New York: Berkley Books.
Seward, Desmond. (1988). *Napoleon and Hitler—A Comparative Biography*. New York: Viking Press.
Shirer, William. (1960). *The Rise and Fall of the Third Reich*. New York: Simon & Schuster.
Speer, Albert. (1970). *Inside the Third Reich*. New York: Macmillan & Co.
Stein, George H. (1968). *Hitler*. Englewood Cliffs, N.J.: Prentice Hall.
Toland, John. (1976). *Adolf Hitler*. New York: Doubleday.

Soichiro Honda

Sanders, S. (1975). *Honda—The Man and the Machine*. Boston: Little, Brown.

Howard Hughes

Bartlett, Donald, and James Steele. (1979). *Empire—The Life, Legend, and Madness of Howard Hughes*. New York: W. W. Norton & Co.
Dietrich, Noah. (1972). *Howard—The Amazing Mr. Hughes*. Greenwich, Conn.: Fawcett.
Higham, Charles. (1993). *Howard Hughes—The Secret Life*. New York: G. P. Putnam & Sons.

Michael Jackson

Gunderson, Edna. (April 20, 1995). "HIStory at Stake." *USA Today*, p. D1.
Jackson, Michael. (1988). *Moonwalk*. New York: Doubleday.
Orth, Maureen. (September 1995). "The Jackson Jive." *Vanity Fair*, p. 144.
Tarrobelli, Randy. (1991). *Michael Jackson—The Magic and the Madness*. New York: Carol Publishing.

Michael Jordan

"Air and Hare." (July 3, 1995). *Newsweek*, p. 39.
"Chicago Bulls Make NBA History as First Team to Win 70 Games in a Season." (May 6, 1996). *Jet*, pp. 52–55.
"The Greatest Returns." (June 1995). *Ebony*, p. 25.
Green, Bob. (1992). *Hang Time*. New York: St. Martin's Press.
Jordan, Michael. (1995). *I'm Back—More Rare Air*. San Francisco: Collins Publishers.
Krugel, Mitchell. (1994). *Jordan—The Man, His Words, His Life*. New York: St. Martin's Press.
Lazenby, Roland. (1996). *Bull Run*. Lenexa, Kans.: Addax Publishing Group.
Levin, Bob. (October 19, 1993). "Master of Midair." *Maclean's*, p. 62.
McCallum, Jack. (October 18, 1993). "The Desire Isn't There." *Sports Illustrated*, p. 28.
"Michael! The Story of Michael Jordan from His Childhood to His Comeback." (Spring 1995). *Sports Illustrated*.
Reilly, Rick. (June 21, 1993). "Smells Like Another Rose." *Sports Illustrated*, p. 74.
Snider, Mike. (June 17, 1996). "Michael Jordan's Bigger Than Basketball; He's a Pop Icon." *USA Today*.
Starr, Mark. (June 14, 1993). "The Gambling Man." *Newsweek*, p. 72.

Martin Luther King Jr.

Clayton, Ed. (1964). *Martin Luther King—The Peaceful Warrior*. New York: Simon & Schuster.

Cone, James. (1991). *Martin and Malcolm and America: A Dream or a Nightmare?* Maryknoll, N.Y.: Orbis Books.
Garrow, David. (1986). *Bearing the Cross.* New York: Random House.
King, Coretta Scott. (1993). *My Life with Martin Luther King.* New York: Puffin Books.
Lischer, Richard. (1995). *The Preacher King.* New York: Osvord Press.

Stephen King

Beahm, George. (1992). *The Stephen King Story.* Kansas City, Mo.: Andrews & McMeel.
Roush, Matt. (September 24, 1996). "King's Double House of Horrors." *USA Today*, p. D1.
Wohlber, Curt. (December 1995). "The Man Who Can Scare." *American Heritage Magazine*, p. 1.

Bill Lear

Rashke, Richard. (1985). *Stormy Genius.* Boston: Houghton-Mifflin.

Mao Tse-tung

Li Zhisui. (1994). *The Private Life of Mao.* New York: Random House.
MacFarquhar, Emily. (October 10, 1994). "A Doctor's Tale on Mao." *U.S. News & World Report*, pp. 48–85.
Payne, Robert. (1966). *Mao Tse-tung.* New York: Pyramid Books.
Terrill, Ross. (1980). *Mao.* New York: Harper & Row.

Karl Marx

Berlin, Isaiah. (1978). *Karl Marx—His Life and Environment.* London: Oxford University Press.
Ivanov, Nikolai. (1978). *Karl Marx.* Moscow, Russia: Novosti Press.
Marx, Karl, and Friedrich Engels. (1848). *The Communist Manifesto.* New York: Washington Square Press.
———. (1867–1879). *Das Kapital.* Chicago: Kerr.

Margaret Mead

Bateson, Mary Catherine. (1984). *With a Daughter's Eye.* New York: William Morrow & Co.
Howard, Jane. (1984). *Margaret Mead—A Life.* New York: Simon & Schuster.
Margaret Mead. (1928). *Coming of Age in Samoa.* New York: William Morrow & Co.
———. (1930). *Growing Up in New Guinea.* New York: William Morrow & Co.
———. (1935). *Sex and Temperament.* New York: William Morrow & Co.
———. (1972). *Blackberry Winter—My Earlier Years.* New York: William Morrow & Co.

James Michener

Hayes, John P. (1984). *James Michener—A Biography.* New York: Bobbs-Merrill Co.
Marnane, Michael, and James Heinen. (1993). "Fostering Moral Growth through Teaching Literature." *Academic Abstracts*, p. 1.
Michener, James. (1959). *Hawaii.* New York: Random House.

————. (1965). *The Source*. New York: Random House.

————. (1982). *Space*. New York: Random House.

————. (1985). *Texas*. New York: Random House.

————. (1989). *Caribbean*. New York: Random House.

————. (1992). *The World is My Home*. New York: Random House.

————. (1993). *Literary Reflections*. New York: Tom Doherty & Associates.

Maria Montessori

Chattin-McNichols, John. (1992). *The Montessori Controversy*. Albany, N.Y.: Delmar Publishers.

Kramer, Rita. (1988). *Maria Montessori—A Biography*. Boston: Addison-Wesley.

Montessori, Maria. (1912). *The Montessori Method*. New York: Schocken Books.

Standing, E. M. (1962). *Maria Montessori*. New York: Mentor-Omega.

Rupert Murdoch

Adams, Bruce. (November 3, 1995). "Fox Outgrows the Bart Simpson Jokes." *San Francisco Examiner*.

Bart, Peter. (February 15, 1993). "Rupert's Rumblings." *Variety*, p. 5.

Donaton, Scott. (June 13, 1994). "Citizen Murdoch." *Advertising* Age, p. 6.

Kiernan, Thomas. (1986). *Citizen Murdoch*. New York: Dodd, Mead & Co.

Martzke, Rudy. (November 1, 1995). "Fox Sports Set to Rival ESPN." *USA Today*, p. Sports 2.

Reibstein, Larry, and Nancy Hass. "Rupert's Power Play." *Newsweek*, p. 46.

Roush, Matt. (November 7, 1995). "Murdoch: Portrait of a 'Pirate.'" *USA Today*, p. 3D.

Sandomir, Richard. (September 4, 1994). "Murdoch and Fox." *New York Times*, p. F1.

Shawcross, William. (1993). *Murdoch*. London: Pan Books.

Sivy, Michael. (March 1994). "Murdoch and Fox." *New York Times*, p. F1.

Tuccille, Jerome. (1989). *Rupert Murdoch*. New York: Donald Fine.

Pablo Picasso

Gilot, Francoise, and Carlton Lake. (1964). *Life with Picasso*. New York: McGraw-Hill.

Huffington, Arianna. (1988). *Picasso—Creator and Destroyer*. New York: Avon Books.

O'Brian, Patrick. (1976). *Picasso*. New York: Norton & Co.

Ayn Rand

Branden, Barbara. (1986). *The Passion of Ayn Rand—A Biography*. New York: Penguin Books.

Branden, Nathaniel. (1989). *Judgment Day: My Years with Ayn Rand*. New York: Penguin Books.

Branden, Nathaniel, and Barbara Branden. (1962). *Who Is Ayn Rand?* New York: Penguin Books.

Rand, Ayn. (1943). *The Fountainhead*. New York: Bobbs-Merrill.

————. (1953). *Anthem*. Caldwell, Idaho: Caxton Printers.

————. (1957). *Atlas Shrugged*. New York: Signet.

————. (1961). *For the New Intellectual*. New York: Signet.

————. (1964). *The Virtue of Selfishness: A New Concept of Egoism*. New York: New American Library.

————. (1982). *Philosophy: Who Needs It?* New York: Signet.

———. (1993a). *The Ayn Rand Letters—1971 through 1976*. Oceanside, Calif.: Second Renaissance Books.

———. (1993b). *The Objectivist Newsletters—1966 through 1971*. Oceanside, Calif.: Second Renaissance Books.

———. (1993c). *The Objectivist Newsletters—1962 through 1965*. Oceanside, Calif.: Second Renaissance Books.

Sciabarra, Chris Mathew. (1995). *Ayn Rand—The Russian Radical*. University Park: Pennsylvania State University Press.

Toffler, Alvin. (March 1964). "Playboy Interview with Ayn Rand." *Playboy*.

Anne Rice

Ramsland, Katherine. (1994). *Prism of the Night—A Biography of Anne Rice*. New York: Penguin Books.

Riley, Michael. (1996). *Conversations with Anne Rice—An Enlightening Portrait of Her Life and Work*. New York: Ballatine Books.

Paul Robeson

Foner, Philip, ed. (1978). *Paul Robeson Speaks*. New York: Carol Publishing.

Gilliam, Dorothy. (1976). *Paul Robeson—All American*. Washington, D.C.: New Republic Book Co.

Robeson, Elende. (1930). *Paul Robeson—Negro*. New York: Harper Bros.

Robeson, Paul. (1958). *Here I Stand*. Boston: Beacon.

Helena Rubenstein

Collins, Amy Fine. (November 1992). "The Reign of Helena Rubinstein." *House & Garden*, p. 144.

O'Higgins, Patrick. (1971). *Madame: The Very Intimate Biography of the Despot of Beauty, Helena Rubinstein*. New York: Dell Books.

Rubinstein, Carin. (October 1992). "*New Woman* Report on Self." *New Woman*, pp. 58–66.

Rubinstein, Helena. (1972). *Helena Rubinstein—My Life for Beauty*. New York: Paperback Library.

Fred Smith

Tucker, R. (October 1986). "Federal Express's Fred Smith." *Inc*. pp. 35–50.

Mother Teresa

Greer, Germaine. (September 22, 1997). "Unmasking the Mother." *Newsweek*, pp. 26–29.

Muggeridge, Malcolm. (1971). *Something Beautiful for God*. New York: Harper & Row.

Royle, Roger. (1992). *Mother Teresa—A Life in Pictures*. New York: HarperCollins.

Tames, Richard. (1989). *Mother Teresa*. New York: Harper & Row.

Nikola Tesla

Cheney, Margaret. (1981). *Tesla—Man Out of Time*. New York: Barnes & Noble.

O'Neill, John, J. (1968). *Prodigal Genius*. London: Neville Spearman.

Tesla, Nikola. (1982). *My Inventions*. Williston, Vt.: Hart Bros.
Wise, Tad. (1994). *Tesla*. Atlanta: Turner Publishing.

Margaret Thatcher

Murray, Patricia. (1980). *Margaret Thatcher*. London: Mackay Ltd.
Young, Hugo. (1989). *The Iron Lady*. New York: Noonday Press.

Ted Turner

Goldberg, Robert, and Gerald Jay. (1995). *Citizen Turner—The Wild Rise of an American Tycoon*. New York: Harcourt Brace & Co.
Whitemore, Hank. (1990). *CNN—The Inside Story*. Boston: Little, Brown & Co.

Mark Twain

Devoto, Bernard. (1964). *Mark Twain—Letters from the Earth*. Greenwich, Conn.: Fawcett Publications.
Kaplan, Justin. (1966). *Mr. Clemens and Mark Twain—A Biography*. New York: Simon & Schuster.
Twain, Mark [Samuel Clemens]. (1917). *The Autobiography of Mark Twain*. New York: Harper International.
———. (1938). *Letters from the Earth*. Greewich, Conn.: Fawcett Publications.
———. (1995). *Joan of Arc*. (1895). New York: Random House.
Young, Thomas, and Ronald Fine. (1968). "Mark Twain." *American Literature: A Critical Survey*, p. 223. New York: American Book Company.

Frank Lloyd Wright

Filler, Martin. (January 1994). "More on the Master." *House Beautiful*, p. 24.
Gill, Brendan. (1987). *Many Masks: A Life of Frank Lloyd Wright*. New York: Ballantine Books.
Goldberger, Paul. (February 13, 1994). "Not an Urbanist, Only a Genius." *New York Times Magazine*, p. 48.
Hatch, Alden. (1974). *Buckminster Fuller*. New York: Crown Publishing.
Margolies, Jane. (June 1992). "Remembering Mr. Wright." *House Beautiful*, p. 18.
Secrest, Meryle. (1992). *Frank Lloyd Wright*. New York: Harper-Perennial.
Wright, Frank Lloyd. (1977). *An Autobiography*. New York: Horizon Press.

Mildred "Babe" Didrickson Zaharias

Cayleff, Susan. (1996). *Babe—The Life and Legend of Babe Didrickson Zaharias*. Chicago: University of Illinois Press.
Herzog, Brad. (1995). "Babe Didrickson Zaharias." *The Sports 100*, pp. 110–14. New York: Macmillan and Co.
Zaharias, Mildred "Babe" Didrickson. (1955). *This Life I've Led: My Autobiography*. New York: Dell.

index

About the Author

Gene Landrum is a high-tech start-up executive turned teacher and writer. He originated the Chuck E. Cheese concept of family entertainment, among other entrepreneurial ventures. After years of interacting with creative and overachieving personalities he noticed they were different and decided to embark on a research effort to determine what made them so. This led him to study some of the world's creative and visionary geniuses such as Bill Gates, Ted Turner, Mother Teresa, Napoleon, Maria Montessori, Albert Einstein, and Walt Disney to see if they had any common characteristics. Landrum's research resulted in a doctoral dissertation on the innovator personality plus six books on entrepreneurship, visionary leadership, and creativity. Landrum lectures extensively on these topics in addition to teaching leadership, marketing, multinational business, organizational behavior, and management at International College in Naples, Florida.

Dr. Landrum is considered a marketing visionary whose success has been a direct result of his Promethean temperament (pragmatic intuitive-thinking). He has an abiding interest in what makes the great tick and his books are inspirational tools for aspiring entrepreneurs, small business owners, parents, teachers, and the gifted. His books are psychobiological studies on what it takes to be great:

Eight Keys to Greatness (1999)
Prometheus 2000: Truth—Vision—Power (1997)
Profiles of Black Genius—Thirteen Creative Geniuses (1997)
Profiles of Power and Success: Fourteen Geniuses Who Broke the Rules (1996)
Profiles of Female Genius: Thirteen Creative Women Who Changed the World (1994)
Profiles of Male Genius: Thirteen Male Entrepreneurs Who Changed the World (1993)
The Innovator Personality (1991)